A Journey into Florida Railroad History

FLORIDA HISTORY AND CULTURE

 UNIVERSITY PRESS OF FLORIDA

Florida A&M University, Tallahassee
Florida Atlantic University, Boca Raton
Florida Gulf Coast University, Ft. Myers
Florida International University, Miami
Florida State University, Tallahassee
New College of Florida, Sarasota
University of Central Florida, Orlando
University of Florida, Gainesville
University of North Florida, Jacksonville
University of South Florida, Tampa
University of West Florida, Pensacola

UNIVERSITY PRESS OF FLORIDA

Gainesville · Tallahassee · Tampa · Boca Raton · Pensacola · Orlando · Miami · Jacksonville · Ft. Myers · Sarasota

A
Journey

INTO

FLORIDA
RAILROAD
HISTORY

Gregg M. Turner

Foreword by Raymond Arsenault and Gary R. Mormino

Library of Congress Cataloging-in-Publication Data
Turner, Gregg M.
   A journey into Florida railroad history / Gregg M. Turner ;
foreword by Raymond Arsenault and Gary R. Mormino.
p. cm.—(The Florida history and culture series)
Includes bibliographical references and index.
ISBN 978-0-8130-3233-7 (alk. paper)
   1. Railroads—Florida—History. 2. Florida—History. 3. Railroads—
Social aspects—Florida—History. 4. Florida—Social conditions. I. Title.
TF24.F6T875   2008
385.09759—dc22   2007050375

The University Press of Florida is the scholarly publishing agency for the
State University System of Florida, comprising Florida A&M University,
Florida Atlantic University, Florida Gulf Coast University, Florida In-
ternational University, Florida State University, New College of Florida,
University of Central Florida, University of Florida, University of North
Florida, University of South Florida, and University of West Florida.

University Press of Florida
15 Northwest 15th Street
Gainesville, FL 32611-2079
http://www.upf.com

Here is an enormous, an incalculable force . . . let loose suddenly upon mankind; exercising all sorts of influences, social, moral, and political. The application of steam to locomotion . . . is the most tremendous and far reaching engine of social revolution which has ever either blessed or cursed the earth.

—Charles Francis Adams Jr., *North American Review*, 1867

Contents

Foreword

A Journey into Florida Railroad History is the latest volume of a series devoted to the study of Florida history and culture. During the past half century, the burgeoning population and increased national and international visibility of Florida have sparked a great deal of popular interest in the state's past, present, and future. As a favorite destination of countless tourists and as the new home for millions of retirees and transplants, modern Florida has become a demographic, political, and cultural bellwether. Florida has also emerged as a popular subject and setting for scholars and writers. The Florida History and Culture Series provides an attractive and accessible format for Florida-related books. From destructive hurricanes to disputed elections, from tales of the Everglades to profiles of Sun Belt cities, Florida is simply irresistible.

The University Press of Florida is committed to the creation of an eclectic but carefully crafted set of books that will provide the field of Florida studies with a new focus that will encourage Florida writers to consider the broader implications and context of their work. The series includes standard academic monographs, as well as works of synthesis, memoirs, and anthologies. And, while the series features books of historical interest, authors researching Florida's environment, politics, literature, and popular or material culture are encouraged to submit their manuscripts as well. Each book offers a distinct personality and voice, but the ultimate goal of the series is to foster a broad sense of community and collaboration among Florida scholars.

Florida railroads have found their champion. Gregg M. Turner has written a highly engaging and meticulously researched study of Florida's railroads from their beginnings in the early territorial period through the modern and postmodern tumult. A prolific author, Turner has written extensively about the enterprise of transportation.

Historically, Florida's long peninsula imposed a tyranny of distance upon settlers. Underpopulated and largely undeveloped, Florida was slow to bridge its vast domain. On the eve of the Civil War, Florida ranked last among southern states in railroad mileage. The decade of the 1880s, however, brought Florida into what the *Tallahassee Weekly Floridian* in 1886 proclaimed "the railroad age." As Floridians fell in love with the railroad, they searched for old and new metaphors to understand it. One writer breathlessly described the new technology as "the resistless chariot of civilization with scythed axles mowing down ignorance and prejudice as it whirls along." In case inhabitants underestimated the power of the modern corporation, the new enterprise even made time stand still. On 18 November 1883, railroads dictated standardized local time.

Few today remember the names, but in the late nineteenth century, grand hopes accompanied the arrival of the St. Johns and Halifax Railroad; the Silver Springs, Ocala, and Gulf railroad; and the Fort Meade, Keystone, and Walk-in-the-Water Railroad. For sheer name value, has any rail line been christened with a more romantic name and route than the St. Cloud and Sugar Belt Railroad, a fifteen mile journey from Kissimmee to Narcoossee?

Turner masterfully traces the evolution of Florida's rail lines from the era of robber barons Flagler, Plant, and Chipley to the age of the Southern Railway, Seaboard Air Line, and the Atlantic Coast Line Railroad Company. Peaking in 1930 with nearly 6,000 miles of rail lines, Florida's railroads—including the fabled Orange Blossom Special that sped passengers from New York City to Miami—entered a decade of financial setbacks and reorganization. Following bursts of passenger increases and government support during World War II, the industry emerged from the conflict with confidence. But new competition (interstate highway, long-distance trucking, and airlines) challenged and succeeded the once vaunted railroads. The author traces the storyline to Amtrak and the contemporary era. Readers will enjoy the journey.

Raymond Arsenault and Gary R. Mormino
Series editors

Acknowledgments

Researching the railway heritage of Florida over many years has required the cooperation of many individuals and organizations. All rendered professional, courteous, and prompt attention. With much gratitude, I wish to especially thank:

James Cusick, curator, P. K. Yonge Library of Florida History, University of Florida; Burt Altman, librarian and archivist, Special Collections, Florida State University Libraries; Eileen Brady, Special Collections head, Carpenter Library, University of North Florida; Paul Camp, Special Collections head, University of South Florida Library; Dan Emerick, Laura Baas, and Cheri Ellison, Florida State Library; Adam Watson, photographic archivist and curator, Florida State Archives; Joan Morris, former curator, Florida State Archives Photographic Collection; and Nick and Debra Wynne of the Florida Historical Society.

I should also like to acknowledge the helpfulness of Cynthia Gandee, Susan Carter, and Amy David of the Henry B. Plant Museum; Jim Shelton, History Department coordinator, Tampa–Hillsborough County Public Library; Ted and Sallie VanItallie, Boca Grande Historical Society; Carole Goad, archivist, Sebring Historical Society; Dawn Hugh, Historical Museum of Southern Florida; Elaine Levey, director, Depot Museum and Historical Society, Avon Park; Christine Best, Sanford Historical Society; Joe Spann, manager, Polk County Historical and Genealogical Library; Ann Shank, Sarasota County History Center; Dorothy Korwek, director of historical resources, City of Venice Archives and Area Historical Collections; Joan Pickett, Jacksonville Historical Society; Jeanette Henderson, Baker Block Museum; Sandra Johnson, Pensacola Historical Museum; Ron Jamro and David Southall, Collier County Museum; Alyssa McManus, Tallahassee Trust for Historic Preservation; Sam Boldrick, Florida Collections manager, Miami-Dade Public Library; Laura Katz Smith, curator, Railroad History Archives, Dodd Research Center, University of Connecticut; and Augustus Veenendaal Jr., senior research historian (ret.), Institute of Netherlands History, The Hague.

I am also indebted to staffers of the Railway & Locomotive Historical Society and the National Railway Historical Society; Larry Goolsby of the Atlantic Coast Line & Seaboard Air Line Railroads Historical Society; Fred Wise, Ed Lee, and Bob Hines of the Rail Office, Florida Department of Transportation; Gary Sease, director of corporate communications, CSX Corporation; Seth Bramson, corporate historian, Florida East Coast Railway; Bonnie Arnold, Andrea Reitor, and Jennifer Paul, South Florida Regional Transportation Authority; and to Susan Terpay, public relations officer, Norfolk Southern Corporation.

Jeanne Hickam and Susan Brady kindly made suggestions to the manuscript.

Legal questions were ably answered by attorney Harry Hendry. Construction and engineering information was supplied by Michael Christiano. Louis Chiappetta furnished valuable financial insights. Inflation figures cited herein are taken from the *Statistical Abstract of the United States*.

Photographic contributions were cheerfully supplied by Fred Clark Jr., Michael Mulligan, Bob Pickering, Ari Rothenberg, David Salter, and Mike Woodruff.

Other individuals who assisted me with research include James Burke, Walter E. Campbell, William E. Griffin Jr., Donald Hensley Jr., Robert Wayne Johnson, William R. Johnston, Stan Mulford, Ken Murdock, Kelly Reynolds, and Russell Tedder.

A special word of gratitude is owed to John Byram, Jen Graham, and Michele Fiyak-Burkley at the University Press of Florida who shepherded this project with skill and enthusiasm.

Lastly, much is owed to my wife, Nancy.

Introduction

*Transportation and settlement always go hand in hand; the former
makes possible the latter, while the latter creates demand for the former.*

—Abbey, *Florida, Land of Change*

If any one American state eventually smiled upon railroads, gave them
a free course over the expanse, and greatly relied upon them to open
up the land to settlers and tourists, it was assuredly Florida. How railroads evolved and developed in the nation's twenty-seventh state, over
whose tracks Florida was hurtled into the Industrial Age and beyond,
is the subject of this work.

Our journey into this fascinating and neglected chapter of Florida
history commences in the 1830s amidst Native American upheaval
and territorial colonization. That this rural and isolated land then had
railroads at all astonished more than one visitor. "Many of them are
little known or completely unknown in the northern part of the United
States," wrote an eminent Prussian engineer in 1839. "Even the geogra-
phers appear to be ignorant of the railroads of Florida, for one looks in
vain for them on the latest maps of North America."[1]

Nevertheless those infant and fragile entities of bygone years were
really a portent of things to come, for within a few short decades the
"iron horse" energized Florida and its economy by furnishing the traveler and shipper with a new and much-needed service: "fast, regular,
dependable, all-weather transportation."[2]

Railroads were indeed the first big business enterprises of America,
but they also proved themselves to be fantastic instruments of change.

In Florida alone, they linked together every important city and town, created new communities, conquered the seemingly impenetrable interior of the peninsula, ushered in untold numbers of settlers and tourists, and conveyed to market—faster than any previous means of transportation—the wealth of Florida's mines, forests, factories, farms, and groves. Their story undeniably had fits and starts, but after Reconstruction new railroad lines were put down at a blistering pace. In fact, the power and influence of the state's railroads and lobby rapidly grew until they practically controlled legislatures and governors.[3]

Perhaps the first public document mentioning railroads surfaced in 1828, when the Legislative Council of the Florida Territory chartered the Chipola Canal Company and empowered it to construct either a canal "or Rail-way" between the Chipola River and the eastern arm of St. Andrews Bay. Although neither project was built, the act confirms that railroads were on the minds of certain Florida visionaries. But who those persons were or where they might have even gazed upon a "Railway" remains an intriguing mystery, as the first railroad in the American South did not open until Christmas Day, 1830! When fully completed three years later, between Charleston and Hamburg, opposite Augusta, Georgia, the South Carolina Canal and Rail Road Company was hailed as the longest continuous operation of its kind in the world.[4]

Another harbinger of note manifested at the 1829–30 session of the U.S. Congress. The delegate from Florida, Joseph White, asked that a survey and cost estimate be made for a line of railroad connecting Augusta with St. Marks, Florida. Although White's petition was eventually nixed, had the line been built it—and not the line out of Charleston—would have become the world's longest railway.[5]

This groundswell of interest helped prompt the legislative council to issue its first railway charter in 1831, though raising capital for the Leon Rail-Way Company proved tortuous. Later a new set of promoters appeared on the scene who recast the project as the Tallahassee Railroad, which was to connect the capital with the ancient Spanish port of St. Marks. The 22-mile route, over which bales of cotton, produce, and merchandise would eventually pass, opened in 1837 using mule-drawn trains. Chronologically it was the second railroad to open on Florida soil, the first having done so the year before between St. Joseph (near

Port St. Joe) and Lake Wimico—a navigable arm of the Apalachicola River.

As we will discover, the railroad heritage of Florida has embraced several periods of development. It began, like that of all other states, with an *era of private enterprise*. By and large, the lines first constructed in Florida connected a river or ocean port with some important interior locale known perhaps for agriculture, lumber, minerals, or trade. Projects having loftier goals followed, beginning in the mid-1850s when America experienced its first railroad boom. But as Henry Poor, the famed railroad analyst and reformer, frequently remarked in his annual volumes of railroad information and statistics: "All the early railroads of Florida were unsuccessful, and speedily upon their opening they went into the hands of receivers from whom no information, as a rule, can be obtained."[6]

For decades, the sparse population of Florida, the lack of smokestack industry, along with a shortage of capital resources served to retard railway development. To remedy matters, legislators passed a stimulus act in 1855 called the Internal Improvement Fund, which bestowed upon qualified companies grants of land and guaranteed the interest on their construction bonds. The scheme worked, and before long Jacksonville was connected with Lake City, as was Fernandina with Cedar Key, Lake City with Tallahassee, and Pensacola to Pollard, Alabama.

But these and other projects came undone during the American Civil War. Much of the network was decimated, and every company obligated to the Internal Improvement Fund defaulted on its construction bonds and sinking fund payments. Thus, the fund's trustees had no choice but to seize and auction the properties, usually at absurdly low prices. The impoverished times and shortage of capitalists lingered throughout Reconstruction. As the American railroad historian John Stover relates: "Of the ten southern states, Florida had the fewest, the weakest, and the poorest railroads in the decade after the Civil War. Limited geographically to the northern third of the state, the railroads in 1865 were bankrupt and minus both equipment and traffic."[7]

Just 84 miles of new track was installed in Florida during the painful years of Reconstruction. As related in chapter 4, the only event of note—and a scurrilous one at that—was a carpetbag fraud committed against the state involving the securities of the Jacksonville, Pensacola and Mobile Railroad Company.

Not until the 1880s did the clouds finally lift. When the new *era of consolidation and system building* emerged in 1880, only 518 miles of track existed in Florida. But when that propitious decade ended, 2,489 miles could be counted—a 380 percent increase.[8] (Georgia led the South with 4,593 miles.) Several factors fueled the renaissance, such as the resumption of state land grants, an influx of tourists, newcomers, immigrants, and farmers; and the work of several spectacular railway developers.

Among the latter who left an indelible stamp upon the landscape was Colonel William Chipley, a powerful figure of the Louisville and Nashville Railroad; the wealthy English capitalist Sir Edward Reed, who became fond of Florida railway securities; Standard Oil mogul Henry Flagler, whose domain became the east coast of the state; and, Henry Plant, who eventually assembled a vast railroad empire below Charleston, South Carolina.

Florida legislators, unable to say no to any new railway project, chartered a plethora of companies in the 1880s and 1890s. Many were needed and justified, others proved redundant or were a waste of capital, and some—such as the one proposed for the sun-baked island of Sanibel—never saw the light of day. But this expansive mood eventually led to overbuilding, cut-throat competition, and a stream of business failures.

As the nineteenth century closed and a new age began, several big out-of-state systems obtained a toehold in Florida, including the Southern Railway, the Seaboard Air Line Railway, and the mighty Atlantic Coast Line Railroad Company—the latter dominating the state's railway affairs until 1967. There were also constructed in this era many logging railroads, which penetrated Florida's great forests and stands of virgin timber.

America's railroads reached their greatest extent (except in Florida) in 1916, when some 254,000 miles of lines existed. Shortly afterward, the United States entered the First World War, and eventually the nation's railroads were controlled by the federal government. The companies were returned to their stockholders in March 1920, thus beginning a glorious chapter in Florida railroad history. A spectacular land boom gripped most of the state that decade, one of the greatest migration and building episodes in American history. The boom generated a tidal wave of freight and passenger railroad traffic, especially for the state's three largest carriers: the Atlantic Coast Line, Seaboard Air Line, and Florida East Coast Railway.

But, as discussed in chapter 8, the so-called Big Three were caught unprepared for the crush of boom traffic. To increase capacity and gain a competitive edge, each firm undertook a bevy of expansion and improvement initiatives. When the Roaring Twenties finally ended, the railway map of Florida then stood at its all-time greatest extent— nearly 6,000 miles when every track, yard, siding, and leased line was factored. Further, the variety and frequency of railway service to, from, and within the Sunshine State reached an imperial level, never again to be repeated.[9]

On the heels of the boom, there surfaced another new period in state railway history: the *era of decline and competition*. Many American railways failed during the Great Depression because of excessive debt, traffic losses, and archaic government regulations. In 1930, the Seaboard Air Line Railway slipped into receivership as did the Florida East Coast Railway one year later.

Where once railroads thrived with little competition, serious inroads were now being made by automobiles, buses, trucks, refrigerated ships, pipelines, and airplanes. In response, railway officials began slashing expenses, reducing payrolls, eliminating unprofitable or little-used lines, and deferring maintenance. To recapture lost traffic, the Big Three began introducing air-conditioned coaches and new services, and even inaugurated streamlined passenger trains.

A big up-tick in business and profits occurred on Florida's railroads during the Second World War, chiefly because so many military installations had been established here. Further, the submarine menace along the Atlantic seaboard generated many extra carloads of petroleum products, lumber, phosphate, sugar, citrus, and vegetables. But after the hostilities, many of America's railroads did not receive their full share of postwar prosperity because the federal government concentrated on building more improved roads and an interstate highway system. Also, truckers successfully captured much traffic formerly belonging to railroads, while airlines were busy converting railroad commuters along with long-distance travelers.

A turning point came in 1958, when Congress passed legislation that relaxed much burdensome regulation and allowed railroads more latitude in ratemaking. There also began a merger movement within the industry. Of significance to Florida was the announcement that two old rivals, the Seaboard Air Line and Atlantic Coast Line railroads, would merge. The marriage, which was not consummated until 1967, produced the Seaboard Coast Line Railroad, which became the nation's eighth-largest carrier with 9,600 miles of track and twenty-three thousand employees.

The railroad map of Florida definitely shrank between 1950 and 1980 as a result of nonprofitable or little-used lines being abandoned. Downsizing aside, however, many firms began integrating technological improvements like radio communications, mechanized track maintenance equipment, and continuous welded rail. The Big Three also began transporting truck trailers on specially equipped flatcars as well as integrating centralized traffic control, which allowed a train dispatcher to remotely activate switches and signals. Even state-of-the-art data processing equipment was purchased.

One problem that continued to plague America's railroad industry was the forced operation of money-losing passenger trains. This burden, too, was greatly eased in October 1970, when President Nixon signed legislation that established the National Railroad Passenger Corporation (Amtrak). Railroads that joined the new organization paid a hefty entrance fee and were thereafter relieved of operating passenger trains. The Seaboard Coast Line Railroad seized the opportunity, but was immediately contracted by Amtrak to operate the latter's service for Florida. In 1984, Amtrak revived a concept formerly offered by the Auto Train Corporation, a firm that transported automobiles and their owners between Lorton, Virginia, and Sanford, Florida.

Our current *era of megamergers and short lines* took root in 1980, after President Jimmy Carter signed the Staggers Rail Act. This landmark legislation eliminated many regulations of the Interstate Commerce Commission, facilitated merger approvals, and expedited track abandonments or expansions. Railroads were also given considerable freedom in selecting what business they wanted and the ability to adjust rates when necessary. In short, the industry was at last to become "market-driven."[10]

Sixteen days after the Staggers Rail Act became law, the Seaboard Coast Line and Chessie System of railroads merged as the CSX Corporation, creating in the process the biggest railroad system in America, with 27,000 miles of track and seventy thousand employees. Other megamergers followed, some of which affected railway transportation in Florida. In recent years, CSX and other firms have sold or leased "marginally profitable" lines to smaller, more cost-efficient operators called "short-line" railroads. Many currently exist in Florida, and they are discussed in the concluding chapter.

There is already one generation in existence, perhaps more than one, to whom Florida's railroad legacy will come as something of a surprise. Indeed, many young people know nothing about railroads whatsoever or have never seen or ridden on a train. Nevertheless the clarion cry of the locomotive whistle awoke Florida. Energy, enterprise, and progress followed the railroad's course; at every stopping place, new life sprang up. As one historian nostalgically reminds us: "Behind the chuffing locomotives and little wooden cars followed the farmer, the miner, the merchant, the immigrant, and all that adventurous company who laid the rails, filled the empty lands, and made the desert . . . blossom like a garden.[11]

1

A Railway Primer

*Without doubt the greatest factors in Florida's progress
are her Railroads.*

—Governor Edward Perry's message to the legislature, 1887

The labyrinth of railway lines that would one day crisscross Florida were not constructed in one fell swoop, nor were they part of any master plan of development. Rather, the state's railroad network evolved over many long decades, with the system not reaching full maturity until the late 1920s. Practically every firm was a unique and separate enterprise with its own set of founders and corporate goals. Rarely did a single entrepreneur or family own, build, and manage a railroad company; therefore, almost every firm had to rely upon the skills and resources of a great many individuals.

Essential to any project, small or large, were its promoters, that cadre of supporters who were deeply convinced of a company's need or usefulness. Whereas the early railways of Florida required just a few goodwill ambassadors, their numbers increased as projects became larger in scope and crossed county or state lines. Their mission, however, remained unchanged: arousing public interest and cultivating investor support. Often the promoter's work took just days or months to complete, but sometimes a year or more was needed if the endeavor did not meet with immediate public favor or failed to attract a sufficient number of investors.

Specifically, the promoters staged public meetings, delivered speeches, appeared at conventions, addressed boards of trade, circulated petitions, met with politicos, and distributed the ever-important promotional pamphlet. The latter usually contained descriptions of the proposed line and the markets to be served, an estimate of cost, a map, and glowing accounts of how investors might be enriched—provided, of course, all estimates and projections came true, which infrequently happened.[1]

A particularly important goal of the promoters was obtaining the support of newspapers and magazines. Promotional copy was readily furnished to editors, and reporters used it to produce articles friendly to the cause. All manner of stories were prepared—from those based on facts to ones fabricated upon rumor or gossip. Promoters even solicited the support of out-of-state newspapers. One of the earliest such articles appeared in 1836, when a New York City newspaper reported on a proposed railway in the Florida Territory as front-page news.[2] The *American Railroad Journal* also ran stories about the early projects in Florida, as did *Nile's Register*, *DeBow's Commercial Review*, and *Hunt's Merchants Magazine*, though at first they never discussed the intrinsic merits or justifications of a particular endeavor.

On occasion, relationships developed between railroad companies and newspapers, giving rise to the latter being regarded as "pro-railroad." The owners and/or editors of these newspapers often received a complimentary railroad pass. Henry Flagler, who founded the Florida East Coast Railway, understood well the power and influence of the press, and eventually owned—among other newspapers—the powerful *Jacksonville Florida Times-Union*.[3]

Infrequently a paper's loyalty to a specific railroad was put to the test, as happened in Fort Myers in the 1920s. That decade, the Seaboard Air Line Railway built into the city and sought support from the prominent *Fort Myers Press*. That paper, though, had a long-standing relationship with the Seaboard's competitor—the Atlantic Coast Line Railroad—that dated to 1904, when it had brought railway service to the old cattle town. The paper's editor essentially shunned the Seaboard, noting that southwest Florida did not need the services of another trunk-line carrier. This forced Seaboard officials to link arms with the *Fort Myers Tropical News* and the *Fort Myers Daily Palm Leaf*, both of which had far smaller circulations.[4]

While the promoters were busily cultivating interest and investors, the railroad's founders were petitioning the legislature for a charter, which gave a legal life to the enterprise. The application for the charter stated the purpose of the proposed corporation, the public advantages that might accrue from its construction, and the powers desired. The charter itself required the passage of a special legislative act. To expedite the requests, legislators passed a general railroad law in 1848 (modified 1878) that established uniform charter clauses along with room for "a few necessary local provisions."[5] Occasionally a charter might create a multipurpose firm such as the Santa Rosa Railroad, Banking, and Insurance Company, which the General Assembly blessed in 1870. The company's principal objective, however, was to construct a rail line between Milton, Florida, and the Alabama state line.

Numerous rights were conveyed by the charter, together with organizational information. The company's formal name was recited, the names of the incorporators, where the proposed route would be built, the amount of capitalization, and when stock subscription books could be opened. (When closed, the stockholders could elect the directors; the directors, in turn, appointed the officers.) Each company was required to hold an annual meeting, at which time a financial report was to be shared with stockholders. Every corporation was given the right to sue or be sued, and to buy, sell, or mortgage its assets. Some charters contained a monopoly clause, extended a tax-free existence, or specified maximum rates or "tolls" that could be charged for the conveyance of freight or passengers. Several early state charters even stipulated that excess profits were to be paid into the treasury of the Florida Territory, or that body politic might have the right to eventually purchase the railroad.[6]

The most important power conveyed by the charter was the right of eminent domain, or the privilege to take all necessary land needed for the new line. To ensure the just recompense of property owners, each railroad had to establish an impartial tribunal to adjudicate disputes. Land that was not purchased was often freely given to a company so that a railway might pass through a specific community or area. Railway officials were also known to extract "inducements" (cash gifts and free land) from town fathers and municipalities, which also aided location decisions.

With charter in hand, the next step for the directors was raising sufficient capital to construct and equip the new line. By nature, rail-

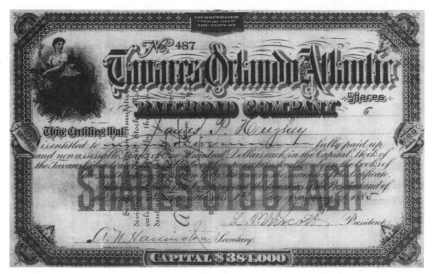

A stock certificate of the Tavares, Orlando and Atlantic Railroad. Stockholders hoped to receive periodic dividends and to have their shares increase in value over time, although this rarely occurred on early Florida railroads. Author's collection.

roads are large and complex enterprises that often required prodigious amounts of capital for their construction. At first, the purchasers of company stock included farmers, merchants, and planters along with banks. Towns, cities, and county governments also acquired shares after the Florida legislature authorized them to do so in 1855. The shares themselves were usually sold on the installment plan, with so much down and the balance due in periodic payments called assessments. Floridians who wished to purchase shares but lacked the cash to do so often supplied a company with a like amount in building supplies or real estate, or they "loaned" their slaves for a specific period during the construction phase of the line.[7]

After local sources for capital were exhausted, railway officials turned to investors and investment houses in northern locales like Boston or Philadelphia—or to those in New York City, where American financial markets were being centralized. Another important source of funds became English and European investors, who began acquiring American railroad securities in the 1850s.[8] Of special significance to Florida were Dutch investors, who eventually obtained important stakes in several railroads.[9]

Although the proceeds from stock sales could "raise up" a corporation and cover the construction costs of a small entity, the financial instrument of choice eventually became bonds. In fact, their popularity became so great that by the 1880s nearly 98 percent of all American railroad projects were funded by this security form.[10] Stockholders, of course, owned the railroad, voted for the directors, received dividends (if the directors declared them), and hopefully saw their shares increase in value. Bondholders, on the other hand, had no vote or say in management. Instead, their reward for essentially loaning money to the corporation was a stream of interest payments and the eventual return of principal. In the process, though, they obtained a proprietary position in the company's capitalization, for bond issues were usually secured with mortgages upon the railroad's assets.[11] As the old maxim goes: "he who finances, controls."

When construction costs were underestimated—as they frequently were—or when it came time to refund a bond issue or to undertake expensive improvements and expansions, a railroad merely floated additional bond issues, creating in the process senior and junior bondholders. Whereas a firm could float an issue on its own, more often than not it used the services of an investment banking house, which, in turn, received attractive fees and commissions. If substantial bond amounts came into play, the lead firm might form a syndicate of underwriting companies that would share in the risk. After all the expenses of a bond issue were paid, what remained was given over to the railroad company.

Practically every Florida railroad eventually issued bonds, and because so many companies experienced financial reversals, the rights of bondholders were tested on more than one occasion. If a company defaulted on paying its bond interest coupon—a clear sign that problems were afoot—the directors almost always first met with the bondholders. If a compromise could not be reached, the firm usually sought court protection. A receivership was established, whereupon the court appointed a receiver or a group of receivers (ideally, experienced businessmen, railroad experts, or company directors) to operate and protect the property while the long-term debt problems were reconciled.[12] During this legal interlude, the railroad was relieved of servicing its bonded debt until a plan of reorganization was approved by the court and creditors.

So as to keep the treasury afloat and the railway operating during the receivership, the court allowed the receivers to issue certificates, which took priority over all other debt including bonds. (Their value was added to the company's total indebtedness.) If the creditors could not agree upon a reorganization plan, then the bondholders could demand that the railway be sold at foreclosure to the highest bidder. As we will see, this often led to the bondholders of old becoming the new owners; or the ailing firm might be moved into bankruptcy court and later sold by its trustees. Proceeds from a foreclosure sale were first applied to the claims of bondholders, then to those of the creditors. Any residual amount was then distributed to the stockholders, who were often wiped out in the process.

Whereas negotiations among bondholder groups, their protection committees, or other interested parties proceeded amicably enough, on occasion fights erupted. This is precisely what happened after the Florida East Coast Railway slipped into receivership in 1931, followed by bankruptcy a decade later. The testamentary trust that owned the railway's stock first advanced millions of dollars to cure bond interest defaults. But when payments ceased, questions arose as to who really owned the company: the stockholders or the bondholders? In time, the dilemma aroused the interest of a powerful and pugnacious Florida businessman by the name of Edward Ball (1888–1981). Ball eventually acquired a majority of certain bonds, waged a bitter and protracted legal battle, and ultimately wrested control of the railway for his employer—the Alfred I. du Pont Testamentary Trust and St. Joe Paper Company.[13]

Once sufficient capital was assured for a project, the directors, in consultation with the chief engineer, began fixing the final route of the railway. This was an especially important decision for the economic fate of communities within the territory to be served hung in the balance. When Florida's first railways were constructed, American civil engineering was still in its infancy. The only real pool of expertise lay with the graduates of the U.S. Military Academy at West Point, who had considerable experience in performing surveys, fixing boundaries, and building fortifications, bridges, and canals. Among those who rendered service in Florida was Lieutenant George Long, who located the Tallahassee Railroad, and Army Captain William Chase, who became president of the Alabama, Florida & Georgia Railroad out of Pensacola. Not only could these officers and their colleagues locate a railway route, but they could also prepare detailed estimates of cost and organize a railroad company along military lines of command—a template that many rail firms follow to this day.

By and large, the engineer's mission was "to reduce his railway as nearly as possible to a level. High ground was to be cut down; embankments were to be raised across the lower lands."[14] The new line also needed to tap as many traffic sources as possible, which meant that several routes had to be surveyed and studied.

No less than twenty possible routes were examined for the Pensacola and Georgia Railroad between Tallahassee and Alligator (Lake City). Edward Cabell, the company's youthful and brilliant president, discussed the advantages of each in the company's 1855 annual report, noting that the very first consideration was the cheapness of construction.

> But it is also quite important to locate the road where it will secure the greatest amount of trade and where it will command stock subscriptions sufficient to build it. We should also endeavor to ascertain whether we can build a road over *any* route, and then whether it will pay after it is built.[15]

Cabell wished his railroad to penetrate a territory having large stands of pine timber (good for future bridges and crossties); to pass through as few swamplands as possible (thus fewer trestles and bridges); and to have land contiguous to the route that was readily adaptable for the production of naval stores, an important traffic commodity. He got his wish.

Since many early Florida railways had to pass through federally owned land, permissions had to be obtained from Congress. Also, projects that crossed the border had to obtain charters from neighboring states. For years, though, no Florida railroad was permitted to enter Georgia or vice versa, for legislators felt that such projects would redirect Florida traffic to Georgia's cities and ports. This prejudice melted during the Civil War, when Confederate military authorities opened the first physical connection from Live Oak northward to Lawton, Georgia, a project that had the support of Robert E. Lee.[16]

After the final route was fixed, the directors hired a contractor and usually held a groundbreaking ceremony. But since so few persons in the South had railroad construction experience, the early contracts in Florida were most often handed to wealthy planters, politicos, or successful merchants who lived along the route. They, in turn, engaged subcontractors who would actually perform the details. The aforementioned Pensacola and Georgia Railroad favored planters and worked around their busy planting schedules. "Should the contract be delayed till after the first of January next, the planters of the country, who we expect will be our contractors, will have made their arrangements for the next year, and can not devote their labor to building our road, as we now hope they will."[17]

A perpetual problem was finding and retaining a sufficiently large labor force. Most construction "gangs" on early Florida projects were comprised of African American workers—usually slaves—who ably performed their tasks with basic hand tools together with mule- or ox-drawn carts and wagons. As noted previously, some had been "loaned" by their masters in exchange for stock shares. Occasionally out-of-state or foreign workers were recruited. Dutch laborers, for example, were engaged for the first railway project out of Pensacola; they demanded two free glasses of beer each working day.[18] A large contingent of Irish, Italian, and Greek laborers, who toiled twelve-hour days for one dollar per hour, helped build the Charlotte Harbor & Northern Railroad between Arcadia and South Boca Grande.[19] An even greater melting pot of workers, from Norway, Sweden, Greece, Spain and the Caribbean, labored on the fabled Key West Extension of the Florida East Coast Railway.

Subcontractors oversaw the grubbing out and grading of the line; the fabrication of trestles, bridges, and culverts; and the installation of crossties and rails. By the 1850s, general contractors were available who could build an entire railroad, recruit all necessary labor, and secure the locomotives and rolling stock. "They did all this for a flat fee," notes one historian, "either on a per-mile or total cost basis, receiving at least part of their payment in railroad stocks or bonds."[20] In this way, a contractor often obtained a financial stake in a new company.

African American workers toiled on many early Florida railroad projects. Some were slaves; others were "free" laborers. This undated scene was snapped somewhere in the Panhandle. State Archives of Florida.

Every infant railway in Florida was built with iron strap rails; that is, longitudinal wooden timbers upon which were nailed iron strap tops. Later, rails made completely of iron appeared. The iron mills of England and Wales supplied most of the requirements, along with spikes, connecting bars, and plates. Their American agents facilitated the purchases, such as Vose, Livingston & Company in New York City, which brokered the iron rails for the cross-state Florida Railroad between Fernandina and Cedar Key. Francis Vose was chiefly paid with Florida Railroad company bonds, whose interest was guaranteed by the state. But when the company defaulted during the Civil War and skipped its interest coupons, Vose sued for restitution. The ensuing litigation hamstrung the Internal Improvement Fund (which guaranteed the interest) for years until a settlement was reached with Vose's heirs.[21]

Iron rails were shipped from abroad in large sailing ships, then offloaded at Florida ports. Rails bound for the aforementioned Florida

Railroad arrived at both Fernandina and Cedar Key, while those for the Florida Southern Railway were brought up the St. Johns River in schooners and unloaded at the railroad's dock in Palatka. The rails were then neatly arranged on flatcars and dispatched to construction sites in so-called work trains.

Though economical to procure, strap rail had one major drawback: the ends often became loose and curled up under the weight of passing trains to form snakeheads, "which often broke through the floor of a passing coach."[22] Solid iron rails, which were not produced in America until the 1850s, could also exhibit deficiencies: they could become brittle with age; ones of inferior quality wore out rapidly, and overweight locomotives could actually crush them. These annoyances vanished when rails made entirely of steel were first imported in 1863. The superiority of such was quickly established, and by 1880 the American steel industry—using a process pioneered by Henry Bessemer that made their production direct and fast from pig iron—was flourishing with orders.[23]

One decision that occasionally perplexed directors was what gauge of track to use for their new line; that is, the distance between the two rails. No fewer than eleven different gauges existed on northern railroads in the nineteenth century, the most prevalent being the standard gauge measurement of 4 feet, 8 ½ inches. Less popular was narrow gauge track, which usually measured 3 feet between the rails. Advocates of narrow gauge proclaimed that their lines were cheaper to build, equip, and maintain. Further, narrow gauge cars and locomotives were usually physically smaller than their standard gauge counterparts, sometimes almost toylike in appearance. (The Disney World theme park in Orlando operates a narrow gauge railroad.)

Southern railroads, too, were bedeviled with gauge differences. Several early lines in Virginia had adopted standard gauge from the outset, as did some firms in North Carolina. However, the broad gauge measurement of 5 feet between the rails proved most popular because the first railway in the American South—Charleston to Hamburg, South Carolina—selected it. Thus, broad gauge track was widely used in Florida. This is not to say that narrow gauge lines were never built here, for indeed many were. Further, the tiny St. Johns Railroad (St. Augustine to Tocoi Landing on the St. Johns River) is thought to have been first constructed with standard gauge track, while the Pensacola & Perdido Railroad (Pensacola to Millview) employed the very rare 6-foot gauge.[24]

Complications naturally arose when railroads of differing gauges met one another and attempted to exchange cars. One solution—also the most time-consuming—was to physically unload each freight car and transfer the contents to one of the firm being met. The more popular technique was to shuttle cars of one gauge onto a special side track, raise up the car ends with a hoist (one end at a time), and swap the wheel sets for those of another gauge. After the conversion took place, the journey resumed. This particular maneuver was performed at several points in Florida such as at Gainesville, where the broad gauge Savannah, Florida & Western met the narrow gauge Florida Southern Railway, and at Sanford, where the broad gauge Jacksonville, Tampa & Key West met the narrow gauge South Florida Railroad. The swapping-out technique could also be applied to passenger cars, but where this was not practicable, patrons had to exit the cars of one train and board those of the opposite firm.

These awkward maneuvers practically vanished in 1886, when almost every southern railroad shifted its broad or narrow gauge track to that of standard gauge. Some 13,000 miles of lines were converted over the course of two days.[25] The Pensacola and Atlantic Railroad (owned by the Louisville and Nashville) and the sprawling Florida Railway and Navigation Company performed the changeover on 31 May, while most all other carriers did so the following day. The cost was estimated at $150 per mile.[26] Those lines owned by Henry Flagler (on the east coast of the state) were not converted until the following year, while several lines of the Plant System did not undergo the transformation until even later. Regardless of when it was undertaken, the conversion greatly facilitated the running of through trains from northern and midwestern cities to the interior of Florida.

With construction advancing, the railroad's board began purchasing its first roster of locomotives and cars. Although many early American railways acquired steam engines from abroad, those in Florida bought them from domestic builders such as Mathias Baldwin in Philadelphia. They were, of course, primitive machines, and most had no cab for the engineer, for "if stage coach drivers could endure the elements, so could engine drivers." In time, though, the locomotives sported an enclosed

THE SOUTH "ADJUSTS" AND "STANDARDIZES." ADOP-
TION OF NORTHERN RAILROAD GAUGE. From *Harper's
Weekly*, XXX (1886), 364.

Most southern railroads adopted standard gauge track in 1886, which allowed for the
efficient exchange of cars and the running of through trains from the North and West.
Some Florida carriers, though, delayed the conversion. Author's collection.

cab for the engineer and fireman, along with a bell, headlight, sandbox, and a functional cowcatcher.

For decades, the locomotive purchase of choice was the "American Standard" type, which had a swiveling front truck (or bogie) comprised of two axles that eased the engine around tight curves; two axles of large driving wheels that furnished the actual pulling power; and no trailing truck of smaller wheels under the locomotive cab. Hence they had a 4–4–0 wheel arrangement. Almost all burned pine wood, each retailed for about $8,000, and many were named after some dignitary, place, or object.[27] Their big balloon smokestacks contained a screen-like spark arrester, though occasionally a hot ember would escape and ignite the clothes of a passenger or cause a trackside fire.

Other popular locomotive designs included the Atlantic class (4–4–2 wheel arrangement), the Mogul (2–6–0), Ten-Wheelers (4–6–0), the versatile Pacific (4–6–2), and the workhorse Consolidation (2–8–0). Certain models were conceived to swiftly haul short trains; others were purposely built to haul heavy long trains at slow speeds. The tractive effort (or pulling power) of a locomotive was determined by many factors, including boiler size, grate area, number and length of boiler tubes, cylinder size, and the stroke of pistons. The bigger the locomotive design, the heavier it became.

As the demand for locomotives increased in America, so did the number of builders. Among the firms that fulfilled orders for Florida railways were Mason of Taunton, Massachusetts; Hinkley of Boston; the Rhode Island Locomotive Works; Rogers, Ketchum & Grosvenor in New Jersey; and the Brooks firm, Grant, Richmond, Norris, and Cooke.[28] (Most joined hands in 1901 to form the American Locomotive Company, or ALCO.) Practically every builder integrated some improvement or advancement to the science and art. Some firms even produced ingenious geared locomotives for logging railroads, of which Florida had many.

Passenger and freight cars were either purchased from out-of-state builders or produced locally in company shops. The first passenger coaches in Florida were really flatcars upon which were fastened wooden benches. A canvas or wooden top (supported by poles) shielded passengers from the torrid sun and downpours. Later, companies selected

Engine No. 46 of the Florida Railway & Navigation Company was built by Rogers in 1885. It had a 4–4–0 wheel arrangement. The so-called American Standard–type locomotive was one of the most popular designs ever conceived. State Archives of Florida.

"long cars" that had a center aisle, reversible wood seats, and room for perhaps sixty persons. Some sported a ventilation stack, toilet, kerosene lights, and a stove. They were connected to one another, as were freight cars, with chains or with dangerous link and pin couplings.

For decades, African American passengers in the South were forced to ride in Jim Crow cars, baggage cars, or coaches labeled "For Colored Only." Northern newspapers greatly deplored this discriminatory practice, which, sadly, continued long after the Civil War. Among those publications that ran stories about the abuses was the *New York Times*, which, on 30 March 1882, reported that a certain Florida railroad had badly mistreated the Reverend Dr. D. A. Payne, who had purchased a first-class ticket and seated himself next to a white clergyman. When Payne refused to give up his seat and ride in the Jim Crow car, the conductor halted the train and physically ejected the college president, who was also a senior bishop of the African Methodist Episcopal Church. The distinguished personage, seventy-one years of age, was compelled to walk for 5 miles, with luggage in hand, back to Jacksonville.

Early train travel had both its advocates and critics. But one class of traveler who often found it vulgar and the social intercourse dreadful were "persons of refinement." The observations of one party has become a classic:

Two poor fellows, who were not much in the habit of making their toilet, squeezed me into a corner, while the hot sun drew from their garments a villainous compound of smells made up of salted fish, tar, and molasses. By and by twelve bouncing working-girls were introduced. "Make room for the ladies!" bawled the conductor. The whole twelve soon made themselves at home sucking lemons and eating green apples. There is certainly a growing neglect of manners! The rich and the poor, the educated and the ignorant, the polite and the vulgar, all herd together in this modern improvement in traveling. Talk of ladies on board a railroad car! There are none. I never feel like a gentleman there, and I cannot perceive a semblance of gentility in any one who makes part of the traveling mob.[29]

A new generation of passenger cars emerged after Reconstruction that were fitted out with large plate-glass windows, hand-carved woodwork, upholstered swivel seats, silk curtains, carpeting, and even silver-plated spittoons. Many were equipped with the Pintsch system of gaslight and safe Westinghouse air brakes.

Two such cars were built in the 1880s for the Jacksonville, Tampa & Key West Railway by the Wason Car Works of Springfield, Massachusetts. Named Palatka and Sanford respectively, their sumptuous interiors featured inlaid cherry woods and Axminster carpets from England, and showcased elegant china and glassware. The most famous builder of all, though, was Pullman of Illinois, whose palace, parlor, and sleeping cars became the industry standard. Often the firm supplied Gilded Age magnates and "captains of industry" with their own private Pullman car; they could often be seen parked on sidings at posh Florida resorts like Palm Beach or at the Belleview Hotel near Clearwater.

Before dining cars appeared on long-distance Florida trains, meal stops were made at stations. Less than thirty minutes were allocated for this purpose, and upon the station platform locals often hawked trinkets and take-away snacks. A passenger traversing the Florida Railroad in 1881 noted that after the towns of Highland, Lawty, and Temples were passed, "the brakeman called out 'Starke, twenty minutes for dinner,' and alighting from the train we proceeded to the Railroad House, kept by Mr. Kleinsmidt. When you go to Starke, do not fail to go to the Railroad House!" Later, on the same trip, the train halted at Otter Creek for another meal, "and what a supper we had!"[30]

Freight cars, too, underwent an evolutionary process. Almost every Florida railway began operations with a mixture of boxcars and flatcars, the former having a capacity of 8 tons by the 1850s. After being introduced, ventilated boxcars were used to convey citrus and vegetables. Salted meats, freshly caught fish, and oysters were packed in kegs and wooden barrels (with ice) and sent to northern markets inside insulated boxcars. Livestock or cattle cars appeared in the 1870s. In the following decade, all-metal hopper cars became available for commodities like coal. Tank cars appeared about the same time; their distinctive "domes" allowing the gas or liquid contents inside to freely expand.

As construction neared completion, the railroad hired its first group of employees, who hopefully became competent and responsible workers. Few applicants, though, had direct railroad experience when Florida railroading commenced, thus firms had to furnish much on-the-job training and offer apprenticeships. New hires with a mechanical aptitude, machine experience, or a background in transportation (stage coaching, the maritime, express package business, etc.) often received preferential consideration. Consistent with southern practice, African American workers had to accept the lowliest, dirtiest, and lowest-paying positions.

Most early railroad companies of the state had just two major departments: operations and finance. (Traffic divisions were added in the 1870s.) Heading the operations side was the company superintendent, and among those reporting to his office—women are never mentioned—were train crews, the chief mechanic, and the road master. Workers under the chief mechanic included shop foremen, mechanics, and tradespeople like carpenters and machinists. It was the road master's responsibility to maintain the physical route of the railway and keep it in a safe condition. This he achieved by assigning a specific portion of the line to a section foreman who, in turn, oversaw a small gang of track laborers. Periodic inspections were made of the route using a hand-pumped car or pedal-operated velocipede.

Because railways paid reasonable wages and did not usually incur shutdowns, employees often remained with a company for their entire working career. (Their offspring would often follow suit.) In time, the more important trades and crafts were represented by unions—the first organized being the Brotherhood of Locomotive Engineers, which was established in 1863. By and large, the rail unions began as fraternal organizations that emphasized sobriety, family, safety, and work ethics. They also offered members low-cost life insurance, which was otherwise difficult to obtain owing to occupational hazards.

Several early Florida railroads owned slaves or hired "free" African American workers.[31] Precise information as to how they were treated as employees is scarce, but it is known that those who behaved badly on the Pensacola and Georgia Railroad were severely punished, as Rule No. 11 of the company's 1858 rulebook confirms:

> Overseers must not strike a Negro with any other weapon than a switch, except in defense of their person. When a Negro requires correction his hands must be tied by the overseer; and he will whip him with an ordinary switch or leather strap not exceeding thirty-nine lashes at one time, nor more than sixty in one day, or for one offense, unless ordered to do so by the supervisor and in his presence.[32]

The railroad's finances were overseen by the company treasurer, whose staff included bookkeepers, auditors, and clerks. The department collected financial data from all others within the firm, whereupon the information was posted to the accounting records and tabulated. The treasurer's reports, in turn, were given to the president, who shared them with the directors and stockholders. Although strategic financial decisions were made by the directors, the treasurer kept a close eye on the company's cash position, assuring that sufficient funds were on hand to pay daily expenses, payrolls, and debt obligations.

The culminating event for any new railroad was the grand opening ceremony. Usually a free excursion was offered to the public over the new route, with celebrants being treated to a picnic or barbecue. At such occasions, railway officials and politicos made speeches; sometimes band music was enjoyed. All this occurred when the South Florida Railroad first opened between Sanford and Orlando in 1880. In fact, the inaugural train even featured a flatcar replete with cannon, which was intermittently fired as the overloaded consist rolled through the countryside. About ten thousand people celebrated the arrival of the first passenger train at Key West in 1912. Later, in 1927, the Seaboard Air Line Railway spared no expense in opening its extensions to Naples and Miami. The company assembled five completely separate sections of its famed Orange Blossom Special passenger train and transported over seven hundred guests and dignitaries from eighteen states and ninety cities—a great celebration in American railway history that lasted nearly a week!

Once opened, the new company got down to the business of making money. Trains began operating on a regular basis according to a published timetable. Most firms initiated service with two daily trains: one in each direction using the same crew, cars, and locomotive. Additional trains were added as business dictated. To save money, some—called "mixed trains"—were assembled with both freight and passenger cars. (Speed was not one of their attributes!) Local trains would stop at every station in search of traffic, while limited or express trains halted only at important settings. Additional revenues were earned by transporting express packages, mail, or running excursions.

The serious money in railroad transportation was made in freight, not passengers. Among the commodities that the early railroads of Florida hauled were lumber, minerals, merchandise, fish, agricultural products, and citrus. Initially the companies set their own rates and tariffs to whatever the market could bear. This authority, though, led to abuses. For example, to the dismay of Florida farmers and growers, the carriers often raised rates just before crops went to market. These and other indiscretions, like the distribution of free passes and rebates to select customers, prompted the establishment of a state railroad commission in 1887. Most of the commission's efforts were directed to establishing "fair and reasonable" rates.

Passengers wanting to ride a train had only to purchase a ticket. The station agent or train conductor then forwarded the fares, and an accounting record, to the treasurer's office. Freight shipments, though, required a "bill of lading," which established a legally binding contract between the railroad and shipper. The document recited all the pertinent information about the article being shipped, including the shipper's name (the consignor) and that of the recipient (consignee). Shipping costs were either paid in advance by the consignor or by the consignee when the goods arrived at the destination. Both parties had a limited time window to load or unload the freight car before penalties (demurrage charges) would apply. Information about the shipment was also summarized on the "waybill," which traveled with every train conductor who became involved with the shipment. Each company would apply special stamps to the waybill, thereby documenting its role in the shipment and eligibility for compensation.[33]

At times, the railroad workplace could be dangerous. This prompted officials to prepare and issue a company rule book, whose cardinal theme was safety. Certain workers, such as train crew members and train dispatchers, had to pass written examinations about the rules before being employed. Employees who violated the rules were either disciplined or discharged. One of the more famous dictums was so-called Rule G (still in force today), which forbade employees to use alcoholic beverages while on duty or report for work inebriated.

Numerous safety appliances and inventions were adopted by railroads in the nineteenth century. The Miller platform, for example, raised the floors of adjoining railway cars to the same level; enclosed vestibules shielded passengers from the elements while moving between passenger cars; the Janney knuckle coupler eliminated dangerous link-and-pin connections; while the safe Westinghouse automatic braking system piped compressed air to cylinders mounted on each car. The telegraph, which greatly aided train dispatching and messaging, became practical in 1847 but oddly enough was only slowly adopted. By 1880, however, some 31 million messages were being sent over 291,000 miles of Western Union wires.[34] Later the telephone appeared, though for years it was used for local calls only. Not until the 1890s did long-distance capabilities truly benefit the railroad industry.

One of the most conspicuous fixtures of railroading, which graced practically every Florida town and city, was the depot or station. It was here that passengers came and went along with freight, baggage, express packages, and mail. The structures themselves varied greatly in design, though most were constructed of wood, brick, or concrete block sheathed in stucco. Their interiors often sported a ticket window, big wooden benches, a cast-iron stove, separate restrooms for the races, a large ticking wall clock, a train arrival and departure board, and possibly a lunch counter. Busy settings also received a freight house, replete with loading platform. Localities served by more than one carrier fre-

The Mediterranean Revival station at Homestead was one of many that the Seaboard Air Line Railway erected in the 1920s and 1930s. By permission of the Atlantic Coast Line and Seaboard Air Line Railroads Historical Society.

quently had several stations, or the various companies might share a common facility. If the setting was a railroad divisional point, then a switching yard might be in evidence as well as shops and a locomotive roundhouse and turntable.

Florida's two greatest terminal buildings were situated at Tampa and Jacksonville. The former, built of brick and stone in the Beaux-Arts style, opened in 1912. Over the decades it fell into disuse, and in 1991 a nonprofit group purchased the property and performed a noteworthy restoration. Amtrak trains today utilize the facility. The magisterial edifice at Jacksonville, which opened in 1919, was also conceived in the Beaux-Arts style. The building closed in 1974, the facility received a complete renovation, and it reopened as the Prime F. Osborn III Convention Center.

As noted, the task of organizing, financing, building, equipping, and operating a railroad was a complex undertaking in the nineteenth century, one that involved persons of vision, large sums of capital, and the expertise and skills of many individuals. We now turn to that first clutch of railroads that were built in Florida during the long-ago territorial era.

2

Panhandle Pioneers

Florida was ceded to the United States by Spain in 1822. Enormous tracts of this spread-out state, in whose warm climate sugar cane and indigo thrive in addition to cotton, remain uncultivated and uninhabited. One is all the more astounded to find railroads actually in operation here, using steam power to transport passengers and freight.

—Gerstner, *Early American Railroads*

The curtain went up on Florida railroad history in the 1830s. Andrew Jackson—no stranger to the "land of flowers"—occupied the White House when the decade began. In fact, Old Hickory was the first American president to actually ride on a train, this on the Baltimore & Ohio Railroad in 1833. "Jacksonian democracy" greatly favored internal improvements like railroads along with the right of American states to charter and aid them. But in no way, according to party philosophy, should the "federal government be found messing into them or sharing the expected profits."[1]

Martin Van Buren, Jackson's able secretary of state, ascended to the presidency in 1836. Possibly the New Yorker was acquainted with the infant railways of Florida. He certainly became acquainted with financial panics, for the one that gripped America the following year crippled the country, shuttered 90 percent of the nation's factories, and brought many railway companies, including those in Florida, to their knees. The "Little Magician" failed to repair either the nation's economy or its banking system, and thus voters did not return him to office.

Four separate governors would come to rule the Florida Territory in the 1830s. William Duval, who had been appointed by President Mon-

roe in 1822, remained in office until 1834. Among other accomplish-
ments, he helped establish a capital at Tallahassee that, in the 1830s,
was still "situated in the middle of a primeval forest with only 1,500
inhabitatants."[2] The lawyer John Eaton, Old Hickory's secretary of war,
succeeded Duval. Then, in 1836, General Richard Keith Call, Jackson's
former aide-de-camp and protégé, took the reins. Call served for three
years, whereupon Van Buren appointed lawyer Robert Reid.[3] Although
each governor perceived railroads somewhat differently, Call became so
enamored of them that he actually ended up owning one.

Throughout the 1830s, Floridians yearned for more transportation
resources, just as they had in the 1820s. But funding internal improvements in such a vast landscape with so few people often proved impossible to accomplish. Thus, the economy grew ever so slowly. As one
historian lamented, "The peninsula of Florida, afflicted with a barren
soil and leading no-whither, is negligible as part of the Economic South.
It is more to be noted perhaps as an obstacle in the coasting trade than
as an economic province."[4]

Upon the territory's eastern coastline were then situated the infant
but growing ports of Fernandina and Jacksonville, from which ships
usually arrived and departed via the Atlantic sea lanes. Farther south
sat the old Spanish city of St. Augustine, which was now alive with citrus production and "strangers" (visitors). Below the peninsula's southern tip lay the thriving island city of Key West, many of whose residents
had grown rich by salvaging wrecked ships. The preeminent port upon
the gulf was Pensacola, whose economy turned on the navy and lumber.
"King Cotton," in turn, drove Apalachicola and its smaller sister, St.
Marks. Less important coastal points were defended by military forts,
while much of the interior of south Florida, an unspoiled wilderness,
was chiefly occupied by Native Americans.

The federal government had sold or granted about 1.5 million acres in
the Florida Territory when the 1830s commenced, this "from a public domain of thirty-five and a half million acres."[5] "Middle Florida" was then
a commercial epicenter, a rich and influential region that lay between
the Georgia border and the gulf, from the Suwannee to the Apalachicola
rivers. Within a few decades, no other area of the South could boast of
finer plantations, so many luxurious homes, or a more prosperous and
contented people. The counties of Leon, Jefferson, Madison, and Gads-

den possessed "almost 50 per cent of the total population of Florida, while Leon County alone rated 10,031 persons."[6] Cotton thrived here, as did produce, tobacco, forest products, and sugar cane. Small wonder that within this bastion of wealth and enterprise, which author Clifton Paisley affectionately calls the "Red Hills of Florida," the first railroads were projected.[7]

Before the iron horse, cotton bales were brought to Tallahassee from the surrounding region and southern Georgia, and conveyed to the port of St. Marks in wagon trains. The journey proceeded at a magisterial pace, for often the big wagon wheels would sink into the deep sandy soil. At St. Marks, the compressed bales were off-loaded and placed aboard shallow-draft vessels that could negotiate the trip down the picturesque St. Marks River. Once clear of its sandbar, they were again off-loaded and stacked into oceangoing ships that sailed for domestic and foreign markets.

Expediting the land portion of the journey played on the minds of certain visionaries who, on 6 January 1831, gathered at the Planter's Hotel in Tallahassee to discuss the practicability of building a "rail-way" between the capital and St. Marks. William Williams was called to the chair, whereupon each of the attendees spoke their minds.[8] Six days later, another convocation took place. It was then learned that the elevation between the two termini did not exceed 180 feet, which the promoters believed to be "a much smaller inclination than on any railroad in this country or in England." According to a local newspaper, the probable cost of constructing such a project with iron strap rails would amount to $3,000 per mile. "If a good charter is obtained from the legislative council, now in session, the stock would be taken and the road could be constructed in a reasonable time."[9] A draft of one was then read, adopted, and subsequently handed to legislators.

The legislative council, which was comprised of the governor and "thirteen of the most discreet persons of the Territory," deliberated little over the application, and on 9 February it issued the first railroad charter in Florida history. Among the incorporators of the Leon Rail-Way Company were Henry Bond, Robert Wellford, Robert Williams, Isham Searcy, John Garey, and Thomas Brown.[10] Two days later, though, Governor Duval vetoed the act because the "letters patent" conveyed a twenty-year monopoly. The matter was reconsidered by the council, and Duval's veto was overridden.

Although the charter did not specify the actual amount of capitalization, it was "never to exceed the amount necessary to complete and continue the company's objectives."[11] The document further stipulated that no more than 12.5 cents could be charged for every 100 pounds of freight the railway conveyed. Also, dividends in excess of 12.5 percent of the stock were to be paid into the territorial treasury. Work had to commence on the Leon Rail-Way within two years and be completed in five; otherwise, the charter would be forfeited.

For whatever reasons, the Leon Rail-*Way* Company was never organized. In its place, there later arose the Leon Rail-*Road* Company without a monopoly clause, an act that Governor Duval quickly approved. The amount of capitalization was now specified ($100,000), and the incorporation of the new firm could commence after $25,000 of stock had been subscribed. But not even this sum could be raised, and, once again, the charter lapsed.

New promoters became identified with the project in 1833, among them the wealthy planter Benjamin Chaires, reputedly the territory's first millionaire. A new promotional tact was even tried: stock was sold without a charter in hand, although subscribers were told that one would be obtained at the next council session. It was, and, on 10 February 1834, the Tallahassee Rail Road Company came alive with a capitalization of $100,000 with rights to double same.[12] Further, the new company could be organized as soon as $60,000 in stock was subscribed. Permission was also given to bridge the St. Marks River. Lastly, there were no restrictions on "tolls" or tariffs the company could charge, and all company profits were to be free of taxes.

Practically every Tallahassean of importance purchased stock in the new company, and by 30 June the requisite sum to organize had been subscribed. The initial issue of one thousand shares of stock was purchased by 110 persons. General Richard Keith Call (1792–1862), a prominent Tallahassee planter, investor, and politician, became president.[13] In fact, Call became the railroad's principal stockholder, retaining control until the Pensacola and Georgia Railroad acquired his shares in 1855.

General Richard Keith Call once owned the Tallahassee Railroad. The former governor of Florida sold the cotton carrier in 1855 to the Pensacola and Georgia Railroad. State Archives of Florida.

Lieutenant George Long, an 1824 graduate of the U.S. Military Academy, was hired by Call and the directors to survey the new line. Long's railroad background was extensive, and after his stint in Tallahassee he became the chief engineer of Louisiana, located the Alton & Mt. Carmel Railroad in Illinois, and later supervised the construction of the marine hospitals in Natchez and Paducah.[14]

Because the proposed railway penetrated lands owned by the federal government, Call sent a "memorial" (or petition) to Congress in December 1834, requesting a 200-foot-wide right-of-way through the property and 100 acres of land at St. Marks for terminal facilities.[15] The Congress, however, granted just a 60-foot easement through its parcels along with 10 acres at the confluence of the St. Marks and Wakulla rivers. Why Washington politicos granted such a stingy appropriation has yet to surface.

According to the *Tallahassee Floridian* of 1 August 1835, the directors hired several dozen laborers to initiate construction on the line. But when the going proved slow, a contract was executed in May 1835 with John and William Gray, railroad contractors of Columbia, South Carolina. Previously, the brothers had built a portion of the first railroad in the American South (between Charleston, South Carolina, and Hamburg) and were currently constructing another Florida railway between St. Joseph and Lake Wimico, whose story will be taken up shortly. The Tallahassee contract with the Grays amounted to $102,000.[16]

That fall, the Gray brothers began advertising for five hundred laborers and two hundred carpenters—the former to be paid twenty to thirty dollars a month, the latter thirty-five to fifty dollars. But the quality of their work ultimately proved unacceptable to the directors, who sued the South Carolinians in Leon County circuit court for $50,000. The suit was later tossed out because it had been imprecisely written.[17]

How, then, was the Tallahassee Railroad finally constructed and operated? Fortunately a most descriptive account was set down by an astute visitor in the spring of 1839. Franz Anton Ritter von Gerstner, Europe's leading authority on railroads, had come to the United States at the behest of the Russian government to investigate American railroads and to compile an encyclopedic work about their construction, equipment, finances, and operations. Only in recent years has an English translation of Gerstner's monumental work—some nine hundred pages long—been published. The work contains invaluable data about Florida's infant carriers and those of other states as well.[18]

Gerstner informs us that the Tallahassee Railroad was built across a very flat terrain that was largely covered with forests. Embankments of the rail line measured 8 feet high in places; cuts were 10 feet wide. He notes that there were drainage issues right from the outset: "When it rains, the earth beneath the track timbers is washed away and the track is thereby displaced. Thus, the road is continually in poor condition and expensive to maintain."[19]

According to Gerstner, the track structure of the Tallahassee Railroad duplicated that which was often used in Virginia. Crossties, upon which the rails rested, were dimensioned on two sides. Each measured 8 feet in width, and was placed on the ground every 6 to 7 feet. (Today's crossties are usually spaced 33 inches apart.) The rails themselves were fashioned of solid wood; each measured 6" x 9" x 8' in length. They were anchored to the crossties using wedges. Atop each wooden rail were nailed iron straps (2.25" wide x .5" thick). The gauge of track, or the distance between the rails, was 5 feet.

Exactly when the Tallahassee Railroad fully opened has been a matter of conjecture. Gerstner states that the 22-mile route commenced operations in 1836, though many sources cite 1837. Two years later, in 1839, the track was extended for an additional 2 miles so as to reach the railroad-owned town of Port Leon. (This necessitated a $30,000 lattice drawbridge to be erected over the St. Marks River.) Station buildings stood at Tallahassee and St. Marks. About halfway along the route, the company constructed a steam sawmill to cut its own track timbers and to provide construction lumber for Port Leon.

At the time of Gerstner's visit, the railroad owned two steam locomotives, built "in New Castle, Delaware," that were not being used owing to the poor condition of the track. Instead, mules and horses pulled the trains. The firm also possessed three passenger coaches, forty-five freight cars ("some with roofs but all with four wheels"), and thirty-five horses and mules. Other assets included a 1,000-acre plantation on which the "primary crop is Indian corn needed for feeding the horses and mules." Gerstner was also told that the railroad owned twenty-three slaves (some worked on the railroad, others on the plantation) along with 4,000 acres of woodlands near the steam sawmill, and a large parcel of land on the Wakulla River where the town of Port Leon was being developed.[20]

The railway's manager disclosed to the visiting engineer that the railroad line itself, the depots, and all the freight and passenger cars were acquired for $107,000. Other acquisitions, along with the steam sawmill, raised this figure to $150,000. When the line was fully completed to Port Leon, the entire cost of the Tallahassee Railroad amounted to $180,000 (2006 dollars: $3,287,391).

Each day a single passenger coach, drawn by two horses, departs from Tallahassee and from St. Mark's. The trip lasts 2-½ hours, and therefore the rate of speed is 9 miles per hour. Freight transport is done in such a way that 2 trains are always dispatched at the same time. Each of these consists of 5 to 8 cars that are coupled together and drawn by 6 horses or mules at 2-½ miles per hour. In every case the horses are changed halfway through the trip.[21]

When the Tallahassee Railroad lacked money, it issued its own currency—called scrip. The bills could not be redeemed for cash, but they could be used to defray transportation costs over the railroad. Author's collection.

A passenger ticket over the Tallahassee Railroad cost $1.50 in 1838, while a bale of cotton (400–500 pounds) was conveyed for seventy-five cents. Passenger fares therefore mounted to seven cents per mile, while freight rates were twenty-three cents per mile. In 1838, the carrier transported four thousand passengers and 8,000 tons of freight. The largest commodity transported was cotton—some 14,000 bales that year. About 5,000 tons of merchandise "went up" to Tallahassee and the southern portions of Georgia from St. Marks. Revenues for 1838 amounted to $43,795. Of that figure, $34,375 was derived from freight, $5,993 from passengers, and $3,427 from warehousing charges.[22]

Gerstner was also told that the railroad made no particular accounting of operating expenses because "the company owns its own Negroes who work on the line. It also owns forests in which it cuts down the timber used in repairing the track, and it saws the same in its own mill. And last, it owns the plantation on which it cultivates feed for its horses, and so on." However, the manager did mention that monthly outlays came to $2,000, or $24,000 a year. When the visiting engineer subtracted that amount from the earnings of 1838, he determined that a net income of $19,795 resulted, or 13.2 percent of the railroad's cost ($150,000). At this interval, the railroad was owned by "five or so stockholders," all of whom "greatly value the worth of their enterprise and are unwilling to sell their shares even at 50% above par."[23]

Another notable who observed the Tallahassee Railroad up close was the French naturalist and scientific traveler Francois Louis de la

In this 1885 scene, a passenger train is about to depart St. Marks for the capital. The dock below the storage building allowed trains to meet vessels. Alvah Harper Collection, State Archives of Florida.

Porte—the Comte de Castlenau (1810–1880). The count, who toured North America between 1837 and 1841, spent a goodly amount of time in middle Florida and prepared eleven lithographs, including one of the railroad station at Tallahassee, a building with the appearance of a barn. His famous "Essay on Middle Florida" includes a description of the railroad, which he declared to be "the very worst that has yet been built in the entire world."[24]

A devastating hurricane visited Port Leon in 1843, which destroyed the company town and carried the railway's drawbridge right up the St. Marks River. Immediately, the southern terminus of the company was changed back to St. Marks. The company town of Port Leon then began to slip into obscurity.

As noted, General Call sold his majority shares to the Pensacola and Georgia Railroad in 1855. Later, the former Tallahassee Railroad passed through a series of mergers and consolidations, eventually being acquired by the Seaboard Air Line Railway in 1899. As the railway network of Florida grew and new commercial centers opened, the importance of St. Marks gradually declined. In 1931, the Seaboard petitioned the Interstate Commerce Commission to abandon the historic line.[25]

However, the axe did not immediately fall, and parts of the route lingered into the late 1960s. Finally, in 1984, the Florida Department of Transportation purchased the abandoned right-of-way, whereupon private citizenry organized the "Tallahassee–St. Marks Rails-to-Trails Coalition." Two years later, the state passed a resolution to convert the line into Florida's first rail-trail. In 1988, the historic thoroughfare officially opened, and ever since the old rail route has been a boon to walkers, bicyclers, joggers, skaters, and horseback riders.

Our survey of territorial railroads shifts now to St. Joseph Bay, near Port St. Joe, and to the old ghost town of St. Joseph. This once-thriving setting owed its brief existence to a bitter land dispute.[26]

Before the Florida Territory had been established, the Spanish government had granted a company of traders a huge tract of land (1.25 million acres) that included the settlement of Apalachicola and the surrounding area. After the cession of Florida to the United States, the validity of the so-called Forbes Grant was legally challenged. The U.S. Supreme Court eventually took the case, ruled for the trading company, and in doing so made squatters out of many persons who held property in "Old Apalach."

The land company was of course willing to sell parcels to the squatters, but at such unreasonable prices that many folks pulled up stakes and started a new community about 30 miles distant on St. Joseph Bay, about a mile from Port St. Joe in an area now known as Oak Grove. The site was especially inviting, for a dry and healthy climate prevailed that was moderated by sea air.

In practically no time at all, the upstart town of St. Joseph arose. Substantial brick buildings soon appeared, along with several palatial homes, banks, churches, shops, a gambling house, barrooms, cheap hotels, warehouses, and even a horse track! The town's principal attraction, though, was its splendid deepwater harbor, something Apalachicola definitely lacked. Eventually, St. Joseph teemed with ships and lusty sailors, and soon became known as "the wickedest City in the Southeast."

But St. Joseph had a handicap too: it was totally cut off from the vibrant and busy Apalachicola River. Steamboats chugged down the commercial artery conveying cotton bales from southern Georgia and eastern Alabama. At "old Apalach," the manifests were off-loaded and placed aboard ships bound for the coastline or foreign ports. The enterprising citizenry of St. Joseph decided to convert their handicap into a challenge, and before long plans were afoot to actually divert the flow of commerce on the Apalachicola River.

The so-called Saints first aspired to build a canal between St. Joseph and some eligible point on the river above Apalachicola proper, the theory being that steamboats would depart the busy stream and use their canal down to St. Joseph. Accordingly, the Saints obtained a charter in 1835 for the Lake Wimico and St. Joseph Canal Company.[27] Within minutes of stock subscription books being opened, some $250,000 had been subscribed. Benjamin Chaires, the wealthy entrepreneur from Tallahassee, became president.

As the weeks wore on, though, the canal's promoters had a change of heart: why not build a railroad instead? Though they lacked the legislative authority to construct one, laborers nevertheless began grading a railway line that October. The territory's legislative council eventually modified the old charter, and the Lake Wimico and St. Joseph Canal and Railroad Company surfaced on 14 January 1836.[28]

The new charter permitted the railroad to also construct a company town facing St. Joseph Bay. Building lots were sold on the installment plan, with one-quarter in cash and the balance being paid, interest-free, over three years. "At the beginning of 1839, three years after the first house had been built in that uncivilized place—a place familiar only to the Indians up to that time—St. Joseph counted sixteen streets and over 1,200 inhabitants. By now the company had already taken in $430,000 for sites purchased."[29]

On paper, the railway-steamboat scheme of the Saints seemed slightly complicated. Steamboats descending the Apalachicola River would turn into what became the Jackson River, whereupon they would transit Lake Wimico and halt at the Bayou Columbus (Depot Creek) dock of the railway. Here, vessels would break bulk. Stevedores would then transfer cotton bales, produce, and merchandise to awaiting rail cars for the 8-mile trip down to St. Joseph. Here, trains would inch out onto the company's 1,800-foot wharf that sat in St. Joseph Bay. Manifests would again be off-loaded and placed aboard oceangoing ships.

The railway's directors hired Major James Graham to survey their di-
minutive line. An 1817 graduate of the U.S. Military Academy, Graham
had previously located several railroads in Virginia and Alabama. Following his Florida appointment, he helped establish the United States–
Canada boundary. The contractors John and William Gray, whom we
encountered on the Tallahassee Railroad, began building the St. Joseph
line in October 1835, aided by one hundred carpenters and two hundred
laborers.[30]

Construction rapidly advanced, and by March 1836 the route was
thrown open to Bayou Columbus. Horses and mules hauled the first
trains, but that summer two Baldwin-built steam locomotives arrived
in St. Joseph from Philadelphia, by way of the schooner *Phrenologist*.
The rail line—the first to open on Florida soil—was formally dedicated
in September.

> On Monday, the 5th instant, a Locomotive drawing a train of
> twelve cars containing upwards of 300 passengers passed over the
> railroad, connecting the flourishing town of St. Joseph with the
> Apalachicola River. The trip, a distance of 8 miles, was performed
> in the short space of 25 minutes. The engineer is confident, from
> the superiority of the road and engine, that the route can be ac-
> complished in eight minutes.[31]

Gerstner, the eminent Prussian engineer, visited St. Joseph in 1839.
He learned that the company's substantial dock in St. Joseph Bay,
whose pilings were sheathed in zinc sheet metal, had cost $75,000. He
was also told that another $12,000 had been expended on the wharf and
buildings for cotton bales at Columbus Bayou.[32]

The company's two steam locomotives were on the property at the
time of Gerstner's visit, as well as six, 4-wheel passenger coaches and
thirty-eight freight cars. During the winter months, freight and passengers were conveyed on the same train.

> As a rule the locomotive was placed behind the freight cars so that
> the cotton bales in the open cars would not be ignited by sparks
> from the stack. The normal speed of travel was 12 miles per hour.

During the slow summer months almost no freight was transported, and horses were used to pull the few passengers.[33]

The Gray brothers constructed the St. Joseph line for $80,000. When the cost of all buildings and rolling stock was factored, this figure rose to $120,000, or $15,000 per mile (2006 dollars: $2,124,159, or $257,786 per mile). Just two curves existed on the route, and the steepest grade was 26 feet per mile. The track structure, which was repeated on the Tallahassee Railroad, consisted of solid timber rails with iron strap tops. The rails themselves rested on crossties that were set 5 feet apart.

Gerstner reconfirms that the railroad was really built to promote the new town of St. Joseph and to increase their real estate values. No fares were charged for the first six months of operations; thereafter they were kept intentionally low. Passengers eventually paid twenty-five cents to ride the line—"if they were Negroes a mere 12 ½ cents."[34] A bale of cotton was transported for fifteen cents. Gross revenues in 1838 amounted to $20,000; expenses came to $13,000, which produced a net profit of $7,000.

Whereas the railroad was judged a success, the steamboat connection left much to be desired. The channel leading from the Apalachicola River was never adequately dredged, snags (tree stumps) abounded, vessels frequently ran aground in Lake Wimico during low water, and Columbus Bayou often silted up. These impediments prompted more than one ship's captain to bypass the connection and steam directly for the port of Apalachicola.

The Saints took the criticisms in stride and eventually hatched a new plan: they would rebuild their rail line to a more accessible point farther up the Apalachicola River; at Iola, 28 miles distant from St. Joseph. By docking and unloading at Iola, vessels could avoid some 70 miles of river navigation down to Apalachicola. A new railway charter was not needed, for the one of old permitted the Saints to build a line to any point on the river.

Many merchants, planters, and investors from the Columbus, Georgia, area rallied behind the Iola project. The construction contract was taken by Benjamin Chaires in 1837, who, in turn, engaged several subcontractors for the work. Shortly afterward, the crippling effects of the nation's first financial panic were being felt. Money became

The first steam engine in Florida was built by Baldwin in 1836 for $7,000. There was no cab for the engineer, much less a bell or headlight. This three-quarter-scale replica was exhibited at county fairs. Author's collection.

scarce, credit dried up, banks closed, and many companies failed. When Chaires asked to be paid for the first section of work, his fellow directors could only issue him company scrip—a paper money promise to pay later—which Chaires refused. Ultimately, all of the railroad's assets were mortgaged to the millionaire, along with all company deeds and notes. Construction of the line then resumed, and by November some five hundred laborers were back on the project. The line opened to Iola in October 1839, at a cost of $300,000.[35]

Gerstner inspected the new route, noting that it started about one and a half miles outside of St. Joseph proper. (The old route through town and the existing dock were retained.) Iola itself was situated on the west bank of the Apalachicola River, near Wewahitchka, about 26 feet above sea level. The rail line passed through several swamps en route to the new northern objective point, and about 5,800 feet of trestle work was needed just to cross Dead Lake. A substantial drawbridge carried the track over the navigable Chipola River, where a railroad wharf was also erected. Additionally, a wharf and several warehouses went up at Iola.

Gerstner mentions that the track structure of the Iola line was more substantially built than the route to Columbus Bayou, but that, initially, a considerable portion was executed in "a poor and neglectful manner" by the subcontractors. Therefore, much had to be rebuilt before the line officially opened.[36] When all wharves, buildings, and rolling stock were added to the outlays for track and bridges, the cost of the Iola route came to $500,000 (2006 dollars: $9,131,643). Once it was opened, the old route to Columbus Bayou was seldom used.[37]

Considerable competition existed among the steamboat lines that plied the Apalachicola River. Thus, to obtain business, the railroad was obliged to keep its rates quite low, to the extent that "its income was barely sufficient to meet operating expenses, and that no dividends could be declared on the original investment."[38] Unfortunately, the railroad's finances continued to worsen.

Convinced that the port of Apalachicola would never vanish, a delegation of Saints eventually met with officials of the Apalachicola Land Company. They proposed that the new Iola line be scrapped, and that a new one be built to connect the two rival ports. St. Joseph, with its deep harbor, would handle all foreign shipments, while Apalachicola would service the coastal traffic and trade. Although there was initial interest in the joint venture, negotiations collapsed.

Another plan promulgated by the Saints bordered on folly: completely tear up the just-built Iola line and replace it with a canal—a ditch 17 miles long and wide enough for two steamboats to actually pass one another.[39] This, too, fell by the wayside.

In 1841, yellow fever descended upon the city of St. Joseph, and it raged with unabated fury. Many residents perished or left the upstart settlement never to return. In the following summer, the Iola railroad was auctioned under court order. What had cost a small fortune to build went for a mere $2,400! The two steam locomotives, all the freight and passenger cars, the wagons and carts, along with the mules, generated an additional $1,300. The purchaser was none other than railroad contractor William Gray, who forwarded the spoils to Monroe, Georgia, where they were used on another railroad project.[40] Two years later, a devastating hurricane hit. As a result, many homes and buildings in St. Joseph were dismantled and brought over to Apalachicola. And before long, "the wickedest City in the Southeast" flickered out of existence.

Little is known about the tiny industrial railroad that operated in territorial days near Bagdad. The historian Dorothy Dodd suspected that the line was constructed sometime between 1838 and 1840.[41] Its owner was unquestionably the manufacturing concern of Forsyth and Simpson, whose mills fronted the Blackwater River. Its rail route ran inland for some 3 miles to nearby Arcadia.

Previously, in 1835, the Pond Creek and Black Water River Canal Company was chartered. Three years later, the concern became known as the Arcadia Railroad Company. Gerstner does not mention the carrier in his voluminous study, possibly because it was not in operation until after his visit. But it was definitely running in 1840, for an area newspaper editor claims he rode the line.[42] In any event, the enterprise was short-lived.

No information has surfaced about its construction or operations, though it is likely that mules hauled the trains and that lumber figured into the traffic mix. Eventually, the Forsyth concern moved its operations to Bagdad, and the site at Arcadia was converted in the early 1850s into Florida's largest cotton mill, one that produced annually more than 600,000 yards of cloth.

This brings us to the only other railroad project begun in territorial days. Throughout the 1830s, Pensacola desired railroad communication with Alabama and Georgia. The project that was eventually conceived was impressive, to say the least, and it would require vast amounts of capital. Gerstner knew about the firm, and had not the panic of 1837 intervened, it quite possibly would have been built.

Situated on the north shore of Pensacola Bay, the port of Pensacola possessed the largest natural, landlocked, deepwater harbor in all of Florida, which prompted the U.S. government to establish a large naval yard here in 1825. The exportation of lumber and naval stores also contributed to Pensacola's reputation. What the city lacked, though, was a railroad to the rich cotton lands of southern Alabama and Georgia. If such a line could be built, "Pensacola would be raised to the status of an important trade town and come into direct competition with Mobile, which is situated much less favorably for maritime commerce."[43]

With this objective in mind, the civic lights of Pensacola began staging public meetings in 1833. The project's prime mover became Captain

William Chase (1798–1870), an officer of the Army Corps of Engineers who had considerable experience building fortifications in the Pensacola area.[44]

The Florida legislature responded by chartering the Florida, Alabama and Georgia Rail Road on 14 February 1834, which was authorized to construct a line from Pensacola to the Alabama border. Chase's team then sought an Alabama charter to advance the project to opposite Columbus, Georgia, on the Chattahoochee River, together with a branch to the state capital at Montgomery. But the branch request "aroused the jealousy and apprehensions of Mobile," which at the time was backing the Montgomery Railroad between Mobile and the capital. Nevertheless, Chase received a charter for the Alabama, Florida and Georgia Rail Road in December 1834. (The authority to construct a branch to Montgomery was not included.) Incorporators of the Alabama firm included many Pensacola figureheads, such as John Cameron, Thomas Blount, and Walter Gregory.[45]

When news of the Alabama charter reached Pensacola, stock subscription books were opened, and $1.5 million was quickly subscribed. On closer examination, though, it was learned that purchasers had only to make a twenty-five-cent down payment on the first installment; therefore only $3,750 of cash was actually raised.[46] Later, on 14 December 1834, the new company was organized with Chase as president. The following February, the Florida legislature repealed the charter it had previously issued, accepted the one recently issued by Alabama, and the project began in earnest.

It now became Chase's mission to raise the serious money for the 210-mile line, all of which led to an intriguing relationship between the railroad and the Bank of Pensacola. The latter had been chartered in 1831 with a capitalization of $200,000. Governor Duval vetoed its act of incorporation, claiming that banks were unsuited to "the genius and spirit of our free institutions."[47] The legislative council felt otherwise, and the veto was overturned. One section of the bank's charter was worthy of note: the personal property of each stockholder was to be pledged *in proportion* to the amount of shares acquired.

Shortly before Duval issued his veto, council members approved an act to increase the bank's capitalization to $2.5 million, and authorized it to issue bonds of up to $500,000. Proceeds from the bond sales would allow the bank's directors to make a substantial investment in the Alabama, Florida and Georgia Rail Road.

But these were no ordinary bonds, for they would ultimately be endorsed by Florida's governor. Moreover, their face amount ($1,000) and interest rate (6 percent) would be guaranteed by "the good faith and credit of the Florida Territory." Thus they became known as "Faith bonds." For every Faith bond issued, the bank was to hypothecate, or pledge, a like amount of bank stock to the territorial government. Again, bank stockholders would be *personally liable* for every bond the institution issued.[48]

Because Florida was still a territory, federal approval was needed to float the bond issue. According to the financial historian Reginald McGrane, the approving act was "laid before Congress on the last day of the session; and as no adverse action was taken, $500,000 [of Faith bonds] were sold on 2 December 1835."[49] Nary a soul questioned how a territorial legislature could extend such a guarantee or pledge its so-called faith and credit. One financier, though, had the courage to say that "Florida was assuming too many obligations for its limited resources and population."[50]

As agent of the Bank of Pensacola, Captain Chase peddled the bonds to several Philadelphia investors who, in turn, resold them in New York and London (via Baring Brothers) and in Holland using the well-established Dutch investment firm of Hope and Company in Amsterdam. The parties who purchased the Faith bonds did so with the understanding that if the bank failed, its stockholders and the Florida Territory would come to their rescue.

But a rather disturbing event occurred in 1838: Florida's legislative council "clandestinely" passed an act that repealed all personal liability of the bank's stockholders. News of the indiscretion was of course never transmitted to the bondholders.[51] Once the proceeds from the issue made their way back to Pensacola, the bank's investment in railroad stock began in earnest.

Much of the proposed railway had to pass through federal land, which prompted the directors to memorialize Congress for a right-of-way and the privilege of taking all nearby building materials. They also requested that an army topographical engineer freely survey the route and that Washington give the railroad a land grant of 600,000

MEMORIAL

OF THE

ALABAMA, FLORIDA, AND GEORGIA RAILROAD COMPANY,

PRAYING

To be allowed to purchase five hundred thousand acres of the Government land, on a credit of six years; and also asking an extension of three years on their bonds for the payment of the duties on certain railroad iron imported by them.

DECEMBER 31, 1838.

Referred to the Committee on Finance, and ordered to be printed.

To the honorable the Senate and House of Representatives in Congress assembled:

The petition of the Alabama, Florida, and Georgia Railroad Company

SHOWETH :

That your petitioners are engaged in the construction of a railroad, from the city of Pensacola, on the Gulf of Mexico, to the town of Montgomery, on the Alabama river; that their enterprise is eminently calculated to ameliorate the commercial and agricultural condition of a large and important section of the southwestern country, now laboring under many evils and inconveniences growing out of the periodical character of the navigation of the rivers, and the remoteness from navigable water courses of the immediate section of country through which their railroad is located; the location being nearly parallel with, and mid-way between, the Chattahoochee on the east, and the Alabama on the west.

That for more than one hundred miles along the line of railroad, Government is almost the exclusive land-holder; which lands have been a long time exposed to private sale, but, from want of a natural outlet for productions, have remained comparatively unsettled, and must continue so, or be developed by railroad communication.

That their railroad, originating at Pensacola, and terminating by branches at Selma and Montgomery, will form the stem of an extensive system of railroads, now under construction, or projected, extending eastwardly and westwardly, and penetrating the most inaccessible districts of Alabama, Georgia, and Tennessee; and that these auxiliary railroads also pass through extensive tracts of Government land, which, for the same reasons as before stated, have remained unsold, but on the completion of the said railroads will be brought into market with great additional value, and thereby add largely to the national revenue.

Blair & Rives, printers.

The promoters of Pensacola's first railroad wanted to purchase 500,000 acres of land from Congress on credit. Sales proceeds were to offset construction costs. Their request was denied. Author's collection.

acres. In return, the Alabama, Florida and Georgia Rail Road would freely transport "ordnance, arms, supplies, munitions of war, as well as troops belonging to, or in the service of, the United States." The Congress, though, granted only a 60-foot-wide path for the track; allowed all building materials to be removed from within 100 yards of same; and approved the free survey. The land grant was denied.[52]

Major James Graham, the same army officer who located the tiny railway out of St. Joseph, surveyed Pensacola's railroad dream. Graham was of the opinion that construction costs would be minimal because of the easy grades and abundance of timber and rock. Chase himself projected a cost of about $1.5 million, or $6,800 per mile.[53] In April 1836, the company requested bids for the first 50 miles of track. Iron strap rail was ordered from England, and six locomotives and numerous freight and passenger cars were purchased from the Proprietors of the Locks and Canal Company in Lowell, Massachusetts.[54]

Finding enough laborers for the big project proved difficult, forcing the contractor to advertise for workers far and wide. Wages amounted to twenty dollars a month, which included room and board. Construction commenced with a skeletal force in May 1836 at the intersection of Broadway and Hancock Streets in Pensacola. By fall, 130 workers of Irish and Dutch extraction had arrived from New York City by ship. The recently ordered freight and passenger cars appeared in October, and in the following month the vessel *Norman* tied up in Pensacola, from Liverpool, England, with 600 tons of iron strap rail. By the summer of 1838, some $600,000 had been expended on the project.[55]

The railroad's promoters also undertook other schemes to raise capital. For instance, they arranged for the new line to begin about one mile from the old city center, in a company town they called New Pensacola. Large parcels of land were acquired here that were eventually subdivided and sold on generous terms. Even a $30,000 hotel was constructed. Soon the setting was alive with activity. "Every business transaction is done and every sale or purchase of real estate is made with reference to the Rail Road," said one newspaper.[56] A public auction of lots, which attracted buyers from far away Cuba and New York City, was held in January 1837.

This euphoric state of affairs was short-lived, however, for on 5 June the Bank of Pensacola closed its doors—a victim of the 1837 financial panic. Work continued on the railroad, but at a far slower pace. To reduce the overall cost of the project, the actual length of the railway was shortened by changing the northern objective point to Montgomery. So as to pay pressing liabilities of the bank, certain equipment of the railroad, such as excess locomotives, iron strap rails, and machinery, were outright sold.

Somehow during this difficult hour the Bank of Pensacola managed to make short-term loans to the railroad. Chase and his fellow directors again memorialized Congress for a land grant, telling politicos that "the Alabama, Florida and Georgia Railroad is a work of a *national character*; and is only not important, but *absolutely necessary* in connection with the general plan of defense for the maritime frontier of the Gulf of Mexico." But again the appeal fell on deaf ears. Railroad construction ceased in 1838, shortly after all the grading and trestlework was completed between Pensacola and the Escambia River.

The spotlight now turned on the Bank of Pensacola. When the bank failed to pay its bond interest coupon in 1840, the United States Bank stepped in "to save the Honor of the Territory." Its director then informed the Florida governor that it was the territory's responsibility to immediately make good on the default. As one historian states: "The Legislature became aghast at the situation."[57]

After weeks of carping and finger-pointing, the legislative council of the Florida Territory decided to repudiate, or cancel, its Faith bonds, claiming that it never had the authority to guarantee them in the first place nor the power to back them. The declaration sent a shock wave through the financial world, one that would cast a long, dark shadow over Florida for years to come. Hundreds of innocent bond owners, many of them in far away Holland, never received a penny more in interest nor a return of principal.

How much capital was lost in Pensacola's railroad-bank debacle will never be known. Certainly railroad stockholders were wiped out, and miles of track stood silent and devoid of trains. These unfortunate events partly explain why the state's first constitution, drawn up years later, stipulated that "the General Assembly shall not pledge the faith and credit of the State to raise funds in aid of any corporation whatsoever."

In retrospect, the legislative council chartered many railroad companies during the territorial era. Except for those just explored, all others remained paper projects. But this did not diminish the public's interest in railroads, for indeed many Floridians remained as convinced as ever that the "iron horse" would one day revolutionize the transportation habits of the land. In time it did.

3

Government Lends a Hand

There is no portion of the Union more advantageously located by geographical position for profitable investment in railroad enterprises than Florida; nor is there one upon the development and population of which such improvements would tell with a more sensible effect.

—Report of the Internal Improvement Board of Florida, 1855

On his very last day in office, 3 March 1845, President John Tyler signed the congressional act that created the State of Florida. William Mosely, a prominent planter and lawyer of Jefferson County, was elected the first governor of the nation's twenty-seventh state, which was then home to some seventy thousand persons. During the next fifteen years, Florida would experience rapid growth, so much so that the population would double by 1860.[1]

Florida's transportation system was unfortunately still in a dreadful state when admitted to the Union. Small wonder that the new state constitution therefore stipulated "that a liberal system of Internal Improvements, being essential to the development of the resources of the country, shall be encouraged by the Government . . . and it shall be the duty of the General Assembly, as soon as practicable, to ascertain by law, proper objects of improvement." Yet, even with this charge, another decade would pass before legislators sprang into action.

Among those who found the dereliction reprehensible was future Florida governor Thomas Brown, whose eloquent chastisement of General Assembly members was repeated in northern newspapers:

> How little this provision of the Constitution has been practically regarded, as your recent journeys from your respective homes in

every part of the State must have painfully reminded you. It is a melancholy reflection, that while the spirit of improvement is pervading every other State—opening new sources of wealth, of comfort, and stimulating human industry in all its varied departments—Florida alone, like the slothful servant who buried his talent, seems well nigh content with inaction and repose on this vital subject.[2]

Merely one railroad existed in Florida when statehood was granted: the rickety but money-making line between the capital and St. Marks. General Richard Keith Call still owned the Tallahassee Railroad. Call himself actually had run for the governorship when Florida became a state, but he lost a close election to Mosely after a hard-fought contest. In the early 1850s, Old Hickory's protégé considered extending his cotton carrier north of Tallahassee into Georgia, where several railroads existed, but the plan never got legs.

The lack of railroad transportation disturbed many Floridians, especially since so many companies had been chartered during the territorial era. At least one state agency had the courage to publicly explain why so few lines had been actually built: "the limited resources of cash capital at the command of our people, and the inability of the State to contribute to their construction."[3]

An important document summarizing the economic resources of the state was prepared in 1852 by Edward Cabell (1816–1896), Florida's youthful and gifted U.S. congressman.[4] Governor Brown obtained a copy of the report, who then distributed it to General Assembly members. Cabell began his encyclopedic assessment by chiding Washington officials for doing so little in Florida. "No part of the Union has been so much neglected," he railed, noting that the flawed policies of the federal government had "greatly retarded the growth and prosperity of the State, and the present backward condition of her internal improvements." Though discouraged, Cabell remained optimistic—in retrospect, prophetic—about the future of Florida:

> Blessed with a genial climate, and a fruitful soil, and advantages for improvement, Florida is destined in time to become a populous and one of the richest and most prosperous States of the Union.[5]

Edward C. Cabell served two terms as Florida's U.S. congressman. The astute lawyer, who lived in Tallahassee, was also president of the Pensacola and Georgia Railroad. By permission of the Library of Congress.

Of the many projects needing to be undertaken, foremost in Cabell's mind was the construction of a railroad directly across the state from Jacksonville to Pensacola. Feeders and branches would stem from the main track so as to service such outlying points as Apalachicola. Cabell estimated that the 350-mile endeavor would require some $4 million in capital, monies that hardly existed then in Florida. Thus, to finance the costly enterprise, the congressman wanted the federal government to give Florida all the alternate sections of land it owned on both sides of the proposed route, which could then be sold by the company and the proceeds applied toward construction costs.[6] It was a classic land grant scheme.

The concept of using land grants to finance internal improvements was again finding favor in America. Florida received 500,000 acres from the federal government's vast holdings when it was admitted to statehood in 1845. Later, in 1850, Congress gifted an additional 10 million acres of "swamp and overflowed lands" the federal government owned here, a figure that rose to nearly 20 million acres by 1900.

But the largesse from Washington came with a hitch: the gifts were to be used only for land reclamation projects. But in the twinkling of an eye, Florida legislators construed that they could also be "lawfully devoted to internal improvements," a decision later greatly derided by future governor Napoleon Broward, who became the state's chief magistrate in 1905.[7]

To administer the gifts, the state established in 1851 an Internal Improvement Board comprised of the governor, certain state officers, and representatives from each judicial circuit.[8] Land commissioners began locating the tracts in the following year, during which time another committee began to investigate how the land might be used to fund internal improvements. Among the latter's six members were Florida U.S. senator David Yulee, the able Tallahassee attorney James Archer, and Jacksonville civic light Dr. Abel Seymour Baldwin. Their findings were submitted to Governor James Broome (1849–53), who then distributed the much-anticipated report to the General Assembly.[9]

Yulee's committee had diligently researched ways to stimulate railroad construction, chiefly by studying the methods employed by other states. Three recurring themes were identified: giving companies outright gifts of money, land, or both; selling state owned tracts and using the proceeds to purchase railroad stocks and bonds; and extending qualified firms state credit.[10] Ultimately the board recommended a plan that blended the first and third strategies together: it proposed that qualified companies should receive gifts of land as construction unfolded, and that the state would guarantee the interest on their bonds. The scheme or mode of aid, the committee insisted, was to benefit "every section of the State."[11]

Transforming the recommendations into legislation fell to Yulee, Archer, and Governor Broome. A draft copy of the bill, which was entitled "An Act to provide for and encourage a Liberal System of Internal Improvements in this State," was appended to the board's report. Both documents received a favorable response, and Broome signed the legislation—arguably one of the most important in state history—on 6 January 1855.[12]

How did the land grant scheme work? When would the state pay the bond interest? What obligations were incumbent upon the companies being aided? The answers to these and other questions were contained in the act's thirty-two sections. The first stated that all lands gifted to Florida would hereafter form the Internal Improvement Fund (IIF), control of which would be irrevocably vested in five trustees: the governor, comptroller of public accounts, state treasurer, attorney general, and the registrar of state lands. They and they alone would manage the tracts, set prices, handle all monies, and so on. Any surplus funds were to be invested in stocks of American companies or in bonds that one day the IIF might issue.[13]

Railroad companies wishing to be aided had only to communicate their intentions in writing to the trustees. Once they had fulfilled certain criteria and received the land grant, the firms—in theory—were free to sell the parcels and apply the proceeds toward the construction costs they incurred. Since railroads usually financed construction with bonds, the state guarantee of interest was intended to make the securities a safer investment—and therefore one more attractive to investors.

Other benefits were also extended. The stock of aided railroad companies would be forever free of taxation; company assets would receive a thirty-five-year tax exemption; company employees would be exempted from military service and jury duty; every firm would receive a 200-foot-wide right-of-way through state-owned lands along with the privilege of taking all nearby building materials; and the state would allow no other railroad to be built within 25 miles of an aided company. Further, the act allowed towns, cities, and county governments to purchase railroad stock.

To obtain the land grant, a company first had to grade 20 miles of its roadbed with crossties. Also, all standing timber on both sides of the track, for a distance of 60 feet in each direction, had to be removed. The roadbed itself was to be of a certain width in cuts and have ample ditches for water drainage. Crossties, upon which the rails were spiked, could only be hewn of certain wood species and had to be cut to specific dimensions. Additionally, any bridge erected along the route could not obstruct the flow of water or impede navigation. The IIF act further stipulated that only "first class" freight and passenger cars could be purchased by the aided roads.

So as to obtain uniform construction standards, all companies had to utilize broad gauge track, and iron rails that weighed not less than 60 pounds to the lineal yard "were to be well fastened to the tie plates and crossties." Also, no grade upon the route was to exceed 45 feet per mile, nor could any curve be greater than 3 degrees. In retrospect, the specifications were not unreasonable and went far to facilitate the exchange of traffic between the various companies.

After specific sections of a new route were completed, the state engineer was to visit each line and certify that the work was properly done. Once this confirmation was transmitted to Tallahassee, the trustees of the IIF could then issue the bond endorsement *provided* the iron rails for the project were located within the state. If a company fulfilled all the foregoing criteria, it would then receive "all alternate Sections of State Lands on each side of their track for six miles," or 3,840 free acres for every mile completed.

The state guarantee of bond interest also came with restrictions. First, the securities had to be registered with the state comptroller. Once they were endorsed by the trustees, the bonds automatically established a first lien upon the railroad's assets. Railroads issuing such securities had four years to fully complete their first 20 miles of track, and eight years to complete the entire project. Each firm also had to supply the IIF with periodic reports of earnings, expenses, and profits. Companies that were willing to conform to the provisions were then authorized

> to issue Coupon Bonds having not more than thirty-five years to run, and drawing not more than seven percent interest, payable semi-annually in the City of New York or Tallahassee, at the rate of eight thousand dollars per mile for the purchase and delivery of the iron rail, spikes, and tie plates, and after the rail has been laid down on the line the additional sum of two thousand dollars per mile for the purchase of the necessary equipment.[14]

Under a somewhat complicated formula, either the company itself or the IIF would pay the bond interest. If the state became involved, then the company had to reimburse the IIF with a like amount of railroad stock. Every firm was also required to make periodic payments into a sinking fund, thereby assuring that monies would be on hand to redeem the face value (or principal amount) of each bond at maturity. If an aided company failed to perform these obligations, the trustees could, after serving a thirty-day notice, take possession and sell the railroad for cash or other securities to the highest bidder. Proceeds from such sales were to be first applied to purchasing and canceling the outstanding bonds, or they were deposited into the sinking fund. The new owners of the railroad were obliged to continue paying any applicable interest and sinking fund contributions.

The IIF act also authorized bonds for certain railroad bridges in the state. For instance, up to $100,000 would be approved for any structure crossing the Choctawhatchee and Apalachicola rivers, as well as the west side of the Nassau River. Also, any railroad erecting a bridge across the Suwannee River could issue $50,000 worth of bonds and receive the state guarantee of interest.[15]

Those that crafted the Internal Improvement Fund act naturally wanted specific railway projects to be built, such as one "from Jacksonville to Pensacola Bay with extensions to the St. Marks River, or the Crooked River on Apalachicola Bay, and to St. Andrews Bay" and another from Amelia Island to Tampa Bay with an extension to Cedar Key. Lastly, the IIF insisted that all aided companies have uniform tariffs or rates of transportation.[16]

About a year after the Internal Improvement Fund act became law, in May 1856, another gift of land sprang forth from Washington, this at the behest of Senator Yulee and Congressman Cabell. Chapter 31 of the United States Statutes stated that any Florida railroad company that constructed a route "from the St. Johns River at Jacksonville to the waters of Escambia Bay, at or near Pensacola; or from Amelia Island, on the Atlantic, to the waters of Tampa Bay, with a branch to Cedar Key, on the Gulf of Mexico; or a railroad from Pensacola to the State line of Alabama" would be entitled to freely receive from the federal government "every alternate section of land designated by odd-numbers for six sections in width on each side of its track." When added to the Internal Improvement Fund gift, such firms would receive a grand total of 7,280 acres for each mile of railroad they completed.[17]

The trustees of the IIF issued their first annual report to the Florida legislature in December 1856. Several weeks after the landmark legislation had become law, the trustees met in Tallahassee to discuss their duties and responsibilities. Rules and regulations were drawn up, and the offices of president, secretary, salesman of land, and treasurer were established.

The aforementioned report also noted that surveyors were still in the field locating the federal tracts that had been gifted to Florida and that several companies had already communicated their desire to be aided by the IIF, namely, the Florida, Atlantic and Gulf Central Railroad, the Florida Railroad, and the Tallahassee Railroad.[18] In fact, when the latter finally issued bonds endorsed by the state, the trustees decided to spend some of their surplus funds on the securities, stating that such action "would give the bonds character in the foreign money markets; as it would show that here, where the operation of the railroad enterprises is supposed to be best known, there is confidence in their success and in their ability to meet their engagements."[19]

The remainder of this chapter describes the first companies that were aided by the Internal Improvement Fund, the firms that formed the very foundation of Florida's future railroad network.

Dr. Baldwin's Company

Jacksonville was a primitive riverside village in 1853 "with only one poor wharf and not a vehicle of any kind to carry passengers or baggage." At least that is how Henry Plant, the future railroad monarch of the South, found the setting. Plant, who eventually did so much for the future transportation gateway of the state, "succeeded in getting some Negro boys to carry his trunk to a poor hotel where he remained just one day.[20]

A more complimentary assessment of the setting, at least from a commercial perspective, had been penned one year earlier by Congressman Edward Cabell: "More than thirteen large lumber mills (mostly steam) are on the river above and below Jacksonville. About 350 vessels annually are loaded with lumber and produce on the St. Johns River. The quantity of lumber annually shipped is estimated at 50 million feet.[21]

Since time immemorial, the St. Johns River had been Jacksonville's lifeline to the outside world. This important artery of commerce made a wide crescent bend at the city, not unlike the Mississippi at New Orleans. In time it became a flourishing port for lumber, shingles, staves, and naval stores. In the 1850s, a movement got under way to develop the western side of the city, and to improve transportation with the hinterland. Many rejoiced in the proposal, for back then a stagecoach trip to Tallahassee meant a back-breaking three-day journey.

Readers will recall that Cabell favored the construction of a railroad between Jacksonville and Pensacola. The physical terrain between the termini was not forbidding, but financing such a grandiose project—at least in the 1850s—was daunting. Such a line was eventually constructed, though in a piecemeal fashion by several companies over many years, the final spike finally being driven home in 1883. That portion of the route between Jacksonville and Lake City, by way of Baldwin, MacClenny, Sanderson, and Olustee, became the mission of the Florida, Atlantic and Gulf Central Railroad.

Dr. Abel Seymour Baldwin (1811–1898), a physician by training and a civic light of Jacksonville, was the company's prime mover. Baldwin also represented Duval County in the state legislature, and his appointment to the Internal Improvement Fund board was no accident. The charter of Baldwin's company, granted in 1851, loosely described the proposed route as being from the St. Mary's River to the Gulf of Mexico. An addendum in 1853 raised the firm's capitalization to $3 million, and redefined the route as being from "some navigable river in East Florida to a Gulf coast point west of the Apalachicola River." While promoters were busily arousing public interest in the project, Baldwin was lining up investor support and helping craft the Internal Improvement Fund Act of 1855.[22]

After the IIF Act became law, Baldwin wrote to its trustees and stated that his company wished to be aided. By now, the route of his railroad had been fixed between Jacksonville and Alligator, a community some 60 miles to the west that, in 1859, was renamed Lake City. The City of Jacksonville, eager to get its first railroad, sold $50,000 of municipal bonds—the first in city history—and used the proceeds to buy railroad stock. Another favorable response came from Columbia County, whose commissioners floated a $100,000 bond issue. Other funds for

This $1,000 bond of the Florida, Atlantic and Gulf Central Railroad (Jacksonville to Lake City) carried the interest guaranty of the Internal Improvement Fund, which made the security more attractive to investors. Author's collection.

construction and equipment were raised through the sale of company stock, bonds, and selling acreage that the railroad would eventually receive from the IIF.[23]

A careful survey of the route was completed in the fall of 1855; construction commenced a few months afterward. Finding a sufficiently large labor force retarded progress, as did a yellow fever epidemic and late shipments of iron rail. In 1857, Baldwin relinquished the presidency to Colonel John P. Sanderson (1816–1871), a prominent Jacksonville attorney. The roadbed was completed to Lake City in August of the following year, whereupon the state engineer inspected the work and issued his certification. This, in turn, allowed the Central (as the railroad was nicknamed) to issue state-endorsed bonds. The proceeds paid for the last of the iron rails.[24]

Few curves existed on the Central route, and just several steep grades could be counted: one near the St. Mary's River, another leading to Hart's station, and a third in the Alachua Trail Ridge. The cost of constructing the roadbed with crossties was close to $181,000, or $3,000 per mile. Though the installation of the superstructure (iron rails, rail joints, tie plates, and spikes) was started in June 1858, "little was done till the locomotive *Governor Perry* blew her first whistle, on the 10th July, and we then regarded the work as fairly commenced." Rails reached Baldwin station in March 1859.[25]

While completing the track to Lake City, the railroad's chief contractor died, whereupon it devolved upon company forces to finish the superstructure. Iron rails for the project, which were forged in both American and English mills, weighed 52 pounds to the lineal yard. The track itself was "well and substantially laid and firmly secured with wrought iron chairs, spiked to yellow pine cross-ties, placed 28 inches from center to center."[26]

The company's first roster of equipment was supplied by the New Jersey Locomotive and Machine Company in Patterson. Among the items purchased were two locomotives and twenty-five assorted freight and passenger cars, for which the railroad paid $28,606. Additionally, the railroad acquired a "first-class passenger car" from the firm of William Cummings in Jersey City. Other outlays were made for a wharf on the St. Johns River ($8,640) in Jacksonville, along with terminal buildings near the intersection of Adams and Clay Streets ($10,800). City fathers gave the railroad a free right-of-way to its new dock, acreage for terminal buildings, together with a thirty-five-year immunity from corporate taxes.[27]

The Florida, Atlantic and Gulf Central opened on 13 March 1860. Two days later a free excursion train departed Jacksonville for Lake City, where celebrants partook of a grand barbecue. On 21 March, the railroad transported the citizenry of Lake City to the company's eastern terminus of Jacksonville, where another reception was tendered. "A pleasing ceremony was carried out at the Judson House where Miss Louisa Holland of Jacksonville and Miss Kate Ives of Lake City mingled the waters of the St. Johns River with those of Lake DeSoto."[28]

From the outset the Central's directors were confident that their company would entertain a large traffic. There were passengers to be transported, along with express packages, mail, merchandise, lumber products, and cotton bales, not to mention cattle, horses, sheep, hogs, hides, corn, fruit, and naval stores. Sanderson estimated that annual revenues to be $128,000, expenses of approximately $108,000, which left a profit of about $20,040 or "upwards of 9.3 per cent on the stock paid."[29]

During its early years, the Central was conservatively and ably managed. As the company's 1859 annual report denotes: "To establish and maintain the credit of the Company has been a primary consideration with your Directors." The latter felt the railroad faced a bright future, especially when its ally to the west of Lake City, the Pensacola and Georgia Railroad, would complete its route between Lake City and Tallahassee. No one, though, could foresee what devastating effects the American Civil War would soon wreak upon the company.

Congressman Cabell's Road

Constructing a rail line from Pensacola to some point on the Georgia border was the initial objective of the Pensacola and Georgia Railroad. Chartered in January 1853, the company's president was the aforementioned Edward Cabell, a graduate of the University of Virginia, a respected lawyer in Tallahassee, and Florida's U.S. congressman (1845–46; 1847–53).

For several years, Cabell and his directors wrestled with funding problems and where the railway's route would be located. After the IIF Act became law, the issues began to melt away. In 1855, the legislature redefined the company's route as connecting Pensacola with Lake City, where it would connect with Dr. Baldwin's firm, which was building westward from Jacksonville. But even the scope of this project overwhelmed Cabell's board, which, in the end, opted to construct a line just between the capital and Lake City. To strengthen its position, the "P & G" would also acquire the old Tallahassee Railroad down to St. Marks. Later, during the American Civil War, the P & G would extend itself west of the capital to Quincy. "The 180-mile gap from Quincy west to Pensacola was left to be built by others."[30]

Locating the route between Tallahassee and Alligator (Lake City) was overseen by Colonel William Griffin, an 1835 graduate of the United States Military Academy. His survey, which was conducted in the company of several fellow officers, commenced in July 1855. That summer proved unusually hot and humid, and most of Griffin's survey party became gravely ill. Substitutes were found, and the engineers returned to the capital in early October.

Griffin determined that Tallahassee was situated about 145 feet above the depot at St. Marks. "This renders it necessary that we should start on our Maximum Grade of forty-five feet to the mile, and even then encounter very heavy work on the first few miles of the Road."[31] Griffin's team ended up surveying twenty possible routes to Lake City, all of which Cabell dissected in the company's 1855 annual report.

Griffin himself possessed a formidable knowledge of railroad construction and was well versed with the construction standards set forth in the Internal Improvement Fund act. But he questioned why any railroad in Florida needed 20-foot excavations and 18-foot-high embankments.

> I regard these widths as unnecessarily great. Not a Road in the Southern country, graded for a single track, has a greater width of embankment at top than 14 feet. The most usual width is 12 feet, which I regard as altogether sufficient, in a country such as Florida, not subject to freezes. I would urge upon the Board to petition the Legislature for an Amendment of the Internal Improvement Act, in several particulars, embraced in the different specifications of the 6th Section. I think all the matters of detail embraced in the different specifications might with safety be left, as usual in other States, to the several Chief Engineers of Rail Roads, subject to the approval of the State Engineer.[32]

Griffin's remarks were likely the first public criticisms of the Internal Improvement Fund. Cabell and his directors no doubt appreciated their chief engineer's forthrightness, for fulfilling unnecessary construction specifications was a genuine waste of capital. At this particular moment, the Pensacola and Georgia Railroad was enjoying the support of Governor Broome as well as David Walker, the registrar of state lands. Griffin's report was dated 25 October 1855. Interestingly, on 14 December, the legislature passed its first amendment to the IIF Act, empowering its trustees to modify any construction standard *provided* the state engineer lent his approval.[33]

Included with Griffin's report were several estimates of construction costs. For example, the chief engineer estimated that a mile of superstructure (crossties, rails, spikes, plates, connecting bars, etc.) would amount to $8,000; surveys, engineering costs, and office and legal expenses would consume another $65,000; and that all necessary real estate, wells, tanks, wood sheds, turntables, road crossings, cattle guards, grubbing, and depots would require about $48,000. Further, the West Point graduate determined that $188,000 would be needed to purchase twelve locomotives and a good assortment of freight and passenger cars, and an additional $50,000 would be needed to fund workshops, engine houses, and all necessary machinery. Lastly, another $31,500 would cover the cost of switches and turnouts. All this, together with a few contingencies, amounted to $438,000. By taking the latter figure and factoring in the cost of all necessary bridges, culverts, trestles, etc. for a particular route, Griffin concluded that the road could be built and equipped for about $1.5 million (2006 dollars: $32,476,649).

The chief engineer reminded the directors that their railway was positioned to "command all the trade of Middle Florida." Of the various routes surveyed though, Griffin felt certain ones "better accommodated the inhabitants owning the most of the wealth of Jefferson and Madison counties." He then posed a pivotal question, one that the directors of any railroad company could not ignore: "Is it not the duty of the Board to take the cheapest and best line—the one best adapted to do the largest amount of business and at the least cost to the company?"[34]

Whereas the directors always felt that the Pensacola and Georgia Railroad would become a conduit for traffic moving between Tallahassee and Jacksonville, Griffin opined that "a connection with Savannah is of equal if not greater importance than the others. Before determining the final route, I think the Board should first select the crossing of the Suwannee River with a view to a Savannah connection."[35]

Detailed maps accompanied Griffin's report, and after much deliberation Cabell's board opted for the survey that ran from Tallahassee to Bailey's Mills, thence to the Madison courthouse, crossing the Suwannee River near Columbus, and terminating in Columbia County at Alligator—the very route that CSX trains of today now utilize.[36]

As noted, Governor Broome supported the P & G and endeavored to sell $800,000 of its stock in middle Florida, but this efforts failed.[37] Undeterred, Cabell got the counties of Leon, Jefferson, and Madison to purchase $375,000 of stock, which supplemented private subscriptions of $149,000. Other funds would be realized once lands from the IIF were received and sold.

Cabell also oversaw the purchase of the Tallahassee Railroad from General Richard Keith Call. The acquisition was made "on the most favorable terms" with a down payment of $4,000; however, the total purchase price paid for the lucrative franchise has not been learned. Cabell then had the old cotton carrier entirely rebuilt. Its strap rail and mule-drawn trains vanished, new iron rails and crossties were installed, and two, 16-ton steam locomotives arrived from builder Mathias Baldwin of Philadelphia. The engines were named for the P & G investors and bankers H. L. Rutgers and General Bailey.

A special excursion train ran down the refurbished line on 13 December 1856. The eighty guests, including Governor Broome and members of the General Assembly, then supped together at the St. Marks Hotel.[38] One year later, Cabell proclaimed that the St. Marks line "is now one of the best paying roads in the country."[39] On another good note, the railroad's shops in Tallahassee were turning out rolling stock for other southern railroads. The concern employed over sixty persons, and in 1860 it produced one hundred freight and eight passenger cars.[40]

While the St. Marks line was being rebuilt, construction simultaneously proceeded on the railroad's main line east of Tallahassee to Lake City. Contracts for the work were given to wealthy planters and merchants along the line, who were compensated with a combination of cash, stock, and bonds. Construction supplies were landed by ship at St. Marks, brought up to Tallahassee by rail, and then dispatched eastward in work trains to various staging areas.

That portion of the P & G route from Tallahassee and Capitola was completed in November 1857. Drifton was reached the following January, together with a short branch north of town to Monticello. Greenville, which was initially known as Station Five because it was the fifth station east of the capital, got the iron horse in 1858. That July, the railway was completed to Madison. Other labor gangs advanced the project west of Alligator. Wellborn was reached in summer of 1858, whereupon the final gap, Wellborn to Madison, by way of Live Oak and Ellaville, was closed. The entire route was opened to the public in December 1860, with passenger trains traversing the line from Tallahassee to Lake City in seven and a half hours.[41]

Prior to the road being completed, Cabell resigned his presidential post and later relocated to St. Louis, Missouri, where he died.[42] He was succeeded by Leon County planter and Savannah native Edward C. Houstoun. Houstoun not only oversaw the last of the construction work but also resolved several financial issues. Cabell's successor, though, deeply regretted that the company never built a connection to Savannah. Moreover, he considered the P & G's agreement with the Florida, Atlantic and Gulf Central Railroad to direct all cotton bales and produce to Jacksonville and not Fernandina to be a "fatal blunder."[43] As the next chapter relates, the wealthy businessman would guide the P & G through the Civil War and the infant years of Reconstruction.

The Dream of Captain Chase

As noted, Pensacola's first railroad venture ended in shambles. Fortunately, though, railroad interest in the great naval and lumber port never really died thanks to the untiring efforts of Captain William Chase, who began agitating for a new project in 1844. Four years later, the army officer made his third appeal to Congress for a new land grant, which was again denied. Later that decade, Chase flaunted his new project before a railroad convention in Montgomery, Alabama. The phoenix finally arose from the ashes on 8 January 1853, when Florida chartered the Alabama and Florida Railroad.[44] That May the company was formally organized with the indefatigable Chase being named president.

The new line, far smaller in scope than the one begun in territorial days, was to stretch for 45 miles between Pensacola and the Alabama border. Private investors subscribed to $116,000 of company stock, while the City of Pensacola bonded itself for $250,000. Other funds would be realized from the sale of land grants made to the company by the Internal Improvement Fund as well as the federal legislation of 1856.[45] Even though the land grants had not yet been deeded to the railroad, the directors signed a construction contract with Milnor, Broughton & Company in February 1856. As headlines in the 22 March *Pensacola Gazette* proclaimed: "Joy to Pensacola! Clear the Track! The

Pensacola's railroad guru of territorial days was Army Captain William Chase, who fought tirelessly to connect the great naval port with Alabama. He lived to see the deed completed. State Archives of Florida.

Railroad Is Coming!" The article also chastised two rival ports: "It will in a few years be necessary for people in New Orleans to send to us for the necessities of life, and Mobile would be desolate only for us."[46]

Groundbreaking ceremonies took place in Pensacola on 12 April at the future depot site on Tarragona Street. Whereas the territorial rail project departed Pensacola in an easterly fashion over swamplands so as to reach the Escambia River, the revived project departed Pensacola northward to Pollard, Alabama. A branch track from the Pensacola would extend southward to the company's dock at the foot of Tarragona Street, which would facilitate the transfer of freight between trains and ships.

Construction of the new line proceeded rapidly, and by July 1856 some 10 miles of the roadbed were declared complete. Negotiations for the iron rails began the following year even though sufficient funds for same were not in hand. Nevertheless, two private investors stepped forward with the requisite capital; they took, in return, a mortgage upon the railroad's assets. In 1859, the land grants from Florida secured an issue of second-mortgage bonds.[47]

These fresh injections of capital allowed completion of the line to Pollard in 1861. On 5 May, using a $30,000 emergency loan from the State of Alabama, Charles T. Pollard finished his Alabama and Florida Railroad between Montgomery and Pollard. The following day, a ten-hour passenger train schedule was inaugurated between Montgomery and Pensacola.[48] The dream of Captain Chase had at last come true.

Dr. Westcott's Vision

History tells us that New Jersey native John Westcott was a man of refinement and numerous talents. Westcott received a civil engineering education at West Point, but later embarked upon a medical career. At one point, he was the surveyor general of Florida. The good doctor also owned a plantation in Tocoi, near the St. Johns River, which boasted extensive orange groves.

Convinced that a railroad was needed between St. Augustine and Tocoi Landing, Westcott and his colleagues obtained a charter from the legislature for the St. Johns Railroad on 31 December 1858. Most of the 14.5 mile line pierced huge stands of virgin timber.[49] Not only did Westcott become the firm's president, but he was probably the only CEO in state railroad history who surveyed his company's right-of-way.

Owing to swamplands, the St. Johns Railroad terminated about 1.5 miles shy of St. Augustine proper, on the west bank of the San Sebastian River. To save money, the company's directors had the line constructed with iron strap rail—a throwback to territorial days. In another frugal measure, the firm opted to have its trains hauled by horses and mules! A solitary coach with "calico curtains" was acquired, which accommodated both freight and passengers.

A journey over the tiny St. Johns Railroad took an unusual amount of time—from four to five hours—as the animals had a tendency to frequently lie down and rest. The one-way fare was two dollars, a somewhat steep charge for such a short distance. Westcott, himself, fielded many complaints about the time-consuming trip and exorbitant rate. His retort never varied: "Quite true, sir, tho' I want to tell you this: you

The horse-drawn trains of the St. Johns Railroad frustrated more than one traveler. Why? Frequently the animals had to lie down and rest in the course of a journey. State Archives of Florida.

will travel longer over *this* line than over any other line in the United States for the same sum."[50]

The railroad's primitive state finally convinced Westcott and his directors to launch a rebuilding program in 1859. Investors were approached in New York City, and a $25,000 mortgage was arranged, all of which paved the way for new iron rails, new passenger cars, and even a steam locomotive. Because the line now conformed to IIF construction standards, the fund's trustees gave Westcott's firm a land grant of 42,086 acres. The rebuilding program was completed just a few months after Fort Sumter was fired upon. As the next chapter relates, Westcott's firm would soon be decimated by Union forces.

Senator Yulee's Railroad

A cross-state railroad connecting the Atlantic Ocean with the Gulf of Mexico had tantalized Florida visionaries since territorial days. Its construction meant that vessels would no longer have to round the peninsula's southern tip and pass through the treacherous waters of the Florida Straits. Further, some 800 miles on the transit between New York and New Orleans would be totally eliminated.

In 1831, the territory's legislative council asked army engineers to locate a line of railroad between the two bodies of water, a request that was ultimately ignored.[51] Three years later, a cross-state railroad company surfaced, the Florida Peninsula and Jacksonville. Nothing materialized. In 1835, a congressional committee "inquired into the expediency of constructing, *at the national expense*, a railroad from Jacksonville, on the St. Johns River, to the mouth of the Suwannee River." This aroused the interest of certain capitalists located in Savannah and Boston. The former got the Atlantic and New Orleans Seaboard Line Railroad chartered in Georgia, though its promoters never applied for a Florida charter. The Boston entrepreneurs, however, sought council support, which, in 1835, issued a charter for the East Florida Railroad Company. But only a partial survey of the route resulted.

On the heels of these endeavors came the Florida Peninsula Railroad and Steamboat Company, which had been given the right to construct a cross-state line from "the St. Johns River to any point between the Suwannee River and Tampa Bay." Little, though, did the company accomplish. The fourth project that garnered attention, the Tampa Bay and St. Johns Railroad, Canal, and Steamboat Company, came alive in 1841. Capitalized at $1 million, a survey was made, and the cost of constructing the 80-mile route, from Palatka to Clay's Landing on the Suwannee River, was estimated at $320,000. However, not a shovelful of dirt was turned.

Finally, in 1842, the cross-state scheme took on a more serious dimension when David Levy, Florida's delegate to Congress in territorial days, persuaded the secretary of war to run a survey for a cross-state railroad. Army engineers conducted the task, who concluded that such a project could be built from the St. Marys River to Cedar Key. And with that pronouncement, the real story of this enterprise began.

Two years later, Levy wrote an open letter to Floridians stating that the 500,000 acres of federal land to be given Florida when admitted to statehood should afterward be sold and the proceeds applied to "the construction of a railroad from the Atlantic to the Gulf of Mexico that

Florida U.S. senator David Yulee founded the cross-state railroad between Fernandina and Cedar Key. Before its completion, however, he had to relinquish financial control to northern investors. State Archives of Florida.

would become the property of the State without the impositions and exactions which a private chartered monopoly would impose."[52] For several years thereafter, Levy did not see himself as the owner of such a company.

Born in 1810, Levy spent his childhood years as a British subject on the island of St. Thomas in the West Indies. His father, Moses, came to Florida after the War of 1812, when the landscape was still under Spanish rule. David was educated in Virginia, after which he helped run his father's plantation near Micanopy. Possessing considerable intelligence and wonderful oratorical skills, Levy later studied law in St. Augustine with federal judge Robert Reid, a future Florida governor. After being admitted to the Florida bar in 1822, Levy decided to practice law in that city's old Spanish setting.

Six years later, Levy's public career began in earnest when he became a delegate to Florida's constitutional convention. A legislative clerkship followed three years later. Then, in 1841, Levy was elected to the U.S. House of Representatives, where he fought vigorously for Florida's admittance to the Union.[53] Statehood was granted in 1845, the same year that Levy became Florida's first U.S. senator. In the following year, he changed his name to David Levy Yulee, in honor of his family's original surname. He would later serve in the U.S. Senate for two nonconsecutive terms.[54]

What attracted Yulee to railroading is not precisely known, though he was undoubtedly aware how railroads were legally privileged and that, given the right circumstances, they could be quite profitable. Over many years, the cross-state railway scheme had played on his mind: "The transit of the trade and travel of the Gulf across Florida became a picture in my mind, the lines of which, more faint at first, were deepened with each year. To achieve this grand result for my State, became a point of ambition. To the realization of the idea, I commenced to apply myself."[55]

But as the years rolled by, the astute politician realized that a once-in-a-lifetime business opportunity was presenting itself, one that private enterprise—and not the state—was better suited to finance and build. The spirit of capitalism no doubt swept over Yulee, and likely intensified after he lost his senatorial seat in 1851 to Stephen Mallory of Key West.

How Yulee's cross-state railway scheme would function was not uncomplicated. After ships departed such gulf settings as Galveston, New Orleans, Mobile, or Pensacola, they would proceed to the railroad's western terminus at Cedar Key, where they would break bulk. Stevedores would then remove the freight manifests and place them in cars of an awaiting train on Yulee's railroad, whereupon it would chug across the peninsula to the company's terminal on the Atlantic Ocean at Fernandina, some 150 miles distant. Again, cargoes would be off-loaded and placed aboard ships for the transit up the Atlantic seaboard or to foreign ports. (The process would be reversed for vessels heading to gulf ports.) If anyone doubted the cross-state railway's potential traffic, Yulee was quick to point to a single statistic: that the value of all trade in one year passing around Florida (en route from New York to New

This bird's-eye view of Cedar Key depicts how the Florida Railroad reached the dock by way of trestlework. Trains met connecting vessels and exchanged freight as well as passengers. Author's collection.

Orleans) was estimated by the U.S. Treasury Department to be $325 million.[56]

In addition to capitalizing on the gulf to Atlantic traffic (and vice versa), Yulee's railway would also exploit the trade that flowed to Cuba, Key West, Mexico, and the Isthmus at Nicaragua. There was also the local passenger and freight traffic that lay east and south of the Suwannee River, where the fertile soil yielded cotton, sugar, tobacco, fruits, and vegetables. Other local revenue generators would include the carriage of livestock, naval stores, and lumber. "There can be no doubt that the local resources on our route will yield a remunerative return upon the cost," claimed Yulee.[57] If one defect could be found with Yulee's cross-state railroad, aside from the labor intensivity of the scheme, it was the fact that the future railroad connected with no other at its gulf or Atlantic terminals.

Fernandina, the proposed eastern terminus of the line, was probably the best deepwater port south of the Chesapeake. The setting largely became known to the commercial world during the American embargo war of 1811–12: "It is said that as many as two hundred square-rigged vessels have been in port there at the same time." Its excellent harbor, landlocked with good anchorage, had 20 feet of water "on the bar" and 30 to 50 feet at the inner harbor. "From the plateau of the town the approach of vessels can be observed seaward as far as a telescope can sight."[58] Acquiring parcels at the inviting setting therefore became paramount, and by 1858 Yulee had quietly obtained title to some 3,500 acres, this before real estate owners could artificially inflate prices.

Years earlier, Yulee had decided upon the location of the cross-state railway's western terminus. In 1834, two citizens of Alachua County—John Gilliland and Edmund Bird—accidentally discovered the Cedar Key islands, and their harbor, while in search of cedar trees. Although neither man obtained title to the remote and uninhabited setting, they later disclosed its location to Yulee, whose "mind immediately adopted it as a Gulf terminus."[59] Again, Yulee went quietly about obtaining title here to nearly 1,000 acres. According to United States Coast Surveys, the depth of water at Cedar Key was between 10 and 12 feet, barely sufficient for oceangoing vessels to use the harbor and meet trains, a fact that was later used by Yulee's detractors.

The first cross-state company Yulee organized—the Atlantic and Gulf Railroad in 1849—failed because his coinvestors found the charter defective in several regards. Amendments were obtained to rectify the problems, but the charter ultimately expired. Yulee, tenacious as ever, pressed on. On 8 January 1852, legislators sanctioned the Florida Railroad Company with a capitalization of $1 million. "I was determined to keep this charter under Florida control," Yulee notes, "and to let the stock pass only as the road was assured."[60]

The new charter stated that the proposed route would begin in East Florida

> upon some tributary of the Atlantic Ocean, having a sufficient outlet to the ocean to admit the passage of sea steamers, and shall run through the eastern and southern part of the State, in the most eligible direction, to some point, bay, arm or tributary of the Gulf of Mexico, in South Florida, south of the Suwannee River, having a sufficient outlet for sea steamers, to be determined by a competent engineer, with the approval of a majority of the directors of said Company.[61]

Two years later, in 1854, Governor James Broome appointed Yulee to the state's new Internal Improvement Board, the very body that would craft the Internal Improvement Fund Act of 1855. Among those rail lines mentioned in the bill deserving of state aid was—conveniently enough—a cross-state railroad between the Atlantic and Gulf. That Yulee's hand was all over the act could hardly be argued, one newspaper going so far as to declare him the "father" of the Internal Improvement Fund, the "Great Projector of a mighty System of Railroads.[62]

By using a recent army survey, the route of Yulee's entity was quickly established. In fact, the survey's creator, Lieutenant Martin Smith, became the chief engineer of the Florida Railroad Company. In March 1855, Yulee notified the IIF trustees that his company wished to be aided. So as to make Yulee's old charter conform to the act, legislators rechartered the firm in December, increased its capitalization to $6 million dollars, and restated its route as now being from "Amelia Island on the Atlantic, to the waters of Tampa Bay in South Florida, with an extension to Cedar Key in East Florida."[63] As the company's principal stockholder, Yulee felt that the extension to Cedar Key should be built first, a decision that would alienate many of his supporters like Governor Madison Starke Perry and certain constituents in the Tampa Bay area who would eventually burn Yulee in effigy.

The Florida Railroad was to begin in Fernandina and proceed across the Nassau River to the mainland. Then the single track would wend its way to Callahan, thence to Baldwin, where it would intersect Dr. Baldwin's firm, the Central. Once clear of the junction, Yulee's road would proceed in a southwesterly fashion for the Trail Ridge district, Starke, and Waldo. Somewhere in this region, likely at Waldo, a divergence point would be selected from which the main line would head for Ocala and Tampa, while the extension would proceed westward to Cedar Key via Gainesville, Archer, and Otter Creek. According to the railroad's 1855 annual report, the cost of constructing and equipping the 142-mile route between Fernandina and Cedar Key was estimated at $2,202,454, or $15,537 per mile (2006 dollars: $47,685,551, or $336,393 per mile). The estimates of both the road's length and its cost would prove incorrect.

Yulee himself drew up a construction contract with Anson Bangs & Company of New York, though for some unknown reason it was short-lived. He then executed a new one with Joseph Finegan & Company on 11 June 1855.[64] Nothing about the early railway construction experience of Joseph Finegan (1814–1885) has surfaced, save that he hailed from Ireland and was known to have been a planter, lumberman, cotton broker, and real estate purchaser for Yulee, especially in Fernandina, where Finegan eventually resided in a forty-room mansion. Finegan also became a brigadier general in the Confederate army and handily won Florida's Battle of Olustee. In 1857, the contractor decided to form a partnership with Colonel Archibald Cole and General Alexander MacRae, the latter formerly the president of the Wilmington and Weldon Railroad in North Carolina. Whether the Florida Railroad contract had initially overwhelmed Finegan has not been learned.[65]

In brief, Yulee's contract with Finegan stated that all work was to meet the standards of the Internal Improvement Fund Act of 1855, that the railroad was to be completed within two years, and that the maximum grade of the route was not to exceed 15 feet per mile. It was also incumbent upon Finegan's firm to fabricate all necessary bridges, culverts, trestlework, pilings, water tanks, depots, as well as the piers at Fernandina and Cedar Key. Also, Finegan was to supply the railroad with its initial roster of locomotives, passenger coaches, and freight cars.

As far as compensation was concerned, Joseph Finegan & Company would receive $20,000 per mile of track completed; $100,000 for the bridge necessary to cross the Nassau River from Amelia Island; and an additional $100,000 for the culverts and water crossings that would be needed at Cedar Key.[66] At Finegan's behest, the compensation was to be paid half in railroad bonds and half in cash. Yulee's firm eventually issued two kinds of bonds: those endorsed by the IIF that were secured with a first-mortgage lien upon the company's assets, and another series, called "free land" bonds, that did not carry the state endorsement but were secured by certain other real estate. (Finegan was paid with the latter.) With a final route length of 154 miles, the potential value of the Finegan contract, including all contingencies and extra expenses, was about $3.5 million, or $22,580 per mile. The Florida Railroad would attempt to raise this amount by floating $1,655,000 of state-endorsed bonds and $1,500,000 of free land bonds, and by selling $345,000 worth of company stock.[67]

After the drawbridge from Amelia Island to the mainland was completed in September 1856, the pace of construction quickened. As each 10-mile section was finished with crossties, the state engineer, Francis Dancy, inspected and certified the work. Dancy then notified the IIF trustees in Tallahassee, who endorsed the company's bonds. As stated in the IIF act, the bond proceeds had to be largely used for the purchase of iron rails, tie plates, and spikes.

This excellent progress continued until 1857, when the nation began to experience another financial panic. Cash became scarce, the demand for American products abroad fell sharply, and a significant downturn occurred in the commercial bond market. American railroads were particularly hard hit, and Yulee's road—not yet opened and producing revenues—experienced a severe cash-flow problem, as did Finegan's construction firm. The railroad's directors therefore had no choice but to pressure Finegan to complete the line to Cedar Key as rapidly as possible.

It was during this difficult interval that an imbroglio occurred on the Florida Railroad. In the summer of 1858, the engineers experienced considerable difficulty in locating a section of the track through the Trail Ridge district below Baldwin, near present-day Highland.[68] The subcontractor laying track, who was fast approaching the troublesome spot, decided to leapfrog the area and install crossties farther along the line that had recently been graded. When State Engineer Dancy later made an inspection of the region, the section in question had been finally located but was hardly in a completed state. Convinced that grading would soon occur and that crossties would promptly be installed, Dancy nevertheless issued his certification as if the work had been finished. Afterward he notified the trustees, who, in turn, endorsed the bonds of the railroad. For the moment, no one in Tallahassee knew of the gaffe.

About this time, Governor Madison Starke Perry (1814–1865) departed his plantation near Micanopy to meet with Yulee and his directors in Fernandina. After pleasantries were exchanged, the state's chief magistrate demanded that Yulee's firm alter its route between Waldo and Cedar Key so that it would pass through Micanopy and not Gainesville. Yulee was dumbfounded by the request, and it devolved upon his fellow directors to explain to Perry why such a change was impossible at this late date. A heated exchange apparently took place, and before long Perry stormed out of the company's offices.[69] The following day, Yulee and the board discussed the possibility of rerouting the company's main line to Tampa via Micanopy, but rerouting the extension from Waldo to Cedar Key and bypassing Gainesville was completely out of the question.

Governor Perry, once an ardent supporter of Yulee, never quite forgot his reception in Fernandina. He then wrote to the senator and demanded that his company immediately begin work on the main line to the more important gulf terminal of Tampa, and to cease construction on the extension to Cedar Key. Yulee wrote back and said the governor could not dictate the affairs of his company. (The railway was then open between Fernandina and Starke; some 35 miles more had been graded toward Cedar Key.) Somehow, Perry now became privy to what Dancy had recently certified as being complete. Whereas the state engineer would eventually be dealt with, the more pressing issue was whether or not Yulee's company had issued bonds with a state guarantee to which it was not legally entitled. Thus began a "war of knives."

As chairman of the Internal Improvement Fund, Governor Perry ordered his secretary to write Dancy for a complete explanation of past events, though for some reason the state engineer never received the letter (or perhaps he did and destroyed it). Since no response was forthcoming, the trustees engaged a consulting engineer—Jonathan Bradford, who had worked on the Pensacola and Georgia Railroad—to investigate the indiscretions and report back any other violations. Then the trustees authorized Perry to seek legal counsel.

Yulee got wind of the impending investigation, whereupon his own directors passed a resolution "to adjust with the Governor or the counsel employed by him, the damages which may have resulted to the Trust Fund." Bradford eventually submitted a lengthy report, and when Perry addressed the legislature in November 1858, he directly and indirectly accused the Florida Railroad of many irregularities, such as issuing illegal bonds, building a poorly constructed bridge from Fernandina to the mainland using state funds, falsely claiming that Cedar Key could admit the passage of sea steamers, and installing track in a poor and inconsistent manner.[70] Legislators were agog at the accusations, especially since they were leveled at perhaps Florida's most distinguished citizen.

Immediately, legislators formed a "Joint Select Committee" to investigate the governor's allegations. A six-week inquiry followed, during which considerable testimony was obtained from both sides and numerous exhibits were laid before committee members. After sorting through the evidence, they issued their report on 10 January 1859. The committee acknowledged that the Florida Railroad had indeed experienced difficulties while laying its track (largely because the crossties had never properly settled into the ground) and that a bond endorsement had been made for a section of railroad not properly completed. But to Yulee's relief, the committee concluded that no irreparable harm had come to the Internal Improvement Fund.

The report also confirmed that bond proceeds for the drawbridge between Amelia Island and the mainland, even though improperly located, had not been squandered. (No judgment was passed upon the bridge's design or safeness, which, according to Bradford, was substandard.) That the waters at the Cedar Key terminal were incapable of admitting sea steamers was also proved false, for data contained in the United States Coast Surveys, relied upon by the railroad but somewhat out of date, confirmed otherwise. Several minority reports of a critical nature were eventually filed, and State Engineer Dancy, who had started the miserable affair, was reprimanded for his "looseness" of manner regarding the track certification.[71]

In 1858, the Florida Railroad Company set off that portion of its route between Waldo and Tampa to a subsidiary called the Florida Peninsular Railroad. Yulee became its president, and the route completely bypassed Micanopy, which no doubt infuriated Perry. Grading of the line began that August, but work ceased when the Civil War erupted.

If the imbroglio with Perry was not enough, a more serious problem now confronted the Florida Railroad: finances. The panic of 1857 had greatly diminished the availability of investment capital in America, especially for railroad companies. Further, northern investors were becoming increasingly skittish about southern projects in light of the sectional issues of slavery. With its cash rapidly drying up and demand falling for company bonds, bankruptcy seemed a real possibility for

Wealthy steamship owner Marshall Roberts provided most of the
funds to complete the Florida Railroad. He was part of a New York
investment syndicate headed by lawyer Edward N. Dickerson, who
had successfully defended the Goodyear vulcanized rubber patent.
Author's collection.

Yulee's company. Further, Finegan & Company could not purchase supplies or meet payrolls because of its own cash problems. On 8 May 1858,
the partnership threw in the towel.[72]

Without a contractor, the failure of the Florida Railroad was a real
possibility. Having no other alternative, Yulee had to bring in northern capitalists to rescue his firm, and quickly. His white knight became
Edward N. Dickerson, a New York investor and eminent patent lawyer.
E. N. Dickerson & Associates not only acquired more than half of the
railroad's stock (obtaining financial control in the process), but they
assumed the construction contract as well. Among those in the Dickerson fold was Marshall O. Roberts, the wealthy president of the United
States Mail Steamship Company.

With nearly $750,000 in fresh capital, completion of the railroad to Cedar Key was assured. In fact, the Florida Railroad fully opened for traffic on 1 March 1861.[73] In time, a telegraph line marched alongside the route and, thanks to Roberts, a mail route contract was obtained between Cedar Key and Havana. About this time, Yulee delivered an impassioned speech to stockholders, remarking that the 154-mile railroad had been built "through a period of many accumulated difficulties."[74] He also noted that a "great civil revolution" was descending upon America. But the ardent secessionist made no reference to his bittersweet feelings about bringing in northern investors and having to relinquish financial control. Without them, though, Yulee's railway dream would have crashed.

4

The Agonies of War, Reconstruction, and Fraud

Railroads shall remain free from toll or other charges upon the transportation of any property or troops, of the State of Florida, or of any other Government legitimately succeeding to the powers, rights, and privileges of the late United States.

—Florida Laws, 1860–61

The bombardment of Fort Sumter in April 1861 marked the formal start of the American Civil War, that "great tragic volume" that John Quincy Adams glimpsed back in 1820.[1] But as devotees of Florida history well know, events of import were occurring long before the cannonade resounded over Charleston harbor.

"The year of 1860 was one of unrest, suppressed feeling, and vague military preparation," notes the historian William Watson Davis.[2] Volunteer military companies were organized in Fernandina and Tallahassee. On 10 January 1861, Florida passed an Ordinance of Secession, the third state to do so, after South Carolina and Mississippi. Less than a month later, the Confederate States of America was organized for "protecting, expanding, and perpetuating slavery."[3] State troops eventually seized the arsenal at Chattahoochee, as well as Fort Clinch on Amelia Island, Fort Marion in St. Augustine, and the valuable naval yard at Pensacola.[4]

Lincoln's strategy for preserving the Union echoed that of Winfield Scott, general-in-chief of the U.S. Army. Scott's so-called Anaconda plan was to physically constrict the Confederacy "by controlling the oceans and Western waters, blockading it from the sea and splitting it along the Mississippi, so that when Union forces finally advanced they would deal with a much-weakened enemy."[5] Jeff Davis, on the other hand, felt that the Union would not fight, though his two exalted generals—Lee and Jackson—knew that victory could only be obtained by "entrapping the Northern army into a decisive battle, ruining it, and then to take Washington and seek a compromise."[6]

The Civil War was the first American conflict to actually involve railroads, and from its outset the North held a superior edge. The twenty-three states of the Union possessed 22,385 miles of railway lines, while the eleven of the Confederacy had but 8,783.[7] Of the $1.1 billion that investors had poured into American railroad securities prior to the war, only $237.1 million had gone for southern enterprises. In almost every instance, northern railways were better built, equipped, maintained, and managed.

During the hostilities, every southern railroad experienced a sharp increase in expenses. Coal shot up in price, as did lubricating oil, glass, and kerosene for coach lighting. Spare parts became difficult to obtain. Labor shortages also existed, and those workers who were available demanded higher wages. But because of cash-flow problems, payrolls were often paid late or sometimes not at all. Iron rails, over which the very trains rolled, became exceedingly scarce, for not a single new one was cast in the South after 1861. This forced Confederate military authorities to impress, or cannibalize, iron rails from already-built routes.

Essential to any railroad company were its steam locomotives, which had to be kept in good running order. Yet, many in the South fell by the wayside simply for lack of parts, routine repairs, or preventative maintenance. The famed Tredegar Iron Works in Richmond produced many prime movers prior to the war, but had to put such orders aside when the Confederacy instead demanded ordnance. No such problems occurred in the Union, where—north of the Potomac—a dozen locomotive manufacturers existed for every single southern producer.

After visiting Florida in November 1861, Robert E. Lee advised its residents to protect not the state's 1,400 miles of coastline but its valuable interior, where beef cattle and agricultural products flourished. It was upon the supply of these commodities (together with sea salt)—in addition to the troops the state provided—that the wartime reputation of Florida would rest. But getting these foodstuffs deep into the Confederacy—at least by rail—often proved very difficult, especially since no track connected Florida with Georgia until the war's end. On the eve of Appomattox, Lee's army was starving because a trainload of food had never reached it, forcing soldiers to eat roots and green corn.[8]

The seizure of Florida's coastal defenses began in January 1862, when the Union warship *Hatteras* entered the almost deserted port of Cedar Key. The "Feds" came ashore and torched five schooners, three sloops, the depot of the Florida Railroad, seven of its freight cars, and a warehouse filled with turpentine. Then the invaders pulled down all nearby telegraph wires. David Yulee, the company's founder, afterward inspected the devastation and comforted what few persons remained.[9]

In early March, a large Union naval detachment descended upon Fernandina, the Atlantic terminus of the Florida Railroad. Just as the lead gunship arrived at the inner harbor, the vessel's master spotted a train steaming for the mainland, loaded with inhabitants and their household goods. A New York newspaper correspondent detailed the pursuit:

> Upon the gunboat approaching the railroad bridge, which connects the island with the mainland, several rifles were discharged from the windows of the cars, which were nearing the bridge at the time, while a small body of the Fourth Florida Regiment of Dragoons, who were mounted, discharged their revolvers, at the same time while riding furiously through the bushes. Captain Stevens of the gunship *Ottawa*, thinking that the train was freighted with soldiers, discharged a shell which struck the rear car—a platform car loaded with furniture—and burst, scattering the furniture on all sides, and instantly killed two young men named Savage and Thompson, who were seated on a sofa. The rebels loosened the last car, and the train immediately proceeded on its way and succeeded in getting over the bridge. Had the gunboat arrived a little earlier it would have succeeded in stopping the train and arresting both David L. Yulee, who was formerly Senator from Florida, and Colonel Joseph Finegan, commander of forces on the island, who were on the train at the time.[10]

This drawing shows Union soldiers commandeering a Florida Railroad train at Fernandina. Bales of cotton and casks of turpentine are being moved about by African American stevedores. Author's collection.

Federal soldiers went ashore and confiscated three of the railroad's locomotives, several platform cars, and large quantities of rice, cotton bales, whiskey, molasses, and naval stores. "The few white people who are left touch their hats or bow as they pass us, but they all have a half-frightened, half hang-dog look, as if they feared some injury.[11]

With the Florida Railroad's gulf and Atlantic terminals now seized, Yulee relocated the railroad's headquarters to Gainesville for the war's duration. Concern then mounted as to whether Union forces would use the rail line to invade the interior of the peninsula. Yulee discussed the matter with military officials, but talks went awry when he discovered that his company's iron rails would soon be taken up and used for other Confederate projects. The former U.S. senator protested vehemently, especially after Florida governor John Milton told Yulee that the "order to impress" would stand and that anyone interfering with the work would be arrested. No stranger to the law, Yulee obtained a court injunction that temporarily halted Milton's efforts, though another scenario would play out in 1864.[12]

The secession of Florida and the formation of the Confederacy took the day-to-day, direct control of the Florida Railroad away from its real owners—Edward Dickerson & Associates of New York. An article in the *New York Times* even suggested that Yulee's hasty withdrawal from the U.S. Senate had been partly motivated by his Florida Railroad investments. For the moment, the Dickerson syndicate was now regarded in the South as enemy aliens.[13] Did Yulee possibly think that his new Confederate government would confiscate the railroad and return ownership to him? No one knows for sure.

The Dickerson crowd no doubt breathed a sigh of relief when Union forces began occupying Florida ports, though their new confidence was shaken when the military eventually withdrew from the settings. Their faith was again renewed when the U.S. Congress passed two confiscation acts (1861 and 1862), which made certain Confederate-owned property subject to seizure by the federal government. The acts of course pleased northern supply houses that had extended credit to southern firms. Among them was the locomotive builder Danforth, Cooke & Company of Patterson, New Jersey, who had sold Yulee's firm two locomotives. Still unpaid, the builder asked federal authorities to confiscate and sell the engines and forward back any proceeds. Marshall Roberts, lead investor of the Dickerson fold, even obtained title to two undelivered steamships ordered by Yulee for use in the Gulf of Mexico.[14] Roberts also attempted possession of the Florida Railroad using several other ploys (like using federal tax commissioner Lyman Stickney), but the efforts failed. After the war, E. N. Dickerson & Associates regained full control. In fact, several of the partners did everything in their power to keep Yulee in prison until "they were satisfied that he would co-operate with them. Only Dickerson himself kept the Associates from completely wiping out the southerner's holdings."[15]

Following the conquest of Fernandina, a federal squadron sailed down to Jacksonville. The vessels anchored at the mouth of the St. Johns River, and a boat was sent ashore for news. "Negroes reported that Jacksonville was being abandoned, and that the fortifications along the lower St. Johns had been dismantled."[16] As nightfall approached, several hundred Confederate troops arrived in the city via the Florida, Atlantic and Gulf Central Railroad, with the mission to destroy all property useful to the enemy. The ensuing conflagration lit the night sky, and flames reduced the railway's facilities to a cinder. As they retreated west, the soldiers then tore up numerous sections of the railroad track.

The federal gunboats *Ottawa*, *Seneca*, and *Pembia* now sailed up the St. Johns with orders to destroy every dock, warehouse, cotton gin, and sawmill. Tocoi Landing, western terminus of the little St. Johns Railroad, was blasted to bits, whereupon the "Yanks" went ashore and destroyed the railroad's cars and sole steam locomotive. Even the company's new iron rails were confiscated, which were then shipped off to the Union supply depot at Hilton Head. Company founder Dr. John Westcott was crestfallen at the carnage, and almost five years would pass before the pint-size carrier would reopen.[17]

Confederate troops withdrew from the great naval port of Pensacola in 1862. Not wishing to leave behind an intact railroad, soldiers confiscated the locomotives and rolling stock of the Florida and Alabama Railroad, along with its iron rails between Pensacola and Pine Barren Creek. The rails themselves were later used on rail projects in Alabama; some were even rerolled into armor for the gun batteries that protected Mobile Bay.

When military authorities announced that they were going to impress all remaining iron rails, company president O. M. Avery dashed off to Richmond and bitterly complained. Though Secretary of the Navy Mallory called the impressments a "damned outrage," in the end the military got its way. Rail was not taken up, however, on the 5-mile Pensacola and Mobile Railroad and Manufacturing Company that opened during the war between Muscogee and Fifteen Mile station, near Cantonment.[18] Avery eventually sought $432,326 for everything the military had seized, impressed, or destroyed.

A less contentious scenario played out in middle Florida during the war, where cotton, tobacco, and foodstuffs flourished. The route of the Pensacola and Georgia Railroad (P & G) penetrated the territory and quickly became a strategic supply artery. Business on the line actually flourished, which allowed management to undertake two expansion measures: extending the main track west of Tallahassee to Quincy, and helping construct the first railroad connection between Florida and Georgia.

For years, Quincy—the seat of Gadsden County and war headquarters of middle Florida—lacked railway service. But thanks to the P & G,

Union gunboats demolished the Tocoi Landing dock of the St. Johns Railroad. Years later, the facility was rebuilt. All seems well in this 1880s view, which features a train and steamboat. State Archives of Florida.

the "iron horse" arrived in February 1862. Iron rails for the project were in the United States Custom House at St. Marks when the war began. When that facility was seized by Confederate authorities, the P & G immediately got its rails, but the company failed to pay certain duties and tariffs, an oversight that sparked federal litigation in 1870.

The purpose of the company's Live Oak Branch (sometimes called the Live Oak–Lawton Connector) was to expedite the movement of troops, munitions, and foodstuffs from Florida into Georgia. Initially, the 47-mile project was a joint venture between the P & G and Georgia's Atlantic and Gulf Railroad. The former built that portion of the line lying between Live Oak and the Georgia border, by way of Madison and Jasper, while the latter advanced the project from the state line to Lawton, now known as Dupont. As early as 1862, the Florida portion was fully graded with crossties, but it lacked iron rails.[19]

About this time, the Confederate military became interested in the undertaking, and Robert E. Lee declared the branch to be "of the greatest advantage."[20] Finding the requisite rails for the Florida portion of the line became a priority, and David Yulee's little-used Florida Railroad again became the target. In March 1862, Florida governor John Milton was authorized to "impress" the latter's iron rails and spikes west of

Fernandina, an order endorsed by Confederate General J. H. Trapier.[21] Yulee, though, refused to cooperate, even after Milton utilized Joseph Finegan as an intermediary. The governor then penned a series of letters that he thought would appeal to Yulee's sense of patriotic duty. But it was for naught. The former senator simply would not agree to the confiscation, claiming he lacked the authority to give away the company's assets.

After nearly eighteen months of wrangling, Milton took up the matter with Jeff Davis and his secretary of war. The removal task was then assigned to the Confederacy's Engineering Bureau, which, in March 1864, ordered Major Minor Meriwether of the Railroad Iron Commission "to proceed south and complete the work in the shortest possible time." Accompanying him was Lieutenant Jason Fairbanks.[22]

Alerted to the removal effort, Yulee secured yet another court injunction. Papers were subsequently served on Fairbanks, but his senior officer advised him to ignore the order and proceed. This he did, but in the company of armed guards! When circuit court judge James Dawkins learned of the defiant response, he instituted contempt proceedings against Fairbanks, who by now had torn up about 3 miles of the Florida Railroad. When Fairbanks failed to appear in court, Dawkins issued an arrest warrant.

A local sheriff scoured the countryside and confronted Fairbanks in Lake City. After the lawman read the warrant, Fairbanks read the order that protected his person and work detail, whereupon his guard detachment threw up a wall of bayonets. Unable to secure his prisoner, the sheriff ignominiously departed.[23] Judge Dawkins, infuriated, now ordered Governor Milton "to vindicate the majesty of the law."[24] Nothing more was done, however. The long-awaited Live Oak Branch, with impressed iron rails, opened for traffic on 4 March 1865, too late to benefit the Confederacy. Within sixty days, its army in Florida would surrender.

Another Civil War event indirectly involving a railroad was the 1864 Battle of Olustee. Union forces came to occupy Jacksonville four different times during the hostilities. During the final invasion, General Truman Seymour had orders to destroy the Suwannee River Bridge of the Pensacola and Georgia Railroad, near Ellaville. To reach the structure, Seymour marched his troops alongside the Florida, Atlantic and Gulf

Before distinguishing himself at the Battle of Olustee, Confederate General Joseph Finegan built a good portion of U.S. senator Yulee's cross-state Florida Railroad. The Irish immigrant was a self-made man. State Archives of Florida.

Central Railroad from Jacksonville to Baldwin, some 20 miles distant, where they arrived on 9 February. The federals then destroyed the railway junction along with a large Confederate supply building containing cannon, camp equipage, cotton, rice, molasses, blankets, hides, salt, flour, sugar, and turpentine.

Eager to bring Seymour's troops into battle was Confederate General Joseph Finegan, former contractor of Yulee's Florida Railroad. Finegan selected suitable ground near Olustee (Ocean Pond), a few miles east of Lake City. Skirmishes forestalled the actual encounter with Seymour's forces, allowing time for Finegan's reinforcements to arrive and entrenchments to be thrown up. On 19 February, Union soldiers were at Barbers station. The next day they walked right into Finegan's trap, and the battle commenced: 5,500 Union soldiers against a force of 4,600. Florida's most famous Civil War encounter ended by nightfall with

Finegan winning handily. Afterward, Seymour's troops made a hasty retreat back to Jacksonville alongside the railway track.[25]

Several other events involving railroads occurred in 1864. In late July, the federal army burned the railroad bridge over the St. Marys River, then tore up parts of the Florida Railroad between Baldwin and Cedar Key. Also, Negro troops of the Union destroyed a fair amount of the Florida, Atlantic and Gulf Central line between Jacksonville and Baldwin. In July 1865, a federal raiding party out of Cedar Key proceeded inland for some 30 miles and burned the Wassassee River Bridge of the Florida Railroad and demolished many portions of the company's track.

With the surrender of Lee and Johnston, the "War of the Rebellion" slowly began to wind down. More than sixteen thousand Floridians ultimately participated in the struggle. About fifteen thousand soldiers served the Confederate Army, while about 1,200 residents would defend the Union cause. The statewide destruction was enormous: "The assessed value of real and personal property in Florida, exclusive of slaves, shrank to $25,000,000 from approximately $47,000,000—a decline of 47 per cent." The emancipation alone wiped out about $22 million in slave values.[26]

The era of Reconstruction (1865–77) was an attempt to rebuild and reform the South politically, economically, and socially, and to recast the subject of race relations.[27] Part of that task was restoring the region's devastated railway industry. Because the southern portion of the United States was so endowed with waterways, and because many portions of the region had developed before railroads even came of age, certain persons felt that the wartime destruction of railroads would not paralyze southern commerce. Such was not the case, for railroads had dramatically altered trade patterns all over the South. Thus, their restoration was absolutely essential for the southern economy to once again function.[28]

The Stars and Stripes was hoisted atop the Florida Capitol on 10 May 1865. Fifteen days later, martial law was declared, whereupon the federal military began managing the state's railroads. Practically every carrier was destitute. Many lines were seriously damaged, their rails had been impressed in numerous localities, and countless engines and cars

The July 1868 issue of *Frank Leslie's Illustrated Newspaper* ran this view of Tallahassee. Union tents are pitched beyond the Pensacola and Georgia Railroad train. Over the capital flies the Stars and Stripes.

exhibited a derelict condition. Further, little maintenance had been performed during the war years, though many postwar repairs would be carried out—gratuitously—by the U.S. military.

Railway transportation in Florida was certainly in a demoralized state, as one newspaper correspondent discovered while journeying between the capital and Lake City.

> The passage from Tallahassee is slow and tedious; the railroad, like everything else in the Confederacy, fallen into decay and ruin. Starting at 7 a.m. on a train of platform cars with no seats, you ride eight miles to a gap in the road, where for three miles the rails have been removed. Here, the freight, baggage, and ladies are transferred to army wagons and hauled round, while the male passengers walk across, under a torrid sun, to the White House, the former residence of a planter named Pettis, now deserted, and subject to occupation by any and all who choose. Here, after an hour's delay, the train from Lake City—a couple of box cars, a cattle car, and dilapidated passenger coach—arrived and took all on board and forwarded us to Lake City, 65 miles from Jacksonville, where we arrived at 4 p.m. After a good supper and a tolerable night at the Hancock House, we were aroused at 4 a.m. to

take the cars back to Tallahassee, 105 miles distant, which took twelve mortal hours to accomplish. Halting now for wood, and then for water; now for breakfast, and finally to actually *rest* the engine![29]

Among those firms hardest hit was the Florida Railroad between Fernandina and Cedar Key. Just 38 percent of the 155-mile route was usable after the war. Rotten crossties abounded, a thick coating of rust covered what iron rails remained, and much of the right-of-way was overgrown with vegetation.[30] David Yulee, the company's founder, was still behind prison bars in Fort Pulaski, near Savannah, Georgia.[31] On 8 May 1865, the railroad petitioned the federal army for a locomotive to replace the one seized by the Confederacy. Weekly service between Cedar Key and Baldwin resumed in July, and to Fernandina in early 1867.[32]

Finances on Yulee's old firm were rickety at best. For example, monies simply did not exist for bond interest coupons or sinking fund obligations owed to the Internal Improvement Fund. In fact, in January 1866, New York investor Marshall Roberts asked the fund's trustees to pay the interest on just one of his many Florida Railroad bonds. Incredibly, not even the IIF had any cash to do so. Other bondholders began to complain, and that November the trustees had no choice but to seize and sell the railroad. The new purchaser became Isaac Roberts (brother of Marshall), who had the deeds made out to Edward N. Dickerson & Associates. Thus, the owners of old remained in control.[33]

The purchase price paid by Roberts, $323,400 for a road that cost well over $1 million to construct, retired many of the Florida Railroad's first mortgage bonds. The bondholders themselves were given two settlement options: $200 for every $1,000 bond they owned (twenty cents on the dollar) or an equivalent amount of railroad-owned land. Francis Vose, a prominent bondholder who had sold iron rails to Yulee's company, refused both offers and sued the railroad along with the IIF and its trustees for the full face value of his bonds, which hamstrung the agency for years until a settlement was made.[34]

In 1869, the Florida Railroad reported revenues of $113,802 and expenses of $195,576, thus a loss of $81,774. In the following year, a deficit of $41,132 was recorded. To fund postwar repairs and improvements, the directors decided in May 1869 to float a new first-mortgage convertible bond issue. Several New Yorkers were named as trustees of the thirty-year, 7 percent issue, which amounted to $2.3 million. Company president Marshall Roberts prepared the prospectus, which described the firm as if it were a veritable gold mine. Interestingly, the document stated that proceeds of the bond issue would be exclusively used for "repairing and equipping the said Railroad, and restoring it to a condition of usefulness."[35]

The new bonds received a weak reception in America. They flourished abroad, however, especially with Dutch investors, who began subscribing in 1871. But the business renaissance described in the prospectus never manifested, which precipitated another corporate reorganization on 18 January 1872. Although the Atlantic, Gulf and West India Transit Company inherited the same rights and privileges, the new firm profited no better. Further, it managed to skip its interest coupon in 1873, a sure sign that problems were foot. In Europe, the $1,000 bonds sank to just 1 percent of par—a mere ten dollars! Dutch investors, enraged, organized a protective committee and dispatched Jacobus Wertheim, a prominent Amsterdam attorney, to America, "to save something from the wreck."[36] A foreclosure sale resulted, and the bondholders of old lost about two-thirds of their investment.

As noted earlier, the tiny St. Johns Railroad was decimated during the war. It managed to reopen, however, around 1870 but remained in a primitive state. An author visiting Florida traveled over the line during Reconstruction and commented:

Two hours strolling about under the shade-less pine trees used up our time while a little asthmatic tea kettle of a steam engine was being tinkered into going condition. It was hitched to two dilapidated boxes on wheels. The railroad itself is more disgraceful than the cars. The rails of pine and cypress (no iron!) were worn, chipped, slivered, and rotten. We smashed one flat to the crossties and had a narrow escape from being capsized into a swamp. We crawled along for nearly five hours, delaying at times to put a new rail on the track, to dip a few bucketfuls of muddy water from a ditch into the boiler, or to cut up a log to furnish nutriment for our wheezy little engine. At last the 15 miles accomplished, we reached St. Augustine tired and worn out. May we never go over that road again![37]

Eventually the St. Johns Railroad was acquired by New York millionaire William Astor, whose son later rebuilt the line. Depending upon traffic, trains on the Astor road were either hauled by a steam engine or the power of horses. Regardless, journeys over the line frequently ground to a halt while the engineer prodded sleeping alligators and bear cubs from the track![38]

Not only did the Florida and Alabama Railroad (out of Pensacola) lack monies after the war, but it was devoid of all locomotives and cars. Further, about 26 miles of its iron rails had been impressed. President O. M. Avery sued to recover the impressed rails and tried to obtain a business loan for equipment purchases. Meanwhile, bondholders were pressing for their interest. The company's largest stockholder, the City of Pensacola, voted to conduct a bankruptcy sale, thinking that a new owner could also fund a much-needed rehabilitation. In March 1868, the line was sold to Ruter, Millington & Company of Kentucky—for the absurdly low figure of $55,000. Because of legal issues, however, formal title did not pass to their reconstituted firm, the Pensacola and Louisville Railroad, until four years later.[39]

The Kentucky owners installed new iron rails, purchased missing equipment, and, by 1870, reopened the line from Pensacola to Flomaton, Alabama, 6 miles south of the old northern terminus of Pollard. They additionally erected an engine house in Pensacola along with new car shops, storage buildings, and a 2,000-foot wharf in Pensacola Bay.[40] Despite the outlays, business on the railway did not materially improve, which prompted another sale in 1872 to lumber merchant Albert Hyer, this time for $66,000. Five years later, Hyer sold out to Daniel and Martin Sullivan, local banking and lumber kingpins, who reorganized the entity as the Pensacola Railroad Company.[41]

Another carrier in west Florida receiving a facelift during Reconstruction was the Pensacola and Mobile Railroad Manufacturing Company, which was completely rebuilt in 1870. That same year, another area firm, the Pensacola and Fort Barrancas Railroad, began conveying traffic between its namesake points via Woolsey and Warrington. In 1873, the Pensacola and Perdido Railroad began constructing an 8-mile line that connected the naval port with the lumber mills at Millview, on Perdido Bay. The little concern generated revenues of $36,220 in 1876 and showed a profit of $3,918. Among its assets were five locomotives, seventy-two freight cars, and one passenger coach.[42]

Our survey of Reconstruction events now focuses on the Florida, Atlantic and Gulf Central, and its close ally the Pensacola and Georgia Railroad. After making postwar repairs, the "Central" began offering weekly service between Lake City and Jacksonville, while the P & G started running three trains a week from Quincy to Lake City.[43]

Owing to a shortage of capital, the Central failed to pay its bond coupons after the war or its sinking fund obligations to the Internal Improvement Fund. The trustees of the IIF, however, made good on the defaults, taking in return a like amount of Central stock. But the advances ceased in 1867, when the arrears exceeded $20,000. The trustees then decided to sell the Central at public auction that September, a decision that distressed President Franklin Dibble, a Jacksonville banker. Immediately, Dibble began discussing a possible consolidation with the company's ally to the west. Although a merger did not evolve, P & G president Colonel Edward Houstoun agreed to work with Dibble "to decrease costs and improve efficiency" on his line.[44]

About this time, a most unsavory figure descended upon Florida, "the most adroit agent of corruption who was ever known in North Carolina."[45] Eager to assemble a speculative railroad combination in the Sunshine State, George W. Swepson (1819–1883) began buying stocks and bonds of the Central in hopes of wresting control. By using the services of a Jacksonville attorney, Swepson secured a court injunction to stop the aforementioned auction. Although the maneuver failed, the trustees of the Internal Improvement Fund agreed to delay the sale until early March 1868.

Ultimately, William E. Jackson & Associates became the new owner of the Central, who paid $111,000 for a company that had $1,270,000 in assets and liabilities of $1,020,000. Outmaneuvered for the moment, Swepson challenged the purchase in court, claiming that the Central was bankrupt at the time of the auction. A federal judge later affirmed it was not.[46] Undeterred, Swepson now hired Colonel Edward Houstoun as his agent to obtain a controlling interest in the Central. This the P & G president accomplished; Dibble was ousted in the process, and

After committing frauds in North Carolina, banker
George Swepson created a speculative venture in
Florida using railroad securities. By permission of
the North Carolina State Archives.

Swepson reorganized the property in July 1868 as the Florida Central
Railroad. He then leased his new acquisition to Houstoun's Pensacola
and Georgia Railroad for ninety-nine years. The first component of the
North Carolinian's "speculation" was now in place.

As noted earlier, the P & G did a brisk business during the Civil War.
In 1865, the company enjoyed revenues of $875,639, incurred expenses
of $406,862, and recorded a gross profit of $468,888—the best perfor-
mance of any Florida railroad company. That year Houstoun journeyed
to New York, where he purchased materials, obtained five new locomotives on credit and enough iron wheels to build twenty-five new freight
cars. He also went shopping for new iron rails, which were readily available from suppliers but only on a cash basis. Even though the P & G's
income statement appeared healthy, recent outlays for overdue bond

interest and sinking fund contributions actually had depleted the company's cash position.

Houstoun needed the rails for the Live Oak Branch that connected Florida with Georgia because the ones that had been "impressed" for the project by Confederate military authorities had by now been returned to their rightful owner, the Florida Railroad Company. Upon his return to Tallahassee, Houstoun began raising cash for the rails, in conjunction with John Screven, president of the Atlantic and Gulf Railroad, who also wanted the Live Oak Branch reopened. The connector reopened in October 1866, and the P & G once again began funneling traffic over the border to Savannah, the favored port of cotton growers.

A greater pressure upon Houstoun was completing his company's route west of Quincy to Pensacola. For years, the citizenry of west Florida had been promised a railroad that would link their part of the state with the capital and the rest of the peninsula. Not only were residents of that region restless, but serious discussions were afoot about annexing the land to Alabama, whose government promised immediate railroad relief.[47] To help raise funds for the western appendage, Houstoun's board decided to sell its Live Oak Branch to the Atlantic and Gulf Railroad, an act the Florida legislature approved on 13 December 1866. However, this action alone hardly furnished all the necessary funds for the project to Pensacola.

While Houstoun was pursuing these objectives, traffic began to decline on the P & G. Expenses increased; profits shrank. Unable to service its bonded debt, the trustees of the Internal Improvement Fund extended a helping hand to the P & G, just as it did with the Central. But the interest makeups eventually ceased, whereupon the trustees announced that they would auction the P & G on 20 March.[48]

Unbeknownst to many, Houstoun had all along been trying to sell his Pensacola and Georgia Railroad, and among those now keen to purchase it was George Swepson. By now, Swepson had reconciled his differences with Franklin Dibble and hired the banker as his agent to acquire Houstoun's companies. (Why Swepson did not deal directly with Houstoun has not been learned.) Dibble won the auction by bidding $1,220,000 for the P & G, along with $195,000 for the former Tallahassee Railroad down to St. Marks. Immediately people began asking: who was George Swepson and where was he getting these kinds of funds?

It is no secret that during Reconstruction the political affairs of North Carolina were controlled by a corrupt Republican government. In 1868, Raleigh banker George Swepson and his protégé General Milton S. Littlefield (1830–1899) joined hands to obtain control of the Western Division of the Western North Carolina Railroad, based in Asheville.[49] Governor William Holden, who was later impeached, got the state to purchase two-thirds of the railroad's stock and, in lieu of cash, proffered $6,367,000 of state bonds, which were to be sold and the proceeds applied to construction costs. The bonds, however, generated just $1,909,486 for the firm owing to market conditions. Little of that amount, though, went into the railroad's coffers. In fact the "sum of $843,633 was personally invested by Swepson in securities of certain Florida railroad companies."[50]

Swepson obtained Houstoun's two firms for $1,415,000 by giving the trustees of the Internal Improvement Fund $807,600 of P & G bonds together with $195,000 of Tallahassee Railroad bonds. The transaction was reprehensible, for the trustees had (1) advertised the auction as a "cash only" sale; (2) they accepted the P & G bonds at their full face value of $1,000 apiece instead of their true depressed market value of about thirty-five cents on the dollar; and (3) they tendered from Swepson a worthless check for over $400,000 to cover the difference. Whether the parties agreed or not, the State of Florida had just been defrauded.[51] Later, Swepson received legislative approval to consolidate Houstoun's two companies into a new entity: the Tallahassee Railroad, not to be confused with the old cotton carrier to St. Marks. And with these maneuvers, the second ingredient of Swepson's "speculation" was now in place.

If anyone wanted the missing rail link built from Quincy to Pensacola, it was Florida governor Harrison Reed (1813–1899). A former newspaperman who had postal department experience, Reed had been elected to office in 1868 as part of Florida's first postwar civil government. The Wisconsin native was confronted with many problems: the state treasury was empty, Florida's railroads were bankrupt, the economy was in shambles, and the school system was defective. Pos-

Union General Milton Littlefield took a shining to George Swepson, who schooled the affable officer in the genteel ways of swindle and embezzlement. Neither man was prosecuted for his Reconstruction misdeeds. Collection of the Railway & Locomotive Historical Society.

sessing more enemies than friends, Reed was forced to work with a legislature that was "largely illiterate and grossly venal." Nevertheless, he constantly stressed the virtues of economy, ethics, and honest government.

There was great pressure upon Reed to connect middle and west Florida with a railroad. The annexation issue was heating up, and several Alabama lights had recently appeared before the Florida legislature promoting the movement. At first Reed supported annexation, but he later reversed himself after two gentlemen told him that they were willing to undertake the big project. Those persons were George Swepson and Milton Littlefield.

Swepson now retreated from the limelight and allowed Littlefield, "a man of singular courtesy and intelligence," to take the reins. A personal friend of Governor Reed and his wife, Littlefield had trained African

American troops during the Civil War. Afterward, the Union officer apprenticed with Swepson in the gentlemanly art of speculation and embezzlement. The Maine native eventually acquired two homes in Florida—the superb mansion of General Richard Keith Call in Tallahassee, and a less fashionable residence in Jacksonville. Once installed, Littlefield began bribing legislators with cash, "free" loans of money, and casks of whiskey and champagne, jewelry, and Cuban cigars. The most recalcitrant legislator found Littlefield's ways charming; his eyes, hypnotic. As one Florida senator chronicled:

> The carpetbag element seemed to be elated, and the hotels and boarding houses in Tallahassee were filled with strangers. The poorest and the shabbiest carpet-bagger could be seen drinking the sparkling champagne and wearing fine beavers. The famous Littlefield was too much engaged to walk, and his carriage was kept at the hotel in readiness to convey him to any part of the city to see the different members of the Legislature. Within ten days twenty-two thousand dollars was distributed by Littlefield as a corruption fund.[52]

In order to construct the missing rail line to Pensacola, Littlefield needed a charter that was packed with incentives. Governor Reed set the stage by calling up a special session of the legislature to consider "An Act to Perfect the Public Works of the State of Florida." Of course, legislators knew what was afoot for the Littlefield "gifts" were in recent memory. Accordingly, on 24 June 1869, the Jacksonville, Pensacola & Mobile Railroad (J, P & M) came alive with a capitalization of $6 million.

Initially, Littlefield wanted $20,000 of state bonds for every mile of the J, P & M route—from Jacksonville to Pensacola—regardless if built or unbuilt. Legislators, though, balked. Littlefield then reworked the bill and asked for $14,000 of bonds for every mile constructed west of Quincy, along with the right to exchange J, P & M bonds with those of the state, dollar for dollar. Legislators found this more palatable *provided* the state obtain a first-mortgage lien upon the railway's assets from Jacksonville to Quincy, which was already built. They also insisted that Littlefield produce clear titles to all the underlying companies whose assets were going to be pledged, a tiny problem owing to the previously mentioned bogus check and the fact that certain deeds were never made out.

Littlefield saw no reason why legislators had to muddy up the charter's final version with a lien clause, or demand certain proofs of title. Rather than complain, the "Prince of Carpetbaggers" decided to pursue a far easier solution: he bribed a state employee to omit the offending clauses from the J, P & M railroad bill just before it was officially recorded in the law books. No voice was raised in protest, though one Florida newspaper later opined that Littlefield's action was "a cunning fraud, boldly and adroitly perpetrated."[53] As an aside, the charter did not consolidate Swepson's Florida Central Railroad (Jacksonville to Lake City) into the J, P & M; thus, for the moment at least, the Florida Central could not exchange its own bonds with those of the state.[54]

The J, P & M was organized in New York City in July 1869. Littlefield was named president. The following May, legislators amended the company's charter and merged the Florida Central into the J, P & M. They also allowed the latter to issue bonds at $16,000 a mile, including for that portion of the railway already built between Jacksonville and Quincy. Thus, Littlefield got what he originally wanted. As the historian William Watson Davis remarked, "state officials had been either fools or knaves, or both."[55]

The J, P & M wasted little time in minting $3 million of 8 percent bonds and then exchanging them —dollar for dollar—with those of the state. The Florida Central Railroad issued $1 million worth as well. Governor Reed questioned the legality of exchanging the latter, but his fellow trustees of the Internal Improvement Fund convinced him otherwise. And with that, the fleecing began in earnest.

Swepson and Littlefield placed most of the Florida state bonds it received with S. W. Hopkins, a New York brokerage house. But just as sales got under way, a disparaging article about them appeared in a New York City newspaper. Sidney Hopkins then shipped off the securities to England, where the picture momentarily brightened until the British press got on to the story. In the meantime, Littlefield sailed for Europe, where he lived large. In his spare time, he peddled the securities in London, Paris, Brussels, Frankfort, and Vienna. John Collinson, a London broker, managed to dispose of nearly $2.8 million worth to a Dutch syndicate. Respectable firms in both Amsterdam and Rotterdam

JACKSONVILLE, PENSACOLA & MOBILE RAILROAD CO.

GENERAL MANAGER'S OFFICE,
JACKSONVILLE, FLA., Dec. 27, 1871.

ON AND AFTER SUNDAY, December 31, 1871, and until further notice, trains will run as follows;

ARRIVE.	ARRIVE.		LEAVE.	LEAVE.
7.50 a. m. ar.	6.00 p. m. ar.	Jacksonville	8.00 p. m. de.	8.30 de. a. m.
6.50 a. m.	5.00 p. m.	Baldwin	9.15 p. m.	9.35 a. m.
4.40 a. m.	2.50 p. m.	Lake City	11.35 p. m.	11.45 a. m.
3.20 a. m.	1.35 p. m.	Live Oak	3.30 a. m.	1.35 p. m.
12.00 a. m.	12.30 p. m.	Ellaville	4.10 a. m.	2.10 p. m.
10.45 p. m.	11.45 a. m.	Madison	5.10 a. m.	2.50 p. m.
8.20 p. m.	10.25 a. m.	Junction	7.00 a. m.	4.10 p. m.
6.00 p. m.	9.00 a. m.	Tallahassee	8.50 a. m. ar.	5.25 p. m.
	7.05 a. m.	Quincy		7.45 p. m.
	4.50 a. m. de.	Chattahoochee		9.50 ar. p. m.

Connects at Jacksonville with Brock's Line of Steamers for all points on the upper St. Johns river. At Baldwin with trains on the Florida Railroad for Fernandina, Gainesville and Cedar Keys. At Live Oak with trains on the A & G. Railroad for all points in Georgia and the North. At Tallahassee with trains for St. Marks.

J. H. GARDNER,
General Manager.

The Jacksonville, Pensacola & Mobile Railroad proved a convenient cash box for Swepson and Littlefield. Later, an English investor, Sir Edward Reed, wrested control of the firm. Author's collection.

then began selling the securities to unsuspecting investors. To impress the foreigners, about $461,000 in interest was paid on them, proving they were a very good investment.[56]

The bond sales eventually netted a few million. After Swepson and Littlefield paid themselves and their henchmen, just $309,000 finally made its way into the coffers of the Jacksonville, Pensacola & Mobile Railroad, barely enough to extend the line for 20 miles from Quincy to River Junction (Chattahoochee). The goal of reaching Pensacola failed.

In 1873, the Florida legislature repealed the bonds it had exchanged with the railroad. Three years later, the Florida Supreme Court declared the entire issue unconstitutional, and thus repudiated the lot. This precipitated a flood of litigation against the J, P & M. At one point, three interrelated cases were being heard by the U.S. Supreme Court.

Amazingly, neither Littlefield nor Swepson were prosecuted for their misdeeds, despite America's highest court accusing them of "the most shameless frauds." At one point, the new governor of North Carolina offered a $5,000 reward to anyone delivering Littlefield to him for prosecution. Florida governor Reed offered a like amount for anyone attempting to kidnap his old friend. And on the sordid tale went.

Reed survived four different impeachment attempts, but owing to technicalities he managed to fulfill his term of office. Interestingly, he revealed in subsequent testimony that he had accepted from Littlefield one of latter's special "loans" of $223,750, about $3,270,000 in 2006 dollars.[57]

In retrospect, the swindle had been balanced on the backs of innocent Dutch investors, most of whom spoke not a word of English but were confident of a certain railway company in far-off Florida.[58] On their behalf, in 1879, the U.S. Supreme Court had a lien placed upon the railroad's assets. As one Florida newspaper summarized, "The Jacksonville, Pensacola & Mobile Railroad has proven itself to be a fraudulent, insolent, arrogant, bold, unscrupulous, and remorseless concern."[59]

5

An Extraordinary Quartet

These railway kings are among the greatest men, perhaps I may say are the greatest men, in America. They have wealth else they could not hold the position. They have fame, for every one has heard of their achievements; every newspaper chronicles their movements. They have power, more power—that is, more opportunity of making their personal will prevail—than perhaps any one in political life, except the President and the Speaker, who after all hold theirs for only four years and two years, while the railroad monarch may keep his for life.

—James Bryce, *The American Commonwealth*, 1890

A railway renaissance in Florida, one long repressed in advancement, began to unfold after the era of Reconstruction. Communities everywhere began clamoring for the iron horse, especially in the peninsula, where a labyrinth of lines would one day be built. As Rowland Rerick states in his *Memoirs of Florida*: "The golden orange was now guiding the footsteps of the immigrants and the lines of the railroad engineer."

Whereas previous state administrations had encouraged railway construction, the inviting atmosphere proffered by Governor William Bloxham (1835–1911) had no parallel. When elected in 1881, Bloxham declared that it was both "his pleasure and duty" to develop internal improvements like railroads, as well as to encourage immigration and to educate the rising generation, "the three great links in the grand chain of progress upon which the State could confidently rely for future growth and prosperity."[1]

A graduate of Virginia's William and Mary College, Bloxham had initially planned upon a career in law, but owing to poor health he instead became a successful planter in Leon County. Bloxham entered public

Railroad builders and developers became enamored of Governor William Bloxham with good reason: he reactivated the Internal Improvement Fund, which distributed attractive land grants. State Archives of Florida.

life before the Civil War, and after serving in the Confederate army his political star began to rise. The staunch Democrat possessed a fine intellect and superb oratorical gifts, and before long members on both sides of the aisle sought his wise and prudent counsel.

The newly inaugurated governor wasted little time in demonstrating his mettle. So as to create revenues for his social programs and to lower burdensome levies, he insisted that railroad companies must pay their proportional share of taxes. Until this time, the myriad firms had refused to do so, claiming that they were exempt under the Internal Improvement Fund Act of 1855. But the state's chief magistrate felt otherwise, believing that only those companies and routes specified in the act should get the exemption, and that all others had to pay. Legislators agreed, whereupon Bloxham's attorney general was ordered "to bring suits against the existing companies to compel payment."[2]

Concurrent with this demand, Bloxham directed his energies to the moribund Internal Improvement Fund—the great dispenser of railroad land grants. Unable to pay interest on defaulted railway bonds, the fund's assets had been frozen ever since the Vose decree was handed down in 1870. Not even Aristides Doggett, the fund's federal receiver, could restore solvency. Thus, the unpaid interest, ongoing legal bills, and daily expenses continued to mount. When Bloxham took office, the encumbrances amounted to $959,934. Bankruptcy of the fund was imminent, and an application was before the federal court to either let the harmed parties manage the fund's vast inventory of lands or let Doggett sell the parcels at public auction to completely satisfy the claims.[3]

Bloxham's solution, one that had eluded prior administrations, was to negotiate the sale of several colossal land tracts (owned by the fund) and use the proceeds to erase the indebtedness. Various parties, such as Samuel Swann, had been pursuing this tact on behalf of the state when Bloxham learned about a youthful and wealthy entrepreneur from Philadelphia. Hamilton Disston (1844–1896) had inherited the largest saw and file manufactory in the world, Henry Disston & Son, which had been founded by his immigrant father.[4] An avid sports fisherman, "Ham" had first visited central Florida in 1877, where he met fellow Republican and capitalist General Henry S. Sanford (1823–1891), who was developing a ready-made city and extensive orange groves near Lake Monroe.[5]

In time, Ham became fascinated with the possibility of draining certain "swamp and overflowed lands" owned by the fund for agricultural purposes. Accordingly, Disston and his colleagues filed an agreement with the trustees of the IIF in early 1881 to drain and reclaim an extensive tract near Peace Creek in exchange for half of the property involved. But when Disston learned that title conveyance could not occur, owing to the encumbrances, the deal started to sour.

Eager to rescue the situation, Bloxham met Disston at a fishing camp to discuss the fund's plight. Knowing that Disston had the means and wherewithal, the pair struck a deal: Disston would purchase 4 million acres of swamp and overflowed lands at twenty-five cents per acre, less than what other state agents were trying to obtain. The two shook hands, and Bloxham publicly announced the big land transaction on 30 May.[6]

Critics howled over the ridiculously low figure, though they were powerless to stop Bloxham because the governor was also chairman of the Internal Improvement Fund. The $1 million in proceeds retired the fund's indebtedness and—to the delight of promoters and developers—the IIF once again began dispensing land grants to railroads and other companies. In all, some 8.25 million acres were gifted during Bloxham's first administration.[7]

Disston became the nation's largest private landowner in the process, and he eventually formed a syndicate to help pay for the purchase, suggesting perhaps that his pockets were not as deep as everyone thought. After combing the land for coinvestors, Ham eventually off-loaded half of his purchase (2 million acres) to a foreign syndicate that was headed by the wealthy English capitalist Sir Edward Reed along with Jacobus Wertheim, a prominent Amsterdam attorney who represented many Dutch investors.[8] In December 1881, Reed set up shop in both Jacksonville and London.

As an aside, once the indebtedness of the Internal Improvement Fund was cleared, legislators began giving away more land to new railroad companies than had been patented to the state from the federal government. As one reader pointed out to the editor of the *Jacksonville Florida Times-Union* (26 January 1884): "The three last Legislatures have granted, or attempted to grant to projected railroads . . . out of a public domain which had never at any time exceeded 14,831,739 acres, the enormous quantity of 22,360,000 acres." Naturally no complaint arose from the railroad quarter, and eventually the gaffe was cured.

About the time of Bloxham's inauguration, Florida was beginning to attract the interest of four spectacular developers, only one of whom was an up-from-the-ranks railroader. Colonel William D. Chipley (1840–1897) had become general manager of the Pensacola Railroad (Pensacola to Flomaton, Alabama) in 1876. A Georgia native and graduate of the Kentucky Military Institute and Transylvania University, Chipley had been thrice wounded in the Civil War. Later, he became treasurer of Georgia's North and South Railroad and went on to serve the Virginia Midland and the Baltimore & Ohio Railroads.[9]

Shortly after his arrival in Florida, Chipley decided that the Pensacola Railroad needed to be succored by a larger enterprise. There was no better candidate, he thought, than the Louisville and Nashville Railroad (L & N), one of America's premier firms, which, at the moment, was on a buying spree. With approval from its owners, Chipley initiated takeover discussions with L & N president Victor Newcomb and his general manager, Frederick DeFuniak. In February 1880, after evaluating the company's books, the L & N purchased the firm for $157,545. The addition pleased Newcomb, who noted in the L & N annual report for 1880 that the transaction "had exceeded all expectations." That year, the new feeder produced profits of $22,364, while $35,343 was declared in the following year.[10]

After acquiring and rebuilding the Pensacola firm, the L & N organized the Havana Steamship Company. Chipley, in the process, became the L & N's area superintendent. Shortly afterward, Chipley went before L & N management with yet another proposal: that the company build the much-desired railway link between Pensacola and River Junction (Chattahoochee), something that the Jacksonville, Pensacola & Mobile Railroad had failed to do. Chipley explained to L & N management that this region of Florida was devoid of railroad service and that it possessed extraordinary stands of timber that represented a tremendous traffic potential. Another inviting factor was that Florida had just reactivated its Internal Improvement Fund, which meant the L & N would receive an attractive land grant.

Chipley's proposal met with acceptance, and the Pensacola and Atlantic Railroad Company came into existence on 4 March 1881. Chipley and DeFuniak became incorporators, and they were named vice president and president, respectively. The Florida legislature, thrilled that a renowned firm like the L & N would undertake the project, bestowed upon the new entity a stupendous land grant: 20,000 free acres for every mile of railroad it would complete. When added to the federal land grant of 1856, the L & N eventually received 2,219,294 acres, practically one-fifteenth of the state of Florida.[11]

To fund construction of the new line, the Pensacola and Atlantic issued $3 million of stock and a like amount of first-mortgage bonds, whose principal and interest was guaranteed by the L & N. So as to maintain a majority control of the subsidiary, "Old Reliable" (a sobriquet of the L & N) subscribed to three-fourths of all P & A stock and purchased every one of the company's bonds.[12]

Work commenced in June 1881, although an official groundbreaking ceremony did not occur in Pensacola until 22 August. The project was divided into three major sections. Local and out-of-state contractors were hired for the work, and at one point more than 2,200 laborers, mostly African Americans, were toiling at a daily rate of $1.50.[13]

Aside from Pensacola, just two communities of consequence existed on the new line when the project began: Milton and Marianna. Almost all of the other settings—such as Crestview, DeFuniak, Bonifay, Chipley, Cottondale, and Sneads—were really children of the railroad. A substantial Victorian station, replete with steeple, was erected in Pensacola at Tarragona and Wright Streets. Milton and Marianna also received framed depots, but most settings got nothing more than a sidetrack with a lowly boxcar serving as a station building. There were no compromises, though, when it came to building the P & A track, which utilized the finest materials, including 60-pound-to-the-yard steel rail. Every wood crosstie, bridge timber, and trestle component was milled from area forests.

Excitement mounted throughout the Panhandle as construction advanced. Although many of its inhabitants knew something about railroads or had ridden on a train, many provincials were totally baffled by the "iron horse." "Some thought it had life," noted a railroad construction worker. "They even asked me if a train could get into the door of a man's house."[14]

By far the greatest engineering challenge was bridging the wide mouth of Escambia Bay, located about 10 miles east of Pensacola. To close the gap, one of the railroad's contractors fabricated a 2.5-mile bridge with a draw span measuring 200 feet wide. A special train from Pensacola eased over the new structure in August 1882. After reaching terra firma in Santa Rosa County, the consist halted, whereupon a round of cheers went up for Colonel Chipley. The special then resumed its easterly trek. Many residents stood at trackside "waving handkerchiefs and other manifestations of rejoicing." On the trip home, Chipley intentionally halted the special on the immense drawbridge. With champagne glasses in hand, the guests detrained and inspected the impressive details close up.[15]

The P & A opened between Pensacola and the Apalachicola River in January 1883. Until the big bridge over that stream was completed in April, freight and passengers were temporarily shuttled across the river by boat, then by wagons and coaches to reach River Junction. Later, two daily passenger trains were traversing the new line. The Atlantic Express and the Gulf Express covered the trip in about six hours. Both halted for a meal stop at the Chautauqua Hotel in DeFuniak, 80 miles from Pensacola. The railroad's accommodation train, which stopped at every hamlet in search of passengers and freight, accomplished the same run in thirteen hours.

The Pensacola and Atlantic Railroad generated $189,098 of revenues in 1883, incurred expenses of $163,796, and showed a profit of $25,302. Land sales furnished another $58,000 of income. However, profits did not cover the interest owed to bondholders. Not to worry! The L & N covered the shortfalls until 1885, when it instituted friendly foreclosure proceedings. The P & A subsequently vanished as a corporation, and the route across the Panhandle became known as the L & N's Pensacola and Atlantic Division.[16]

During the late 1880s, the L & N became interested in shipping Alabama coal out of Pensacola. It subsequently enlarged its coal car fleet, extended its Muscogee Wharf at Pensacola, and dredged the channel to a depth of 28 feet. Additionally, the L & N board ordered two oceangoing steam tugs and several barges and invested in Export Coal Company. Soon ships were steaming out of Pensacola for Latin American ports with coal, lumber, salt, rice, sugar, bricks, phosphate rock, fertilizer, and manufactured goods.[17] To facilitate the influx of new rail traffic, the L & N opened a 100-acre switching complex in Pensacola (Goulding Yard) in 1896.

A number of small railroads surfaced in west Florida after the L & N established a presence; all depended upon "Old Reliable" for connections to the outside world. One firm the L & N actually purchased was the unfinished Alabama & Florida, which, in 1902, it proceeded to complete between Georgiana, Alabama, and Graceville, Florida. About halfway along its route was located Duvall, Alabama. By installing rails down to Florala, the L & N obtained a handy connection with Florida's Yellow River Railroad for Crestview, a lumber concern that was opened in 1894 by sawmill operator W. B. Wright.

When the Louisville and Nashville Railroad opened its Pensacola & Atlantic subsidiary across the Panhandle, all of west Florida rejoiced. A colossal land grant was then extended to the firm. Author's collection.

Colonel William Chipley, who did so much for breaking the railroad isolation of west Florida, eventually became the L & N's land commissioner for the state. He also served as mayor of Pensacola, ran that city's board of trade, became a state senator, chaired the Democratic State Executive Committee, and organized the annual Florida Chautauqua event at Lake DeFuniak. Chipley died suddenly in 1897 at age fifty-seven. Though Chipley is buried in Georgia, a splendid obelisk to his memory now stands in Pensacola's Plaza Ferdinand VII.[18]

Although he did not achieve Chipley's notoriety in Florida, English capitalist Sir Edward Reed (1830–1906) made substantial investments in Florida land and railroads. History, though, will forever remember him as a renowned authority on naval architecture. As previously noted, Sir Edward figured into the Disston land purchase, using his 2 million–acre holdings to form the Florida Land and Mortgage Company with offices in both Jacksonville and London. Local managers actually communicated with Reed's office, in London's smart Westminster, using a secret telegraphic code.[19]

Without question, Reed's career was unique. He had trained as an apprentice in England's Sheerness Royal Dockyard, where his outstanding abilities were quickly recognized. Later he attended a select school for mathematics and naval architecture at Portsmouth, from which he graduated in 1852. His first appointment, overseeing dozens of draftsmen, bored him, and he discharged his frustrations by writing poetry. He then took over the editorship of a popular mechanical magazine. In 1854, Reed offered the British Admiralty a design for an armored frigate whose concept was far ahead of its time. Afterward he helped form the Institution of Naval Architects. Before long, the Admiralty began to take Reed's abilities seriously, and he was subsequently commissioned to design several ship prototypes. When the First Lord of the Admiralty retired, Reed became chief constructor of the British navy.[20]

But Reed's star was just rising. After the American Civil War, he began to receive design commissions from many foreign countries. By using complex calculations and careful experiments, Reed unveiled several novel principles that improved armor, turret guns, ballast, and hydraulics. In the late 1870s, when his investments in Florida railroads were just beginning, he entered the political arena by representing England's Pembroke and Cardiff districts, all the while serving on several

C.B.

CHIEF CONSTRUCTOR OF THE NAVY.

and Vice President of the Institution of Naval Architects.

Sir Edward Reed infrequently visited Florida and thus was regarded as a shadowy figure. The wealthy investor though had figured into the Disston land purchase and owned several railroads here. By permission of the National Portrait Gallery, London.

parliamentary committees. He was twice knighted and, in 1876, became a Fellow of the Royal Society.[21]

It is not known why such a distinguished personage became so involved with Florida railroads, but Florida certainly has always presented an inviting field of investment opportunities for foreigners. No doubt Reed's naval commissions generated substantial fees that, in turn, provided investment funds. Further, Reed likely had investment advisors who were knowledgeable about American railroads, for many U.S. companies attempted to sell their securities in England and on the Continent. Lastly, the various investment firms abroad were in constant communication with one another. For example, one of the many trading partners of Barings of London was Hope & Company in Amsterdam. When Dutch investors were defrauded by the infamous Jacksonville, Pensacola & Mobile Railroad (see chapter 4), they selected Jacobus Wertheim as their representative. Reed and Wertheim knew one another, and both played a role in the Disston land syndicate.

Shortly after forming his Florida land company, Reed the railroad investor became Reed the railroad owner. His first acquisition was the old Florida Central Railroad—Jacksonville west to Lake City—which he purchased at auction in January 1872 for $395,000. The following month, Reed picked up the Jacksonville, Pensacola & Mobile Railroad—Lake City west to River Junction, which had been mired in litigation since the 1870s. (Reed and Wertheim had large stakes in both companies.) That same month, the Florida legislature allowed Reed to consolidate his two purchases as the Florida Central and Western Railroad.[22] To manage its affairs, Reed brought in an experienced railroader and ex-army officer from Kansas: Major Benjamin S. Henning.

The Florida Central and Western operated a rail system between Jacksonville and River Junction, along with branches to St. Marks and Monticello. Shortly after its creation, the company issued a descriptive guidebook about the so-called Floral City Route that proved popular with newcomers, farmers, and immigrants, all of whom were flocking to Florida in record numbers. Many of these persons needed to purchase land, and Reed's land company stood, of course, at the ready. But Reed himself envisioned a far larger empire, and he now set his sights on the railroad founded by U.S. senator David Yulee.

As noted in chapter 4, the Florida Railroad was reorganized in 1872 as the Atlantic, Gulf and West India Transit Company. Back then the firm ran a cross-state rail line between Fernandina and Cedar Key (by way of Waldo and Gainesville) and owned a subsidiary (the Peninsular Railroad, chartered 1876) that was to complete the main line to Tampa. The latter had actually been constructed from Waldo down to Ocala, via Hawthorne, Lochloosa, Citra, and Anthony, a region endowed with numerous citrus groves and vegetable farms. To capitalize on the tourist attraction of Silver Springs, the railroad additionally had a 2-mile branch constructed (near Ocala) to the popular setting. The Peninsular Railroad, including its Silver Springs Branch, opened for business on Independence Day, 1880.

Advancing rails south of Ocala to Wildwood and Panasoffkee became the objective of yet another subsidiary: the Tropical Florida Railroad, which surfaced in January 1881. The remote and woodsy location of Wildwood got rail service in June 1882. Curiously, its residents first feared the railroad's arrival, believing that once trees were felled for the track, heavy winds would blow along the right-of-way and destroy crops. The terrain along the Tropical Florida route was far from forbidding, but the company's contractor spent a considerable amount of time overcoming the mushy Panasoffkee Swamp, into which the track occasionally sank. To the delight of villagers, the iron horse chugged into Panasoffkee proper on New Year's Day, 1883.

While this construction work unfolded, events of a different nature were taking place with the parent firm, which was based in Fernandina. The Atlantic, Gulf and West India Transit was experiencing financial problems, to the extent that it was skipping its bond interest coupons. Bondholders naturally became irate, ultimately insisting that a foreclosure sale take place. One did, and the new owners—really the bondholders of old—paid a mere $320,000 for a property that had cost well over $1 million to build and equip. As was so often the case, the company's stockholders were completely wiped out in the process.

The new owners reorganized themselves as the Florida Transit Railroad in April 1881. Later that year, one of its security holders took the leadership helm: Sir Edward Reed. Two years later, Reed consolidated the Peninsular Railroad and the Tropical Florida Railroad into the Florida Transit, whereupon he renamed everything the Florida Transit and Peninsular Railroad. Joining Sir Edward in controlling the new enterprise were his old bondholder friends from Holland.[23]

Reed now controlled a railroad fiefdom that embraced the cross-state route between Fernandina, Waldo, and Cedar Key; a trunk line down the peninsula from Waldo to Panasoffkee along with a branch into Silver Springs; and he owned the Florida Central and Western between Jacksonville and River Junction. The astute Englishman now decided to place his various holdings under one umbrella. Accordingly, in 1884, the Florida Railway and Navigation Company—the state's first true railroad system—emerged.[24] Reed also persuaded the owners of two other firms to join the big merger: the unbuilt Leesburg and Indian River Railroad, and the Fernandina & Jacksonville Railroad (F & J). The former had the right to construct a line from Wildwood eastward to the lakeside setting of Leesburg, to some point on the Indian River on the east coast. The latter, which opened in April 1881, furnished a shortcut from Hart's station (renamed Yulee) directly into Jacksonville proper. Interestingly, the American railroad financier Edward Harriman held a large stake in the F & J, as did the wealthy New York banker Bayard Cutting.

For reasons later explained, Sir Edward retreated from the scene after organizing "Navigation," though he continued to operate his big land company in Jacksonville. Among the directors sitting on Navigation's board were Harriman and Cutting, along with Edward Dickerson.[25] Even former U.S. senator David Yulee was given a seat, despite his stating to the *Florida Times-Union* on 23 May 1886 that he had totally withdrawn from all railway activities in 1881—"my advanced age requiring repose."

When created, Navigation owned 509 miles of lines. The company's Western Division extended from Jacksonville to River Junction with branches to St. Marks and Monticello; its Central Division connected Fernandina with Cedar Key; its Southern Division descended from Waldo to Panasoffkee with a branch to Silver Springs; the Jacksonville Branch connected Hart's station with the growing gateway of Jacksonville; while its Leesburg Branch would one day connect Wildwood with points east. Further, Navigation owned the DeBary-Baya Steamboat Line, whose fleet of seventeen vessels serviced the St. Johns River and the popular maritime route between Fernandina and Savannah. Navigation certainly dominated the railroad affairs of Florida. But the real question was whether the behemoth could service the big debt load it had inherited from all the underlying companies.

At first it seemed that Navigation might very well succeed. For example, in 1884 it reported earnings of $1,001,589; expenses of $616,392; and a net profit of $385,197. Practically all of the latter, however, went to pay bond interest, with a mere $41,297 remaining for operations. No dividends were paid to stockholders.[26] By issuing more bonds the following year, Navigation extended its Southern Division south of Panasoffkee down to Terrell and completed its Leesburg Branch from Wildwood over to Leesburg and Tavares. In 1886, the company once again extended its Southern Division from Terrell down to Plant City; created a short branch into Sumterville proper; built a connecting track at Jacksonville to unite its Jacksonville Branch with its Western Division; and opened an appendage from Fernandina to Amelia Beach, which the company used as a storage track for most of the year.

In retrospect, the cost of these expansionary measures merely added to Navigation's financial problems, as did a brief national financial crisis. Foreign capital invested in American railway securities had reached nearly $1.5 billion in 1883, but owing to recent rate wars, parallel building projects, and financial mismanagement, a decline began in 1882. Foreigners began selling off their American railway investments to the tune of $25 million annually, which possibly explains why Sir Edward Reed retreated from the American railroad scene.

Florida Railway and Navigation skipped its interest coupon in 1885, which greatly upset the Dutch bondholders. Their new representative, a director of the Rotterdam Bank named Pieter van Weel, immediately sailed for America to inspect Navigation's books for irregularities.[27] In the following year, the conglomerate slipped into receivership with railroad executive Colonel H. Reiman Duval—a paragon of integrity and respectability—being named receiver. During this legal interlude, the company was spared from servicing its bonded debt. Bayard Cutting, himself a large bondholder who was chairman of Manhattan's Central Trust Company, ironed out a reorganization plan with the creditors, all of which paved the way for a new entity to surface in 1888: the Florida Central & Peninsular Railroad Company. What became of this carrier

The Florida Railway and Navigation Company—the state's first conglomerate—was cobbled together by Sir Edward Reed in 1884. Nicknamed "The Key Line," it was once the largest rail system in the state. Author's collection.

will be taken up in chapter 6; suffice it to say that Sir Edward Reed's efforts of prior years laid the foundation for an important future player in Florida called the Seaboard Air Line Railway.

Chipley and Reed certainly played important roles in Florida railway history, but Henry Plant and Henry Flagler left a more profound stamp upon the Florida landscape. An extensive literature about each has surfaced over the decades that underscores that the two men had more similarities than differences.

Beyond sharing the same Christian name and sporting generous moustaches, each man was greatly influenced by his religious upbringings—Plant a Puritan Congregationalist, Flagler a Presbyterian. Each man also raised one son, neither of whom inherited his father's exceptional business acumen. Both Plant and Flagler were Republicans who had made their initial fortunes in other industries. Interestingly, both first came to Florida not to make money but to restore the health of their sickly wives. And each assembled an empire in the Sunshine State comprised of railroads, steamships, land companies, and hotels. The two men began the development of Florida late in life, when most Gilded Age figures had retired or gone on to their reward. Lastly, both men left behind complicated estates and trusts.

Henry Bradley Plant, who was nearly a decade older than Flagler, was born in 1819 in the seaside village of Branford, Connecticut.[78] Fatherless at age six, Plant was raised by his mother in an atmosphere of love and thrift. After completing the eighth grade, the somewhat restless farm lad became a "captain's boy" aboard steamboats plying the waters between New Haven and New York City. This led to an apprenticeship in the express package room.

Plant married in 1843, and the couple raised one son, Morton. Desiring more of a home life, Henry left the world of steamboats to eventually manage the New York office of Adams Express Company—the nation's largest such firm. In 1853, Ellen Plant contracted a lung disorder. Her doctors suggested she convalesce in Florida, whose climate they claimed had restorative qualities. The couple sailed for Jacksonville—their first visit to the South—and Ellen's health improved. The annual winter respites continued, and along the way Henry became enamored of southern ways, so much so that he became superintendent of Adams

Express at Augusta, Georgia. His mission now was to aggressively scour the southern states for business, meet key transportation officials, and gain a thorough knowledge of railroad services.[29]

Ellen Plant died of tuberculosis just before the Civil War. Fearful that the Adams firm's southern assets would be confiscated during the upcoming hostilities, its directors sold them to Henry Plant, who organized the Southern Express Company. This was a watershed mark in Plant's career, reminiscent of Shakespeare's observation that "there is a tide in the affairs of men which, taken at the flood, leads on to fortune."

The Connecticut Yankee—no advocate of Civil War—now made an offer to Jeff Davis: if Davis would allow Plant to remain in the South and continue running Southern Express, the latter would freely carry packages that were destined for southern soldiers, along with the Confederacy's important papers, currency shipments, and payrolls. Davis approved the plan and gave Plant a Confederate passport. He also exempted Southern Express employees from the draft and named Plant's firm the official "Collector of Tariffs."[30]

By and large, the war years proved quite lucrative for Southern Express. Owing to poor health, Plant departed the Confederacy late in the conflict and convalesced abroad. He eventually returned to New York City, remarried, and purchased a substantial Manhattan brownstone. He also renewed friendships of old, including one with Connecticut native General Henry Sanford, who was developing citrus groves and a brand-new city near Florida's Lake Monroe.[31]

Plant was always convinced that, after the war, the South would rise again as an economic power. The key, he felt, would be good transportation resources. Flush with funds from Southern Express, Plant decided to enter a business arena far more lucrative than the express package business: railroading. By acquiring destitute southern railroads and constructing new ones, the so-called Plant System began to unfold below Charleston, South Carolina.

To help finance his new field of interest, Plant organized the Plant Investment Company (PICO), drawing into his inner circle many wealthy and conservative investors such as William Walters and Benjamin Newcomer of Baltimore, the New York financier Morris Jessup, and Standard Oil kingpin Henry Flagler. Plant's "cash box" both invested in

Connecticut native Henry B. Plant first made a fortune in the express package industry. He then created an empire of railroads, steamships, and hotels. In its salad days, the Plant System employed nearly twelve thousand workers. Author's collection.

and purchased railroad lines along with steamboats, marine facilities, land, and hotels. In 1887 alone, PICO had assets of $14.6 million (2006 dollars: $313,946,330).[32] Although not a railroader by training, Plant had the wisdom to surround himself with a cadre of railway specialists, along with many financial and legal experts.

Plant's first purchase occurred in 1879, when he acquired the 237-mile Atlantic and Gulf Railroad; its crescent-shaped route connected Savannah, Georgia, with Bainbridge (on the Flint River) by way of Jesup, Lawton, Valdosta, Thomasville, and Climax. Plant renamed the enterprise the Savannah, Florida & Western Railway (S, F & W). Of considerable importance was the company's branch that descended the main track at Lawton (renamed Dupont) for Live Oak, Florida, which Confederate military authorities had completed during the waning days of the war. The branch allowed trains from Savannah to reach the growing Florida gateway of Jacksonville, though in a roundabout manner via Lake City and Baldwin. A year later, Plant snapped up the Savannah & Charleston Railroad, which operated between its namesake cities.

Eager to reduce the circuitous route from Savannah to Jacksonville, Plant built a shortcut from the S, F & W track at Waycross directly into Jacksonville by way of Boulogne, Hilliard, and Callahan. The cutoff, which became known as the Waycross Short Line, was constructed by convict labor leased from the State of Florida. It opened on May Day, 1881. In the following year, the S, F & W began running through trains between New York and Jacksonville via the cutoff, which were comprised of Pullman palace and sleeping cars.[33]

Plant even fashioned a third entrance into the Sunshine State so as to tap the fertile Apalachicola River valley. Climax, Georgia, was situated just east of Bainbridge. Plant's henchmen obtained charters for a short branch that descended to River Junction (Chattahoochee), which was soon to be served by the Pensacola and Atlantic Railroad. Sir Edward Reed's Florida Central and Western Railroad also serviced the setting, whose main track headed easterly for Tallahassee, Lake City, and Jacksonville. The feeder from Climax was completed in April 1883. A few months earlier, the Pensacola and Atlantic finished its route from Pensacola.[34]

Prior to the Civil War, the wealth and population of Florida was chiefly concentrated in middle Florida. As one publication noted, "The people here lived like nabobs, and devote themselves with equal zeal to the cultivation of cotton and amenities of social life." But the fortunes of war changed all this, and after Reconstruction newcomers, tourists, and farmers began venturing into the peninsula. Some came for the climate, others out of curiosity. Orange and lemon groves were set out; experiments were conducted in citrus culture; and the production of early winter vegetables for northern markets became a practical success. The region, though, lacked one ingredient: a network of railways. It was a deficiency that Plant—and others—were keen to correct.[35]

Plant's invasion of the peninsula began simply enough. He would extend the Live Oak Branch of his Savannah, Florida & Western below Live Oak to Gainesville. By using "front men" and dummy corporations, the project opened in 1882 to New Boston, which sat aside the Suwannee River. (Locals renamed it New Branford, in honor of Plant's birthplace.) Schedules of the Savannah, Florida & Western were arranged so that trains could meet steamboats plying the Suwannee River. Plant's contractor then connected New Branford with Fort White, High Springs, and Newnansville, where workers encountered something quite unexpected: a competitor.[36]

The Florida Southern Railway was busily constructing its narrow gauge route between Palatka and Lake City by way of Rochelle and Gainesville. The company also possessed the right to build south of Rochelle to Tampa Bay and Charlotte Harbor. Boston capitalists controlled the entity, who opened the Palatka-Gainesville branch in October 1881. Learning that the company was short of funds, Plant waved a carrot: if they would allow him to purchase a controlling interest, Plant would allow the Bostonians to remain in office and permit construction to proceed down the peninsula to Charlotte Harbor—but not to Tampa Bay, where Plant had other plans. Plant's fellow New Englanders approved the plan, and the *Gainesville Bee* newspaper confirmed the takeover on 8 December 1883.

Plant's contractor now removed the narrow gauge rails between Newnansville and Gainesville, widened the roadbed, and installed broad gauge track, such as what was used on the Savannah, Florida & Western. Residents of Lake City did not take kindly to this, however, for it meant that the Florida Southern would not connect their setting with Charlotte Harbor. Litigation ensued, but Plant smoothed ruffled feathers by building a branch to Lake City from the Fort White area. No doubt Plant viewed this as a minor inconvenience, more than offset by the generous land grant that the Florida Southern would eventually receive after completing the line to Charlotte Harbor: some 2.7 million acres, the biggest railway land grant in state history.

With its treasury refreshed, the Florida Southern resumed construction below Rochelle to Ocala and Leesburg, using narrow gauge track. In 1884, Pemberton Ferry (renamed Croom) got the iron horse. Nearby Brooksville got nothing—that is, until city fathers paid railway officials a $20,000 inducement, whereupon a branch track was hastily built. (Service to Croom began in January 1885.) Endless groves of oranges dotted both sides of the Florida Southern track in this part of the state, which prompted the company to advertise itself as the "Orange Belt Route." Another Plant entity, the South Florida Railroad, completed its sibling's track between Croom and Bartow by way of Lakeland.

While progress was being made to Bartow, laborers simultaneously began building the Florida Southern's "Charlotte Harbor Division" that departed Bartow in a southwesterly direction to what became Punta Gorda. Albert Gilchrist, a future Florida governor and resident of Punta Gorda, surveyed parts of the route, which in many places paralleled the Peace River. After rails reached Arcadia, the directors of the Florida Southern operated a special train over the company's route in the presence of Governor Edward Perry and his cabinet. At Zolfo Springs—one of many settings that the railroad literally created—the train halted on the Peace River Bridge for dinner:

> The elegant narrow-gauge Pullman car that was our new home seemed perched like a bird on the top-most twig of a tree; twenty feet or more below flowed the dark waters of the river; around was the forest of somber pine and cypress; stretching away from either end of train were the slender lines of steel track, apparently touching each other in the dim distance, while to the whispering winds among the pines were added the liquid trills of a saucy mockingbird which swayed and sang in a tree-top close by. Everybody enjoyed the scene fully as well as the cold turkey and the sparkling Mumm champagne.[37]

Rails reached the southern terminus of Trabue—where the Peace River flows into Charlotte Harbor—in June 1886. (In the following year, the setting was renamed Punta Gorda.) Colonel Isaac Trabue, a Kentuckian, had given the railway a considerable amount of land here, hoping that the iron horse would help transform the rough-and-tumble hamlet. The first through train from Bartow arrived on 24 July. Workers also installed a 4,200-foot dock into Charlotte Harbor so that Florida Southern Railway trains could meet Morgan Line steamboats bound for Tampa, Key West, and Havana. A subsidiary of the railway, the Florida Commercial Company, erected a posh hotel called Hotel Punta Gorda.[38]

The aforementioned South Florida Railroad, which was also chiefly founded by New Englanders, was to link Lake Monroe with Tampa Bay, and had the authority to construct a branch to Charlotte Harbor. Groundbreaking ceremonies took place in Sanford on 10 January 1880, with General Ulysses S. Grant, an old friend of Henry Sanford, throwing out the first shovelful of dirt. Later that year, the line opened to Orlando, which was then considered a haven for rheumatics. Intermediate stations along the route included Longwood, Maitland, and Winter Park. The line was subsequently extended to Kissimmee in March 1881. Henry Plant received a personal invitation to ride the inaugural train between Sanford and Kissimmee. As the trip got under way, Plant asked South Florida Railroad president James Ingraham how he might obtain a controlling interest in the company. Ingraham's board eventually agreed to a takeover, and, on 4 May 1883, an *Associated Press* dispatch announced that the company had sold a 60 percent majority interest to the Plant Investment Company.

Curiously, another firm also possessed the right to bring the iron horse to Tampa. In fact, the Jacksonville, Tampa & Key West Railway possessed a better land grant than Ingraham's company. Big on plans but at the moment short on funds, Plant made another of his many irresistible offers: if the firm with the imposing name would sell its unbuilt franchise between Kissimmee and Tampa, Plant would purchase a large quantity of its construction bonds that would allow the firm to begin building its own route between Jacksonville and Sanford. The bait worked.

Plant paid $30,000 for the desired franchise, and shortly afterward the Connecticut Yankee—true to his word—became a major bondholder of the Jacksonville, Tampa & Key West Railway. But there was one catch: the 74-mile route between Kissimmee and Tampa had to be quickly built, for the land grant on this segment was about to expire. Plant's railroad adjutant, Colonel Henry Haines, now swung into action and recruited numerous contractors for the project. Work commenced at both Kissimmee and Tampa. An army of workers soon began clearing vegetation, grading the right-of-way, installing bridges and trestles, and spiking into position iron rails, all at breakneck speed. The opposing work gangs met each other east of Lakeland at Carter's Kill, on 22 January 1884, just a few days before the land grant was to expire. Shortly thereafter, Plant ran an inaugural train into Tampa, where much merrymaking took place. Among those riding the special was Florida governor William Bloxham and his entire cabinet.[39]

Tampa was home to just seven hundred souls when the railroad arrived. Rows of unpainted houses fronted its sandy streets. Nevertheless, the railroad precipitated an economic boom, just as it did in so many other Florida communities. New industries popped up such as wholesale fish dealers and cigar makers, who now sent their products and goods to northern markets by train.

Plant eventually extended his South Florida Railroad to Port Tampa—another Plant creation!—which became the largest phosphate shipping terminal in the world, where twenty-seven ships could be accommodated at once. The Plant System of steamboats departed the setting as well, for such points as the Manatee River, Fort Myers, Key West, Havana, the West Indies, and Mobile, Alabama. In 1891, Plant opened the palatial Tampa Bay Hotel—today a national treasure and home to both the University of Tampa and the Henry B. Plant Museum. As Plant modestly summarized the situation to the *Florida Times-Union* on 5 January 1892, "It seemed to me that about all South Florida needed for a successful future was a little spirit and energy which could be fostered by transportation facilities."

Though Plant made substantial investments in the Tampa area, he also continued to expand his railroad fiefdom. In 1883, his South Florida Railroad leased the Sanford & Indian River, a citrus feeder that connected Sanford with Orono and Lake Jessup. (Expansions later brought service to Oviedo and Lake Charm.) Two years later, the South Florida firm built a branch from Lake Alfred down to Bartow—the "City of Oaks." A new branch from Pemberton Ferry to Inverness opened in 1891, while a year later the company leased the little rail line founded by Hamilton Disston: the St. Cloud & Sugar Belt Railway (Kissimmee to St. Cloud and Narcoossee). Lately, this region had become home to several lumber and naval store operators, as well as sugar growers.

Another entity Plant enlarged was the Florida Southern Railway. A branch was installed from its main track to serve Micanopy. Others connected Proctor with the orange center of Citra. In 1885, the company leased the St. Johns and Lake Eustis Railway, which had been founded by New York millionaire William Astor. The line commenced in the village of Astor, located on the west bank of the St. Johns River, and proceeded down to the Lake Eustis area, a region fast becoming known for lumbering, agriculture, and citrus. The narrow gauge line opened in 1881 between Astor and Fort Mason, where steamboat connections were had for Leesburg via lakes Eustis and Harris. A few years later, the route was pushed down to Tavares and Lane Park. Plant died in 1899, but three years later the Florida Southern acquired yet another protoplasm: the 6-mile Yalaha & Western, which ran between the lumber and turpentine setting of Okahumpka to the burgeoning citrus center of Yalaha.

The aforementioned Jacksonville, Tampa & Key West Railway finally opened between Jacksonville and Sanford in February 1886, by way of Green Cove Springs, Palatka, and DeLand. Coal magnate Robert Coleman of Cornwall, Pennsylvania, spearheaded the project. Several branches and connecting tracks emanated from its main line. Coleman additionally leased a few firms, including the Atlantic Coast, St. Johns and Indian River Railway (which ran to Titusville), and the Sanford and Lake Eustis Railway, whose track departed Sanford for Tavares by way of Mount Dora.

Despite its ability to convey passengers and freight faster than any steamboat on the St. Johns River, Coleman's company produced mixed financial results. Burdened with debt, the company entered into a receivership in 1893. Bond interest was later skipped, several disastrous freezes impacted citrus revenues, and yellow fever epidemics literally scared passengers away. After five court attempts to sell the "Tropical Trunk Line," the Plant Investment Company took charge in 1899, whereupon the property was recast as the Jacksonville and St. Johns River Railroad.[40]

The Plant System's biggest component was the Savannah, Florida & Western Railway, which also pursued a course of expansion. In the late 1880s, the firm opened a branch between Thomasville, Georgia, and Monticello, Florida, giving the latter setting a direct northern connection to the outside world. Other branches were built between High Springs and Archer, and from Morriston to Juliette.

In 1895, the Savannah, Florida & Western acquired one of the more colorful operations in Florida: the Orange Belt Railroad, whose 156-mile route meandered across the peninsula from near Sanford to St. Petersburg by way of Sylvan Lake, Claroona, Winter Garden, Lacoochee, Dunedin, and Clearwater. Peter Demens, a sawmill operator at Longwood, was the company's prime mover. Pinellas Point became the railroad's ultimate western terminus, which Demens renamed St. Petersburg in honor of his Russian birthplace.[41]

From the outset, the Orange Belt firm was fraught with problems. Construction delays occurred, land grants were forfeited, workers rioted

The Plant System of railroads, which was situated below Charleston, South Carolina, embraced over 2,200 miles of track. Much of it was located in Florida. In 1902, it was acquired by the Atlantic Coast Line Railroad. Author's collection.

for back wages, and finances occasionally collapsed. Creditors forced a sale in 1893, and the new owners reorganized the backcountry wanderer as the Sanford & St. Petersburg Railway. Two years later, the Plant Investment Company took the reins, which passed it over to the Savannah, Florida & Western.

Another property the S, F & W obtained was the Silver Springs, Ocala and Gulf, which operated between Ocala and Dunnellon. Owned by New York capitalists and opened in 1897, the line owned a small spider web of lines that tapped area phosphate and limestone traffic. A year later, service was extended past Dunnellon to Homosassa, then to Inverness. Henry Plant obtained a financial stake in the company, but it was not acquired by the S, F & W until 1901, the same year that the latter picked up the 13-mile Tampa and Thonotosassa Railroad, which had opened between its namesake points in 1893.

To tap the phosphate traffic of central Florida, the Savannah, Florida & Western purchased the rail line of the Winston Lumber Company. Initially constructed as a logging road, Plant extended the taproot into the so-called Bone Valley to serve the phosphate mines at Pebbledale, Phosphoria, and Tiger Bay. After being mined and processed, trainloads of the mineral made their way out of the phosphate district to Port Tampa, where it was off-loaded into the holds of oceangoing ships. Other carloads of phosphate departed the state in regular trains bound for northern and midwestern markets.

Occasionally the Plant Investment Company directly purchased a rail firm, such as the Florida Midland. Organized by New England capitalists, the line departed the Lake Jessup area for Ocoee, Dr. Phillips, Harpersville, and Kissimmee. Construction commenced at Longwood in 1886. In the following year, a branch was built from Apopka to Rock Springs. Work simultaneously progressed on the main line, south of Ocoee, to the hamlets of Windemere and Isleworth. The iron horse finally reached Harpersville in 1889; Kissimmee, a year later. The movement of timber and agricultural products furnished most of the company's revenues. PICO absorbed the Midland in 1896.

The Savannah, Florida & Western also gathered up rail lines (or built new ones) in Georgia, Alabama, and South Carolina. The myriad acquisitions and projects greatly enlarged the Plant System map, which, by 1902, boasted over 2,200 miles of track, a remarkable achievement for the system's founder who began his working career as a lowly captain's boy.[42]

Henry Morrison Flagler, the remaining member of the quartet, was born 1830 in Hopewell, New York, the son of a poor Presbyterian minister. Flagler quit school at age fourteen and later clerked at a general store in Ohio for five dollars per month. He married the owner's daughter in 1853. Mary Flagler's uncle was Stephen Harkness, the whiskey-distilling king of the Buckeye State. Flagler himself eventually became a commissioned merchant, and before long he was sending grain and produce to his aggressive Cleveland agent and friend, John D. Rockefeller.

After accumulating about $50,000 in savings, Flagler moved his family to Saginaw, Michigan, where he tried his hand at the salt business. The endeavor proved disastrous when salt prices collapsed at the close of the American Civil War. Not only did Flagler lose his capital, but he incurred debts of a like amount. He returned to Ohio and for the next few years lived an impecunious existence, often skipping lunch to save money. He also greatly reflected upon the vagaries of capitalism.[43]

In time, Flagler removed his family to Cleveland, where Henry again began selling grain. He also renewed his friendship with Rockefeller, who, by now, had tossed his hat into a new arena: oil refining. In fact, Rockefeller was forming a partnership and invited Flagler to join. Stephen Harkness advanced the requisite $100,000 contribution, insisting that Henry become the partnership's treasurer. News of Rockefeller's new firm broke in March 1867. Flagler intensely devoted himself to the new business. He and Rockefeller lived on the same street in Cleveland, and both walked to and from work each day discussing business affairs. In 1870, Mary Flagler gave birth to a son, Henry Harkness Flagler. Afterward, her health deteriorated and she became an invalid.

Transportation costs greatly affected the profitability of oil refining. In short order, Flagler became the partnership's master of negotiations and contracts. Cleveland was then served by the mighty New York Central, the Erie, and the fabled Pennsylvania railroads. As Rockefeller's eminent biographer states: "Flagler played these three railroads against each other in seemingly endless permutations."[44] The usual technique was for Flagler to negotiate a preferential rate with the railroad's president—adjutants would never do!—by guaranteeing not only a minimum daily number of car shipments but assuming all liability for fire and any accident. The offer would have made any CEO's mouth water.

After striking a deal with one carrier, Flagler would then disclose the details to the president of another, so as to obtain an even better deal. Other refiners emulated Flagler's methods, but in the end no other firm could match his partnership's minimum daily carloads, which might amount to sixty cars a day. When a competitor was about to fail, Flagler descended on the scene with ready cash to purchase the distressed firm, naturally at below-market prices. Such were business practices in the "Age of Bare Knuckles."

Flagler eventually convinced Rockefeller that their partnership should "go public" in order to raise funds for expansion. Standard Oil Company evolved, and in 1877 Flagler moved his family to New York City, where the new company was headquartered. Poor health, though, continued to plague Mary Flagler, and thus, during the winter of 1877–78, the couple made their initial journey to Florida for rest and recuperation—just as Henry and Ellen Plant had done many years before. Mary died of tuberculosis in 1881. Two years later, Flagler married his wife's nursing attendant, Ida Shrouds, an actress of sorts who later became mentally incapacitated. (Ida was thirty-five; Henry, fifty-three.) The newlyweds eventually honeymooned in Florida, a land that continued to fascinate Henry.

On the couple's next visit, in February 1885, Flagler's affair with America's oldest city began in earnest. After arriving in Jacksonville in his private rail car—he was then worth about $20 million—the couple made their way across the St. Johns River in a ferryboat to South Jacksonville. There they boarded a train of the Jacksonville, St. Augustine & Halifax River Railway, a narrow gauge outfit that had opened in 1883. Again, the weather and charms of St. Augustine played on Henry's imagination. The Gilded Age mogul eventually purchased several real estate parcels, the couple left in April, and Henry reappeared the following month with his advisors and an architect. The stupendous Ponce de Leon Hotel (now Flagler College) opened in January 1888, an architectural marvel that helped convince the nation that Florida was not just for semi-invalids but a pleasure playground as well. Another Flagler hotel opened nearby for the less wealthy, and the master also acquired a third, already-built hostelry.[45]

From the outset, Flagler realized that his target audience—wealthy northerners—would not patronize his triumvirate unless good transportation was available. Although the Jacksonville, St. Augustine & Halifax River Railway proved useful in conveying construction supplies for the hotels, it nevertheless was a decrepit operation known for poor service. Flagler's clientele would demand better. To improve matters,

After a successful and lucrative career with Standard Oil, Henry M. Flagler began developing the east coast of Florida. Among the Flagler System holdings was the Florida East Coast Railway. State Archives of Florida.

Flagler joined the railway's board in 1885, and relieved the company's president, Jerome Green of Utica, New York, of his $300,000 controlling interest. Flagler then had the line totally refurbished. Its narrow gauge track was widened to standard gauge, new cars and locomotives were purchased, and the time-consuming ferry across the St. Johns River was, in 1890, replaced with a magnificent steel drawbridge. Only then, according to the noted historian and author Seth Bramson, could all-Pullman deluxe trains depart New York and arrive in St. Augustine proper.[46]

But Flagler's interest in railroads had hardly ended, and before long he began a buying spree. As mentioned in chapter 4, William Astor acquired the little St. Johns Railroad, between St. Augustine and Tocoi

Landing on the St. Johns River, around 1870. His son rebuilt it. Halfway along its route was situated Tocoi Junction. From there, the Astors built a new line down to East Palatka, a more prominent shipping point on the St. Johns River for vegetables, citrus, and lumber. They named their new enterprise the St. Augustine & Palatka Railway. Flagler bought both properties in the late 1880s.

Another area operation attracting Flagler's attention was the St. Johns & Halifax, which, by 1886, was operating a 51-mile logging line between East Palatka and Daytona via Tomoka and Ormond. Its owners even had a bridge installed across the St. Johns River so as to reach Palatka proper, thereby obtaining a handy connection with the Florida Southern Railway as well as the Jacksonville, Tampa & Key West Railway. The railroad's owners eventually converted the company's narrow gauge track to standard gauge and arranged for a branch to be built directly into Ormond Beach. Flagler acquired the outfit in May 1888. In 1892, a 3-mile branch was built from the company's main line in order to reach San Mateo, a pretty village setting containing lovely frame houses and many fine orange groves.[47]

In a curious turn of events, Flagler allowed the Jacksonville, Tampa & Key West Railway to manage his rail properties because, he said, "I have so many irons in the fire."[48] In reality, Flagler had taken a shine to coal millionaire Robert Coleman, the railway's youthful and ambitious president. The relationship with Coleman's firm was short-lived, however, for when the "Tropical Trunk Line" became mired in debt and litigation, Flagler decided to withdraw from the consortium.[49]

After he obtained the charter of the Florida Coast & Gulf Railroad, Flagler's conquest of the east coast now began in earnest. In 1892, he had the unbuilt firm reorganized as the Jacksonville, St. Augustine & Indian River Railway, partly to take advantage of Florida's new land grant policy of 8,000 acres for every mile a new railroad completed. The new firm also became an umbrella, or holding company, for Flagler's growing list of properties. To oversee its day-to-day operations, Flagler hired away two of Henry Plant's top lieutenants: Joseph Parrott and James Ingraham. The former became president of the railway while the latter handled land sales and industrial development.

Flagler's immediate goal was to tap the rich agricultural traffic that radiated from the Indian River region, an area renowned for its citrus, pineapples, and lumber. To reach it, workers advanced rails of Flagler's reorganized company from Daytona southward past New Smyrna, Titusville (head of navigation on the Indian River) to Rock Ledge, where the iron horse arrived in February 1893. Service commenced to Fort Pierce the following January, another burgeoning shipping center known for fish and citrus that was situated 240 miles below Jacksonville. Later in 1894, the railway reached what would become West Palm Beach.

Long before the railroad arrived at West Palm Beach, Flagler had personally reconnoitered the palm-covered island that lay on the opposite shore of Lake Worth. At its northern tip, Flagler envisioned an exclusive enclave for the nation's bluebloods, and to that end he began acquiring parcels for the future Palm Beach.

To accommodate wealthy winter tourists at Palm Beach, Flagler erected the colossal, 500-room Royal Poinciana Hotel. Construction materials for the magisterial edifice were floated down the Indian River from Eau Gallie to Jupiter, carried some 8 miles across land by the little Jupiter & Lake Worth narrow gauge railway to Juno, and then loaded into vessels for the transit to Lake Worth. Flagler's own railway did not open to West Palm Beach until March 1894, a month after the grand facility opened. To reach the hotel, guests were ferried across Lake Worth until 1895, when a wooden bridge allowed trains to directly service the stratified setting. Thereafter, the private rail cars of the socially elite crowded the side tracks. In early 1896, Flagler opened a second hotel there, facing the Atlantic Ocean, that eventually became known as the Breakers.[50]

Flagler now faced a rather important decision: whether to advance his railroad south of West Palm Beach to Miami. At that moment, Dade County contained just 257 persons. There were no wagon roads to Key Biscayne; the valuation of all real estate therein amounted to less than $20,000; and mail for Miami was still being delivered from Lantana on a semiweekly basis—the postal carrier literally walked the route using the beachhead.

Prior to his departure from the Plant System, James Ingraham had examined a good deal of lower south Florida in 1892. His employer, Henry Plant, was then toying with the idea of connecting the two coasts by rail. Flagler became privy to the plan, and realized that if his own rail line did not penetrate Miami, then possibly a competitor would seize the day.

Flagler's thinking was also being influenced by a plucky widow and large landowner named Julia Tuttle, who lived in the confines of old Fort Dallas, near the Miami River. Interestingly, Ingraham had met Tuttle in 1890 at a dinner party in Cleveland. She mentioned to him that she was about to remove her family and effects to Miami, so as to develop a large property on the Miami River that she had inherited from her father. She told Ingraham: "Someday, someone will build a railroad to Miami, and I will give to the Company that does so one-half of my property for a town site. Perhaps you will be the man." Ingraham responded: "Miami is a long ways off from Tampa, but stranger things have happened, and I may yet call on you to fulfill this offer."[51]

After moving to Miami, Tuttle wrote to Flagler and asked that he extend his railroad to her remote yet beautiful setting. The requests, though, went unheeded until the great freezes of 1894–95, when countless citrus groves perished along Flagler's rail route. Biscayne Bay, however, escaped the devastation, and to prove it Tuttle sent Flagler a box containing orange, lime, and lemon blossoms. Flagler soon relented and visited Tuttle, and her neighbor William Brickell, in June 1895. By nightfall of the first day, Flagler had made the decision: in exchange for certain parcels of land, he would extend his railway down to Miami, help establish a city, and erect a sumptuous new hotel.

The Army Corp of Engineers surveyed the rail route south of West Palm Beach, and that September construction workers—mostly prisoners leased from the state—were on the scene. Labor camps, along with staging areas for materials, were established at various points along the right-of-way. Where possible, steamboats delivered supplies via local waterways. The thick vegetation was grubbed out, the roadbed was smoothed, manifold bridges and trestles were fabricated, and the new steel rails were rapidly spiked.

To Tuttle's delight, the 70-mile extension opened in April 1896. In July, Miami was incorporated, and Flagler became the city's first benefactor by funding sidewalks and paved streets, stringing electrical lines, and installing water and sewage works. He also donated land for churches and municipal buildings. And true to his word, Flagler opened the doors of the stately Royal Palm Hotel in January 1897 on a scenic, 15-acre site at the confluence of the Miami River and Biscayne Bay.

Shortly before the work to Miami was begun, Flagler changed the name of his company to more accurately reflect the territory it served. The Florida East Coast Railway continued to expand even after the route to Miami opened. In 1896, the company acquired the Atlantic & Western, which departed New Smyrna for the picturesque inland settings of Lake Helen, Orange City, and Blue Springs. Four years later, the Jacksonville & Atlantic was picked up, whose track emanated from South Jacksonville for the Atlantic Ocean beach community of Pablo. (Eventually the line reached Mayport, at the mouth of the St. Johns River, where substantial docks and wharves were built.) The Southeastern Railway was brought into the fold in 1902, which connected Titusville with the Lake Monroe community of Enterprise, by way of Maytown. A year later, the Florida East Coast Railway built a new extension south of Miami in order to serve the agricultural lands of the Cutler Ridge district. The taproot reached what became Homestead in 1904.[52]

Flagler, whose energies seemed inexhaustible, also found time to expand his various land companies, steamship lines, and chain of hotels. In 1901, at age seventy-two, he divorced his second wife on grounds of incurable insanity, a Florida law he arguably promulgated and financed. On 24 August of that year, the aging tycoon married thirty-four-year-old Mary Lily Kenan. For a wedding present, he presented the "short, buxom and attractive woman" with a 55-room Beaux Arts mansion in Palm Beach, named Whitehall, which is today home to the magnificent Henry Morrison Flagler Museum. The Rockefellers, though, did not attend the marriage ceremony. According to Rockefeller's biographer, the couple had—years before—distanced themselves after Flagler's propensity for young women, princely possessions, and extravagance had manifested.[53]

Flagler's culminating career achievement was not realized until 1905, when the Florida East Coast Railway began building its famed Key West Extension. Later hailed as one of the world's greatest engineering marvels, the colossal undertaking has recently become the subject of several books, including one by the noted American novelist Les Standiford.[54]

In brief, Flagler wished to link the Florida mainland with the island city of Key West, by having rails hopscotch over keys and opalescent water. Constructing the breathtaking scheme had tantalized visionaries for decades, a serious attempt having been floated by the Great Southern Railway Company during the era of Reconstruction.[55]

In the end, though, it was Flagler who had the means and wherewithal to complete the daunting challenge. Flagler certainly believed in the growing importance of the nation's trade with Cuba, and the role that Key West would play when the Panama Canal would be completed (which did not occur until 1914). In the spring of 1905, at age seventy-five, Flagler confidently, but incorrectly, predicted that the company's Key West Extension would be completed in 2.5 years. Further, he told Henry Walters, the patrician chairman of the Atlantic Coast Line Railroad Company, that the project would cost $7.5 million—a far cry from the near $30 million that was eventually spent (2006 dollars: $626,203,396).[56]

Using in-house management rather than an outside contractor, "Flagler's folly" experienced a goodly number of logistical, supply, construction, and labor problems. Only 22 miles of the route was on terra firma; the remainder rested atop bridges of various descriptions. The route between the mainland and Knight's Key was, in many ways, admirably suited for the location of a rail line, affording good alignment and demanding comparatively little bridging, the longest stretch of water being at the lower end of Long Key, where a concrete viaduct with graceful arches, 2 miles in length, was eventually built. Below Knight's Key was a water gap nearly 7 miles wide. A few miles farther sat Bahia Honda, where a bridge 5,100 feet long was needed. "These three structures, together with a concrete arch bridge, 2,573 feet long at Boca Chica, a few miles north of Key West, were the principal bridges as originally planned, although later it was found necessary to provide additional arch structures."[57]

Most construction supplies were brought down from the mainland as needed, including potable water. Hurricanes destroyed completed sections of the route and seriously disrupted production schedules. At Key West, no land for the railway's facilities existed, forcing engineers to reclaim underwater materials using hydraulic pumps. The effect of seawater upon the manifold concrete bridges required constant moni-

This publicity photograph depicts the Havana Special halting on Long Key viaduct of the Florida East Coast Railway. Once built, the company's Key West Extension was hailed as the "8th wonder of the World." Author's collection.

toring. The steel girders of other bridges were coated with the company's familiar yellow paint, so that corrosive decay could be quickly detected. The warm, moist sea air even prompted engineers to coat the steel rails with a special solution of kerosene, cement, and refined coal tar.[58]

Recruiting and retaining a sufficiently large labor force was a never-ending chore. Workers of many nationalities appeared for the work, and virtually every imaginable building trade was represented. Try as the railway did to furnish acceptable wages, housing, food, and proper medical attention, charges of unfair labor practices were leveled against the company. At one point, a sensational trial over peonage unfolded, but in the end the Florida East Coast Railway and its labor agencies were acquitted.

Flagler played banker to the Key West Extension project, but when costs proved exorbitant, the Florida East Coast Railway issued $12 million of mortgage bonds. The 1909 issue, which investment banker J. P. Morgan & Company syndicated, was secured with a first lien upon both the existing and all future lines the railway would ever construct.[59] At that moment, laborers were toiling furiously on the final 45 miles between Knight's Key and Key West, a critical segment that alone would require $4 million to complete.

On the morning of 22 January 1912, almost seven years after the work had begun, the first through passenger train from the mainland arrived in Key West. Flagler and his invited guests were greeted by "the roar of bursting bombs, the music of bands, shrill whistles, the cheers of thousands, and the waving of flags."[60] Behind the special was another Pullman train bearing a congressional delegation, foreign diplomats, army and navy officers, and other dignitaries. After alighting from his car, Flagler was guided along a footpath lined with American Beauty roses and singing children. The infirm chairman proclaimed that he could now die a happy man—"My dream is fulfilled."

Flagler fell down a staircase at his palatial mansion in Palm Beach on 15 January 1913. He never fully recovered from the fall and died there on 21 May. A simple funeral service followed at Memorial Presbyterian Church in St. Augustine, which Flagler had built in memory of his daughter.

About a year afterward, another tribute went off at the Royal Poinciana Chapel in Palm Beach. Pink carnations, asparagus ferns, and palm branches smothered the sanctuary; dozens of dignitaries and social bluebloods packed the pews. The service, which commenced with the reading of Tennyson's immortal poem "Crossing the Bar," was conducted by the Reverend Dr. George Morgan Ward, a former attorney and past president of Rollins College. The chapel's tall, blue-eyed, athletic cleric—who once told Flagler that he did not deliver cream-puff sermons to the idle rich—proffered a eulogy of simple words, reminding all that a great figure in Florida history had gone to his reward.

6

Regulation,
System Builders,
and Federal Control

The interests of the railroads and the people, of the carriers and the shippers, are the same. The bonds that unite them are indissoluble, only death can divorce them. A prosperous people make prosperous railroads. They each lay golden eggs for the other, and neither should be killed. They must live by helping each other, and must not be allowed to slay themselves by cutting each other's throats.

—*Second Annual Report of the Railroad Commissioners of Florida*, 1889

As discussed in the previous chapter, the work of Flagler, Plant, Reed, and Chipley helped launch a new period in Florida railroad history, the *era of consolidation and system building*. During that auspicious interval, which lasted until the late 1920s, many new rail lines were opened, the state's first railroad commission was organized, and several big out-of-state systems obtained a presence in Florida. Also, all of America's railroads were placed under federal control during the First World War.

Throughout this same period, countless newcomers, farmers, and immigrants moved to the Sunshine State. Many new communities were established in the process along with countless businesses and manufactories. New farms and groves arose too, and the tourist industry flowered as never before.

Because the automobile and airplane were either not yet invented or still in their infancy, the demand intensified for more railroad transportation. But the rush to create these new lines came at a price. A number of firms ended up being poorly constructed, undercapitalized, or without their anticipated traffic. Overbuilding resulted, as did cut-throat competition. Whereas the 1880s proved to be the greatest era in Florida—and the nation—for the most new railway lines, the 1890s became the worst for receiverships and failures.[1]

It was during the final two decades of the nineteenth century that the power and influence of Florida's railroad industry and lobby reached imperial proportions. Abuses unfortunately resulted, all of which aroused public feelings of mistrust and ill will. As one historian summarized it:

> An antagonism against the railroads had grown up among the people, largely based on the high rates for passenger and freight transportation, charges of discrimination, the contest of some of the roads against taxation, and the absence of a law under which owners of livestock killed on the tracks could recover damages.[2]

Among those keen to curb the industry's arrogance was the Farmers Alliance—it surfaced in 1887—whose able spokesperson became Florida U.S. senator Wilkinson Call (1834–1910). General Edward Perry (1831–1889) of Pensacola was governor back then. On one hand, the tall handsome lawyer who had valorously defended the Confederate cause at Fredericksburg, Chancellorsville, and the Wilderness wanted more railroads built, declaring in his 1887 legislative message that they were "the greatest factors in Florida's progress." But he also desired reform, and to that end he and others helped persuade legislators to establish the state's first railroad commission on 7 June 1887.[3]

The act establishing the commission was patterned after the one Georgia had passed a decade earlier. The Florida commission was to be comprised of three persons appointed by the governor and confirmed by the Senate. Their appointments were good for four years, each was to be paid $2,500 a year, and in no way could a commissioner be connected with a railroad company or own railroad securities. Although the trio recommended by Perry had no practical railroad experience per se, all were paragons of integrity and respectability, "in no sense aspirants for political preferment."[4] Among those first appointed was George G. McWhorter of Milton, who had to relinquish his post as chief justice of the Florida Supreme Court. By law, the commission was charged with establishing fair and reasonable rates of railway transportation and to

When this map was prepared in 1894, Fort Myers and Miami were still without railroad service. In fact, few souls occupied south Florida, and those who did were mostly Native Americans. But all this soon changed. Author's collection.

expose and punish those firms that practiced discriminatory measures. Upon these dictums the Florida commission would distinguish itself.

The commissioners soon discovered that the existing rates and tariffs of Florida's railroads were often perplexing. Virtually every company subscribed to the freight classification charges of the Southern Railway and Steamship Association, which fixed rates and classes until the practices were outlawed by the Sherman Antitrust Act of 1890.[5] After obtaining a working knowledge of the matrix, the commissioners, in September 1887, ordered every carrier to appear before them in order to establish "just, reasonable, and uniform rates."

The meeting was partly a revelation, for McWhorter's group (he became the commission's first chairman) learned that most of the companies had irregular earnings and numerous financial problems, which partly explained why the companies adjusted rates with little or no warning to whatever the market could bear. Nevertheless, the commission ordered a reduction in passenger tariffs to three cents per mile and fixed uniform freight rates, actions that the attendees of course found unpalatable. As to fixing rates on goods shipped to other states, the commission was severely limited, for in 1886 the U.S. Supreme Court had ruled (in *Wabash Railroad Company v. Illinois*) that the rights of states to regulate so-called interstate rates was severely limited and that they could not enact direct burdens. This created a dilemma for railroad commissions throughout the land and partly explains why the Interstate Commerce Commission was organized.

When the Florida commission act had been framed, legislators established a Board of Revisers to adjudicate any disputes between the commission and the railroads, comprised of the attorney general, comptroller, secretary of state, treasurer, and commissioner of agriculture. As noted, the first round of tariffs and rates ordered antagonized the carriers, who immediately registered their displeasure with the revisers. However, the tribunal sided with the new commission, and did so in almost every subsequent dispute. This is not to say that the commission's decisions were lopsided, for when conditions warranted, it raised certain passenger and freight tariffs.[6]

Owing to poor health, McWhorter resigned his commission chairmanship in early 1891. Governor Francis Fleming, a known friend of Henry Flagler and Henry Plant, announced that he would appoint his personal secretary, Edward J. Triay, to fill the vacancy. Triay had railroad connections, and years later he became a labor agent for the Florida East Coast Railway. The state's most powerful newspaper declared the proposed appointment "distasteful."[7] Other dynamics were in play. Certain politicos and newspapers felt that the commission itself was costing too much money to maintain, though its annual expenses were less than $10,000.

Several historians confirm that other elements were attempting to outright abolish the commission, namely William Chipley, Henry Flagler, Henry Plant, and the Farmers Alliance, which felt that having no commission was better than having one with a biased member.[8] All this led to an awkward dilemma: either legislators had to approve Fleming's controversial nominee, or they would vote to abolish the commission. Fleming refused to withdraw his candidate, and in the summer of 1891 there came to an end "one of the most intelligent railroad commissions that had yet come into existence in the United States."[9]

For the next six years, no regulatory body oversaw "just and reasonable rates" of railway transportation in Florida. The discriminatory practices resumed with gusto, and in general the companies had a field day. Among those outraged was the up-and-coming politico Napoleon Broward, who became governor of Florida in 1905. In an open letter to the press dated 20 July 1894, Broward accused four railroads of running an interstate monopoly that was costing Florida hundreds of thousands of dollars annually: "The companies manipulated local rates on oranges so as to receive an additional twenty-four dollars per carload, or about eight cents a box." Rate discriminations for phosphate shipments from mine to port were also flagrant.[10]

The public's wrath mounted, and eventually the demand for a new railroad commission swept over both houses of the legislature. The commission act of 1897, though, packed more punch than its predecessor. Its regulatory and investigatory powers were enlarged; the commissioners themselves were now to be elected by the people (one was to be a lawyer, another to have railroad experience, the third had to be connected to agriculture); while the Board of Revisers was abolished, and in its place the carriers could now appeal commission decisions in courts of law.[11] The railroad lobby naturally felt the new act went way too far. Even the nation's foremost railroad trade magazine became aghast at the powers extended, noting "that the State of Florida has served notice on the world that it desires no more money invested in railroad building. We can cheerfully promise she shall have none."[12]

The new commission's first order of business was to meet with the carriers to discuss "just and reasonable rates." The Southern Classification rate system, which had been established by the Interstate Commerce Commission after its founding, was now in force. The Florida commission generally followed its directives, but on occasion it tweaked rates for vegetables, oranges, lemons, and forest products. Occasionally, commission decisions were challenged, such as when the carriers tried to abolish the "mileage books" of frequent passengers, which the commission felt was an unauthorized rate increase. (It thus ordered a reduction in passenger fares from four cents per mile to three.) On balance, relations between the parties remained amicable enough, though some firms, such as the Louisville and Nashville Railroad and the Florida East Coast Railway, often ignored commission rulings.[13]

In subsequent years, Florida's second railroad commission also regulated trolley lines, telegraph and telephone companies, motor transportation carriers, express companies, sleeping car companies, boat line operators, along with bridge and canal firms. In 1947, it was renamed the Florida Railroad and Public Utilities Commission; in 1963, it became the Florida Public Utilities Commission. Two years later, the Florida Public Service Commission (FPSC) surfaced. American railroads were deregulated in 1985, and the FPSC relinquished its jurisdiction over the industry. Today at the state level, Florida's railroads are monitored and assisted by the Rail Office of the Florida Department of Transportation.

About the time Florida's second railroad commission got legs, the Sunshine State was attracting the interest of several big out-of-state railroad systems. A foretaste of things to come had surfaced in the early 1880s, when the mighty Louisville and Nashville Railroad obtained a toehold in the state. Now, the Seaboard Air Line Railway, the Atlantic Coast Line Railroad, and the Southern Railway began flexing their muscles.

The "Seaboard" began life as an alliance of several post–Civil War railroads that connected Portsmouth and Norfolk, Virginia, with Atlanta, Georgia. In 1898, the consortium was acquired by the Richmond banking house of John L. Williams & Sons and the Baltimore investment firm of Middendorf, Oliver & Company. John Skelton Williams, later the U.S. comptroller of the currency, headed the alliance that, in February 1899, purchased the majority shares of the 940-mile Florida Central & Peninsular Railway (F C & P), whose story was briefly touched upon in chapter 5 and to which we now return.

The F C & P surfaced in 1889 as a reorganization of Sir Edward Reed's Florida Railway and Navigation Company—the state's first conglomerate. As stated in the first F C & P annual report, "The traffic of the new road is practically limited to the products of a single state, Florida, and that which comes into the State for consumption and its local and tourist travel."[14]

Prior to its absorption by the Seaboard syndicate, the F C & P had undertaken a number of expansion projects. In 1890, for instance, it finally completed its main line from Plant City to Tampa, while in the following year there opened a taproot, south of Archer, to serve the Early Bird, Eagle, and Standard phosphate mines. Also, a new phosphate feeder was finished in 1892 that connected Sydney (near Plant City) with the Alafia River Mineral Lands Company. Another appendage in the same region linked Turkey Creek with Durant.

Acquiring property for the important Plant City–Tampa leg proved somewhat problematic. Although citizens of Tampa donated a right-of-way and bought $40,000 of company notes, a certain segment of the new line had to pass through an old military reservation occupied by squatters. The latter naturally protested the railroad's invasion and threatened to obtain a court injunction. But the railroad's contractor—one step ahead of the court—managed to install the necessary crossties and rails in the course of a single weekend, which angered locals even more. But the ruffled feathers were quickly calmed after railway officials appeared on the scene and distributed a few cash gifts. After the 22-mile leg was completed, the F C & P received a U.S. land grant of 35,000 acres; Florida chipped in 32,000.[15]

The company's endeavors hardly ended with the aforementioned projects. In 1891, the F C & P purchased the Tavares, Orlando and Atlantic Railroad for $176,600, thereby obtaining a route out of Tavares down to the burgeoning community of Orlando, by way of Ellsworth, Zellwood, Plymouth, and Apopka. A year later, the F C & P leased, then later purchased, the 16-mile East Florida and Atlantic Railroad between Orlando and Oviedo, whose track it eventually extended to Lake Charm.[16]

The F C & P's biggest initiative, though, came alive in 1892, when Florida legislators empowered the company to build an extension north of Yulee station (formerly Hart's Road, above Jacksonville) to the Georgia state line. A subsidiary firm—the Florida Northern—was organized in Georgia to advance the project onward to Savannah. When completed in 1894, the 116-mile Savannah Extension, which cost $1,925,456 to construct, actually made the F C & P an intrastate railway system.[17] That same year, Florida's largest railroad company completed a 7-mile branch between Summerfield and Lake Weir, and purchased the tiny 2-mile Fernandina and Amelia Beach Railway.

Prior to its absorption by the Seaboard, the F C & P also undertook many improvement and betterment projects. For example, the company's extensive marine facilities at Fernandina were enlarged, and a new and large phosphate storage elevator was installed. Further, several substantial warehouses were erected on the company's property along Bay Street in Jacksonville, which were ultimately leased to such firms as Anheuser Busch Brewing, Clyde Steamship Company, and Armour Meat Packing. New stations arose too, as did water and coaling facilities. New locomotives and cars were also purchased, and many miles of new steel rail were installed.

One of the more remarkable sights on the F C & P main line was situated between Hawthorne and Citra, below the southeast shore of Orange Lake. Here, the track bisected a mammoth orange grove that contained over seventy thousand full-bearing trees, the largest such setting of its kind in the state. Practically every passenger train passed through the perfumed setting in daylight hours, including the Flying Cracker, which hauled elegant Pullman parlor cars.[18]

But the 1890s was not all glitz and glamour. The financial panic of 1893 created an unprecedented commercial depression in America, one that greatly reduced earnings of the Florida Central & Peninsular Railway and prompted a reorganization, resulting in the Florida Central & Peninsular Rail*road*. Then, in 1895, disastrous freezes descended over

The within Index and Township Map of Florida is the best, most correct and only comprehensive map of the State ever published, showing Fruit, Vegetable, Tobacco and Phosphate Belt; showing locations, etc.

INFORMATION FOLDER—AUGUST 15, 1893.

15059   The Matthews-Northrup Co., Complete Art-Printing Works, Buffalo, N. Y.

From the ashes of the Florida Railway and Navigation Company, there arose the Florida Central & Peninsular Railroad in 1888, whose main line later reached Savannah, Georgia, and then Columbia, South Carolina. Author's collection.

the state. "On December 28th there came a blighting cold which destroyed a crop of four million boxes of citrus fruit worth $5–6 million, worth $800,000 in F C & P revenues."[19] Another unusual cold wave swept over the landscape the following February, "which cut citrus trees to the ground and destroyed a large crop of vegetables worth $100,000 in company revenues." All this greatly reduced income. In 1895 alone, less than $5,000 in profit was recorded on revenues of several million! In the following year, a loss of $111,883 was sustained.

Since revenues could not be substantially increased or expenses cut much further, it was becoming evident that the Florida Central & Peninsular needed the resources of a larger system, one that served more markets and had deeper pockets. Thus, takeover discussions were initiated by the wealthy New Yorkers W. Bayard Cutting and R. Fulton Cutting (who owned a majority of F C & P stock) with banker John Skelton Williams of Richmond, Virginia, whose railroad syndicate purchased their shares in 1899.

The Seaboard Air Line Railway, which was formed with twenty separate companies having 2,600 miles of track, drew its first breath on 14 April 1900. In the following month, the company operated two celebratory trains over the new system from Richmond to Tampa. A thirty-two-piece band accompanied the celebrants, a steamboat tour of Tampa Bay was made, and a twenty-one-gun salute greeted Williams and his entourage when they returned home.

Immediately the company inaugurated a year-round train to the Sunshine State—the Seaboard Fast Mail—and ordered two thousand cars for the anticipated freight business. During the 1902–3 winter season, the Seaboard Florida Limited began service with a club car, two Pullman sleeping cars, and a ten-section observation car, whose interior was resplendent in highly polished mahogany, nickel, and brass. The luxury train, whose many patrons included steel mogul Andrew Carnegie, was lighted throughout by electricity generated by a dynamo located in the baggage end of the club car.

One of the first activities the Seaboard undertook in Florida was executing a traffic agreement with the United States and West Indies Railroad and Steamship Company, whose construction bonds the Seaboard owned. The 51-mile feeder connected Durant with Parrish, Palmetto, and Sarasota, the first train having arrived at the latter setting

The Seaboard obtained a Florida presence by acquiring the Florida Central & Peninsular in 1899. Immediately the company began operating through train service between New York and Florida. Clever ads announced the service. Author's collection.

on 22 March 1903.[20] A few months later, the ponderously named firm was reorganized as the Florida West Shore Railway. As the 1903 annual report of the Seaboard denotes: "The country traversed by our Florida West Shore subsidiary is exempt from frost and is admirably adapted for the growing of oranges, lemons, grapefruit, pineapples, bananas, and early fruits and vegetables of every kind." Spurs emanated from its main track to serve the agricultural settings of Terra Ceia, Ellenton, and Manatee. Later, the Seaboard extended the main track east of Sarasota to Fruitville, where citrus and vegetables were also grown in abundance.

Three other entities the Seaboard acquired during the early 1900s included the Plant City, Arcadia & Gulf, the Tallahassee, Perry & Southeastern, and the Atlantic, Suwannee River & Gulf. The first was built as a logging line between Plant City and Welcome by the Warnell Lumber & Veneer Company. After purchasing the taproot in 1905, the Seaboard rebuilt the line so as to reach the phosphate-rich Bone Valley of central Florida. Spur tracks were later installed to the mining towns of Coronet and Nichols.

The second entity, which ultimately became the Seaboard's Covington Subdivision, began life as the Florida, Georgia & Western Railway, a log and lumber carrier out of Tallahassee that reached Lake Como in 1891. A series of ownership changes occurred, and in time the route was extended farther east to Wacissa. In 1906, the Seaboard reorganized everything as the Tallahassee, Perry & Southeastern, and eventually extended the track to Covington and Waylonzo. Three years later, the 38-mile firm was formally acquired by the Seaboard.[21]

The Atlantic, Suwannee River & Gulf, which the Seaboard picked up in 1908, was another regional logging and lumber operation. The company operated between Starke, Buda, and Wannee, and built a branch from Buda down to Norwills.

In addition to acquiring existing companies, the Seaboard extended many routes. For example, in 1911 the Archer–Early Bird branch was advanced down to Dunnellon, Hernando, and Inverness, where seemingly inexhaustible beds of hard rock phosphate and limestone existed. Simultaneously, the Seaboard enlarged its presence in the Bone Valley to serve the mining towns of Agricola, Mulberry, Bartow, Pembroke, and Juneau. In 1914, the company completed its Lake Wales Extension from Bartow eastward to Lake Wales, Baynard, and Walinwa. Four years later, another Seaboard subsidiary—the Kissimmee River Railway—opened for business between Walinwa and Nalaca.

Bertha Palmer, a wealthy Chicago widow and socialite who was developing much of what would become Sarasota County, persuaded Seaboard officials to extend their track at Fruitville down to Bee Ridge, Laurel, and Venice, where she envisioned a ready-made resort city. The railway obliged, and the iron horse arrived in Venice in the fall of 1911.

Huge stands of longleaf pine existed below Venice, and before long the Manasota Land & Timber Company began operations. Its company-owned railroad penetrated area forestlands, and trains brought the cut pine logs to the millhouse in Manasota, which was later renamed Woodmere. Finished lumber was then dispatched up the Gulf Coast Railway track to Venice, from where the Seaboard relayed the traffic to Tampa, where manifests were off-loaded to awaiting ships.[22]

The Seaboard's big marine facility in Tampa, located on Seddon Island, was opened in 1909. A Seaboard subsidiary, Tampa Terminal Company, managed the facility, along with the loading of phosphate and bulk cargo. To obtain more regional traffic, the Seaboard acquired in 1912 the Tampa Northern Railroad between Tampa and Brooksville. (Branches served Tooke Lake and Centralia.) A year later, in order to reach St. Petersburg, the Seaboard acquired a controlling interest in the Tampa & Gulf Coast, whose line also serviced Port Richey, Tarpon Springs, and Clearwater.[23]

Hardly remembered today is the East & West Coast Railway, a Seaboard subsidiary that opened for business in 1915 between Arcadia and Bradenton by way of Myakka City. Numerous naval stores and lumber operators were situated along its route, including the Manatee Crate & Lumber Company, whose logging trains had running rights over the East & West Coast track. The Seaboard furnished the "E & W" with all necessary locomotives and cars. When area timberlands played out in the early 1930s, the backcountry wanderer was completely torn up.

One of the last additions the Seaboard made before the historic land boom of the 1920s was the Florida Central & Gulf. Organized in 1916, the company's sole purpose was to acquire the Standard & Hernando Railroad (S & H) of the Dunnellon Phosphate Company. The S & H connected the various phosphate mines around the Hernando area with

Port Inglis, where a dock on the Withlacoochee River was maintained. At Dunnellon, the firm made a handy connection with the Seaboard, which purchased the outfit in 1919. At that moment, the 41-mile phosphate hauler owned three steam engines, 154 freight cars, and one passenger coach.

During 1901, its first year of operation, the Seaboard posted revenues of $10,426,279. Profits, though, only amounted to $252,676. By 1917, revenues climbed to $30,345,146, yet profits were a paltry $854,067. Heavy expenses plagued the firm, and the cost of servicing the company's long-term debt extracted a heavy toll from income. Nevertheless, President S. Davies Warfield remained confident about the railroad's earnings potential, convinced as ever that its costly investments in Florida would, in time, eventually pay off.

An even larger out-of-state system that obtained a Florida presence in the wee hours of the twentieth century was the Atlantic Coast Line Railroad. This came about largely as a result of a long-standing relationship between the founders of the "Coast Line" and Henry Bradley Plant, whose career was discussed in the previous chapter.

Like the Seaboard, the Coast Line system evolved from dozens of smaller firms that stretched along the Atlantic seaboard below Richmond, Virginia. The company's prime mover was William Walters, a Confederate sympathizer and successful Baltimore produce merchant. Convinced that the South would again become an economic power after the Civil War, Walters and his inner circle of investors began acquiring railways that had earnings potential and could help form a confederation, or system that could one day convey early winter vegetables and fruits to northern markets and transport winter-weary tourists to warmer climes.[24]

Henry Walters, the only son of William, became general manager of the Coast Line in 1884. Like his father, Henry was reticent and possessed remarkable business acumen. Both the father and son shared a passion for collecting fine art, and the magnificent Walters Art Museum in Baltimore thrives today as never before.[25]

In the late 1880s, Henry persuaded George Pullman to finance and construct two special train sets for service between New York and Jacksonville. The New York and Florida Special was comprised of drawing room, dining cars, and sleeping cars that boasted electric lights, enclosed vestibules, steam heat, blue upholstered seats, and rich wood interiors of bird's-eye maple and Spanish mahogany. Operations commenced on 9 January 1888, with the trains covering the 1,074-mile trip in thirty hours flat. The service, which became an instant hit, coincided with the opening of Henry Flagler's opulent Ponce de Leon Hotel in St. Augustine. After Flagler bridged the St. Johns River in Jacksonville in 1890, the "Aristocrat of Winter Trains" ran directly into America's oldest city.

For years, friendly relations had prevailed between William and Henry Walters and Henry Bradley Plant, even to the extent that they invested in each other's enterprises. Their respective systems met at Charleston, South Carolina, where traffic was exchanged. The Plant System forwarded early winter vegetables, citrus, phosphate, and passengers, while the Coast Line handed off all manner of northern manufactured goods, mail and express packages, and countless winter tourists.

The citrus traffic became so extensive that the Coast Line founded the Atlantic Coast Despatch, a fast freight service that utilized specially built refrigerator fruit cars. To further stimulate interest in the Sunshine State, the Coast Line funded a guidebook, *Florida: Its Scenery, Climate and History*, which the American author Sidney Lanier was commissioned to write in 1875.

Prior to inaugurating its sumptuous New York and Florida Special, the Coast Line was operating two popular passenger trains between New York and Florida: the Coast Line Florida Mail and the West Indian Limited. Demand for more train service arose, and two additional year-round Florida consists were added in 1910: the Gulf Coast Limited and the Palmetto Limited.[26]

William Walters died in 1894, whereupon Henry became chairman and the Coast Line's principal stockholder. Five years later, Henry Plant passed, but legal complications prevented his vast estate—comprised of railroads, steamship lines, land companies, and hotels—from passing to his heirs until several years later. Overtures to purchasing the railroad portion of the empire were communicated to Henry Walters by Robert Erwin, the trusted confidant and legal brains of the Plant System.[27] Walters, though, hardly needed convincing, for the purchase

Henry Walters, the patrician chairman of the Atlantic Coast Line Railroad, oversaw the Plant System purchase in 1902. Afterward, numerous improvement projects were carried out in the Sunshine State. By permission of The Walters Art Museum, Baltimore.

would not only be a natural extension for the Coast Line, but it would give the latter a much-needed presence in the Florida marketplace.

Walters came back with an offer that, after some fine tuning, pleased the widow Margaret Plant, though she insisted that the purchase price be made with cash and not railroad securities. This demand slightly delayed matters, but on 1 July 1902 she sold the railroad empire—comprised of 2,235 miles of lines—for $46,563,898, or roughly $20,800 per mile. At the closing table, the Coast Line assumed all Plant System railroad debt while Margaret received the remaining proceeds in Atlantic Coast Line Railroad stock, which she immediately exchanged for a check.[28] Thus, with a pen stroke, the Coast Line doubled in size and instantly became the dominant railroad player in Florida, a position it would retain until 1967. If the transaction did not dazzle the American railroad world, the next move by Walters did. Several months afterward, the Coast Line purchased a majority stock interest in the sprawling Louisville and Nashville Railroad. And with that coup, the Atlantic Coast Line Railroad Company owned or controlled some 9,000 miles of track.

Although he was hardly known or seen in Florida, primarily because he was so reticent, Henry Walters ordered many expansion and improvement programs for the Sunshine State. One of his first initiatives was to extend the Coast Line south of Punta Gorda (then the southernmost point of the system) down to Fort Myers. For years, civic and business leaders of the "City of Palms" had wanted railroad service, but Henry Plant had lent a deaf ear. Now, city fathers were willing to give the Coast Line a free right-of-way through the old cattle town along with suitable grounds for a station and terminal facilities. The 28-mile extension, which G. W. Baxter & Company of Jacksonville built for $309,000, opened amidst considerable fanfare on 10 May 1904. Immediately, the seat of Lee County began to experience an economic boom. Tourists and newcomers started to pour in, while carloads of ocean and lake fish departed Fort Myers for northern markets along with crates of citrus and vegetables as well as cattle.[29]

Other initiatives approved by Walters included the installation of new drawbridges on the company's main route between Jacksonville and Sanford; converting the narrow gauge track of the old Orange Belt Railroad to standard gauge between Trilby and St. Petersburg; erecting new terminal facilities at "St. Pete"; and building new phosphate mine spurs in the Bone Valley of central Florida. Further, the switching yards at Jacksonville and Lakeland were enlarged, and all main line tracks within the state received new 85-pound (to the yard) steel rails. Lastly, orders were placed for many new locomotives along with freight and passenger cars.

Walters also realized that many Plant System stations needed repairs or outright replacement, and that certain communities lacked facilities for the conduct of business. Accordingly, new structures opened in 1905 at Punta Gorda, Alligator Creek, Samville, Tice, Fort Myers, DeLeon Springs, Wauchula, Wallkill, and Moffets. To handle the influx of yellow pine traffic at Jacksonville, the Coast Line also built a substantial new dock facility on the St. Johns River, calling it the Jacksonville Export Terminal. Later, new freight facilities were constructed in St. Petersburg, while new combination freight and passenger depots were completed at Tarpon Springs, Winter Garden, Kathleen, and Juliette. Still more stations opened in 1908 at Leesburg, Dunnellon, Doctors Inlet, Apopka, Newberry, Satsuma, Duke, Edgar, and Homeland.

The Plant System purchase included not only railroads but extensive parcels of real estate, most having been gifted to the underlying companies by the State of Florida. Walters placed the portfolio with a Coast Line subsidiary—Atlantic Land and Improvement Company. "Alico" oversaw many construction projects in Florida, including the building of a new phosphate elevator at Port Tampa. Alico's real estate holdings of were scattered about the state. Those concentrated in south Florida contained vast stands of timber, which conveniently furnished the Coast Line with a supply of wood for crossties, bridge timbers, railroad cars, stations, and other construction projects.

Other railways that the Coast Line purchased in the prewar period included the 86-mile Jacksonville & Southwestern (J & S), founded by the Cummer lumbering family. The J & S connected Milldale (near Jacksonville) with Newberry by way of Baldwin, Raiford, Lake Butler, and Burnetts Lake. After acquiring the concern in 1904, the Coast Line extended its track past Newberry to Wilcox in 1907; two years later, it reached the burgeoning lumber and turpentine center of Perry. Another logging line addition was the 47-mile Florida Central, whose route connected Thomasville, Georgia, with Fanlew, Florida, by way of Fincher, Capitola, and Cody.

In the fall of 1910, the Coast Line began constructing its Haines City Branch from Haines City southward to Lake Hare and Sebring. Citrus and vegetable growers—along with many lumber operators— abounded in the "Scenic Highlands" of the state. Residents cheered the railroad's arrival, as the *Sebring News* of 1 August 1912 confirms: "At a quarter of five in the afternoon, accompanied by the camp meeting melodies of the Negro tracklayers, the screaming of the whistle on the engine and the cheers of our residents, the last spike, in the last rail, was driven. This long anticipated climax marked the beginning of a new era of promise for Sebring."

During the prewar period, the Coast Line also purchased the Sanford & Everglades Railroad, a 12-mile feeder that linked Sanford with Mecca Junction; it extended the old Winston and Bone Valley Railroad past the mining town of Tiger Bay to Fort Meade; Archer was connected to Morriston; and Dunnellon was linked with Wilcox. During the prosperity of 1916, Coast Line directors voted to extend the Haines City Branch below Sebring down to Immokalee, an up-and-coming timber and agricultural market, this by way of Palmdale, Harrisburg, and Goodno.

In conjunction with the extension to Immokalee, Walters ordered the Coast Line's contractor to build a branch from Harrisburg, on Fisheating Creek, to Moore Haven, on the western shore of Lake Okeechobee. Previously, the mayor of Moore Haven—the daughter of a Midwest railroad executive—told Coast Line officials that the region's mucklands were producing fantastic yields of vegetables, but what the town lacked was railroad transportation. Apparently though, the Moore Haven Branch of the Coast Line was not very well constructed. Trains did manage to rock 'n' roll over the line, even at slow speeds. The editor of the *Moore Haven Times* complained that riding on the railroad's Muck City Express was like "being with a shy young girl afflicted with the St. Vitus dance."[30]

Another branch project of significance was the Tampa Southern Railroad. The unusual number of citrus and vegetable growers situated in Manatee County, together with the productive phosphate mines east of Palmetto, prompted the line's construction. David Gillett, a former Tampa mayor and owner of Buckeye Nurseries, became president of the concern. At first, the press nicknamed Gillett's operation "The Ghost Line" because no one knew its real owner. The company's route commenced in Uceta (east of Tampa) and descended to Ruskin, Gillett, Palmetto, down to Bradenton, where rails arrived in 1920. Although chapter 8 will offer more details about this firm, suffice it to say that the firm's real owner was the Atlantic Coast Line Railroad!

Other projects the Coast Line completed in this period included a state-of-the-art creosote plant in Gainesville and more stations; orders were also placed for additional cars and engines. In 1917, Coast Line revenues stood at $44,063,331, net income amounted to $10,701,294 that year, and stockholders received 7 percent dividends. The Atlantic Coast Line Railroad then owned 807 locomotives, 698 passenger cars, and 30,777 freight cars. By any measure, it was a growing, impressive operation.

The remaining big out-of-state system that obtained a Florida presence in this era—albeit a small one—was the Southern Railway. Chartered in 1894, the company's maze of tracks connected Alexandria, Virginia, with Columbus, Mississippi; Chattanooga through Atlanta to Brunswick, Georgia; from Memphis through Chattanooga to Bristol, Virginia; from Selma, Alabama, to Rome, Georgia; and from Danville, Virginia to Richmond.

The Southern Railway was conceived by the investment banker J. Pierpont Morgan, together with his railroad securities specialist Charles Coster and legal brain Francis Stetson. Samuel Spencer, a railway executive of exceptional experience and a former president of the Baltimore & Ohio Railroad, became the Southern's first president. When organized, the company owned some 4,300 miles of lines, 19,694 cars, and 623 locomotives. In 1895, after its first full year of operation, the Virginia-based corporation declared revenues of $17,114,791, expenses of $12,062,854, and net earnings of $5,051,937.

To obtain its Florida presence, the Southern purchased an ownership interest in the Georgia Southern & Florida Railroad (G S & F) in 1895. As the Southern annual report for that year remarked: "The Georgia Southern & Florida originates a large lumber, fruit, and melon business in Georgia and reaches the fruit growing regions of Florida, partially by its own rails, but to a much greater extent through its terminus on the St. Johns River at Palatka, Florida, and its connections at several points with the most important railway systems in that State."

Spencer allowed the G S & F to maintain its corporate identity and kept all of its senior officers on the payroll. But try as he did to obtain a stock majority in the firm, Spencer admitted in the same 1895 annual report that, because of technicalities, the investment in the G S & F did not quite produce a majority stake, although it came very close. Nevertheless, the acquisition made money, and Southern directors "have every reason to be satisfied with this investment."

Who, then, was the Georgia Southern & Florida? In 1884, the Florida legislature chartered the Macon & Florida Air Line Railroad, empowering it to construct a route from the Georgia border down to Tampa or Charlotte Harbor, along with a branch to the St. Johns River. In 1881, Georgia had chartered the Georgia Southern & Florida Railroad to advance such a project from the state line up to Macon. The two entities merged in 1888 and retained the name of the Georgia concern. Company goals were later revamped, with a line from Macon to Valdosta resulting. By 1890, the Macon Construction Company had advanced the route from Valdosta southeasterly to Palatka, Florida, via Jennings, Jasper, Lake City, Lake Butler, and Sampson City.

But the cost of creating the so-called Suwannee River Route, coupled with some misuse of funds, pushed the company into bankruptcy in 1891. A new G S & F emerged four years later, and many of the receiver's certificates, which were convertible to the new company's stock and bonds, were purchased by the Southern Railway. Later, in 1902, the Southern allowed its G S & F subsidiary to acquire two connecting lines: the Atlantic, Valdosta & Western and the St. Johns River Terminal.

The Atlantic, Valdosta & Western connected Valdosta with Jacksonville by way of Crawford. Because of topographical issues, the 107-mile route twice entered Florida in order to reach Jacksonville—first at Sargent, again at Kent. The company, which was affiliated with the G. S. Baxter Lumber Company of Jacksonville, was regarded as a progressive carrier. Its route, for example, was equipped with 70-pound (to the yard) steel rail, while company locomotives were the first in Florida to carry electric headlights. Timber and wood products were the company's traffic mainstays.

Organized by the Atlantic, Valdosta & Western in 1901, the St. Johns River Terminal Company serviced a variety of industrial customers at the port of Jacksonville. Operations commenced with about 7 miles of track, though within a few years the company added another 19 miles. The firm also developed industrial sites. Connections with the parent firm were made at the busy Jacksonville interchange point of Grand Junction.

"Now, therefore, I, Woodrow Wilson, President of the United States, under and by virtue of the powers vested in me . . . do hereby . . . take possession and assume control at 12 o'clock noon on the 28th day of December, 1917, each and every system of transportation . . . within the boundaries of the continental United States." And with that pronouncement all 693 railroad companies in America came under control of the United States Railroad Administration.[31]

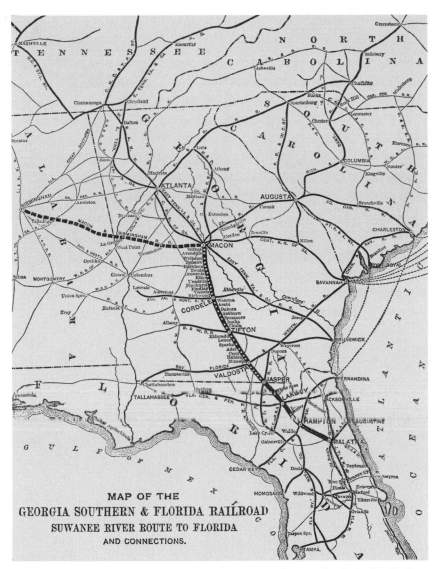

MAP OF THE

GEORGIA SOUTHERN & FLORIDA RAILROAD
SUWANEE RIVER ROUTE TO FLORIDA
AND CONNECTIONS.

Palatka was the southernmost point of the Georgia Southern & Florida Railroad. The firm chiefly conveyed lumber, citrus, and general merchandise from the St. Johns River area to the Peach State. Author's collection.

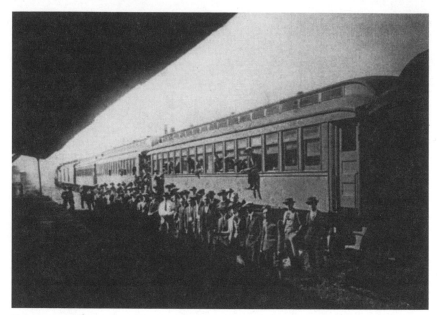

Enlistees of the First World War—many in suits and ties—pose for the camera before departing Gainesville in 1917. After basic training, it was off to Europe, where many soldiers perished. State Archives of Florida.

America had tardily entered the First World War (1914–18). The ongoing atrocities, such as the sinking of *Lusitania* and the resumption of unrestricted submarine warfare in early 1917, finally prompted President Wilson to ask for a Declaration of War on 2 April 1917, less than a month after his second term began. Congress obliged four days later. The cost of fighting it, excluding lives, was astronomical: ten times greater than that of the American Civil War, or about $112 billion, not counting the few billions America loaned to Allied governments.

Harnessing the American economy for wartime purposes was not an easy task. Essential to the process was the unqualified cooperation of the transportation industry, especially the nation's railroads. When federal control was enacted, America's railroads were not only at their all-time greatest extent, but they were transporting their largest traffic ever.

At first, the nation's railway companies attempted to organize themselves for the war effort. A Railroad War Board was established, which studied ways to effectively use the national car fleet, discontinue needless passenger trains, alleviate congestion, systemize settlements, and how to best transport lumber and steel for the army and navy. Unfortunately, universal agreement upon such issues could not be garnered. Labor shortages also complicated matters, and many firms were experiencing financial problems. Consequently, in December 1917, the Interstate Commerce Commission recommended that the carriers be taken over by the government.

The U.S. Railroad Administration (USRA) surfaced that same month. William McAdoo, secretary of the treasury, became director general of railroads, and among his inner circle of consultants was Henry Walters, chairman of the Atlantic Coast Line Railroad. To meet the pressing demands of wartime production, the USRA soon ordered 100,000 railroad cars and 1,930 steam locomotives.

Every railroad in Florida and elsewhere came under USRA control, and not until March 1920 were they returned to their rightful owners—the stockholders. The USRA compensated each using a Standard Return (or rental fee), which was based on a three-year earnings average from 1915–17. Certain railroad executives found the plan acceptable, but many others did not, and before long hard feelings developed. Among those angered by the plan's unfairness was S. Davies Warfield, chairman and president of the Seaboard Air Line Railway. Further, the USRA promised to return the carriers in roughly the same condition as when taken. Such was not the case, and many were given back in a much-worn condition, which further angered executives.

Florida's railroads experienced considerable uptick in traffic during the war years. Extra carloads of citrus, vegetables, lumber, and phosphate were transported, along with soldiers, war material and building supplies. The federal government funded several military projects in the state, such as the 8-mile spur at Arcadia that led to a nearby aviation training facility called Carlstrom Field.

In retrospect, America's experiment in "nationalization" proved to be a costly venture—nearly $1.2 billion—and therefore it was not repeated in the Second World War. Shortly after the companies were returned to private ownership, a historic land boom began in Florida. The war years, though, had sidetracked many much-needed expansions and improvements, thus Florida's biggest railroads were caught unprepared for the crush of boom business. But as chapter 8 relates, these deficiencies were soon erased.

7

Vignettes

The railroad line to Boca Grande also brought the manifold benefits of a nascent but prosperous resort industry, a source of wealth proving increasingly significant with the introduction of Pullman service to Jacksonville in 1911 and the subsequent opening of the railroad-owned Gasparilla Inn.

—Schwieterman, *When the Railroad Leaves Town*

In 1939, after months of patient and careful research, the Railroad Commission of Florida determined that 564 railroad companies had been chartered since the 1830s. Of that figure, 251 lines actually had been built, although many had been subsequently abandoned or broken up. The remaining 313 firms never got beyond the paper stage. Of those that were constructed, however, 154 lines were still in operation but not under their original names. In fact, as a result of sales, receiverships, bankruptcies, consolidations, and mergers, there existed in 1939 only twenty-two companies.[1]

Space limitations preclude a portrait of all 251 lines built; nevertheless, this chapter is devoted to some of the more memorable players of bygone days, almost all of whom have vanished. This survey—an arbitrary and informal one at best—commences in west Florida and proceeds across the Panhandle to Jacksonville, whereupon it descends the peninsula.

Nestled in the northwest corner of the state was the Escambia Railroad of Alger-Sullivan Lumber, which opened in 1901.[2] Its tracks chiefly penetrated the dense forestlands of nearby southern Alabama, though the company's headquarters and sawmill complex—the largest east of the Mississippi River—were situated in Century, Florida, where connections were made with the Louisville and Nashville Railroad (L & N).

After the great longleaf pine trees were felled, the trimmed logs were hauled to the company's nearest rail spur in high-wheeled wagons hauled by oxen. (The company owned 250 of the beasts along with numerous horses.) Special geared steam locomotives often collected the loaded log cars and then assembled them into trains. Conventional rod engines then hustled the traffic off to Century—formerly known as Teaspoon—for processing.

Another area logging railway was the Pensacola & Andalusia, a narrow gauge operation owned by Skinner & McDavid Lumber. Its 18-mile route, which serviced the timberlands of Santa Rosa County, departed Molino (where connections were made with the L & N) and headed for Centennial via Chumuckla. In this same region was the rail operation of Escambia Land & Manufacturing. Two rail lines departed the company's headquarters at Pace: one headed down to the L & N junction near Mulat, another northeasterly to Chumuckla. The lumber concern acquired the aforementioned Pensacola & Andalusia around 1904.

Another firm relying upon the L & N for connections to the outside world was the Pensacola and Perdido Railroad, whose track connected the docks in Pensacola with Millview. Owner Henry McLaughlin later combined the firm with other holdings to form the Pensacola, Alabama & Tennessee, a grandiose project he and his colleagues hatched in 1892. But the dream only got as far as Muscogee, where a large sawmill and rail line of Southern States Lumber existed. Logs and lumber were the company's traffic mainstays, and occasionally the outfit ran passenger trains. But the lofty goal of linking Pensacola with Memphis never materialized.

Another of the many projects conceived by McLaughlin was the Pensacola, Mobile & New Orleans, which managed to construct just 23 miles of track from Parker station (between Millview and Muscogee) to Pomona, Alabama, a destination far short of New Orleans. Later, in 1918, McLaughlin organized an umbrella firm to contain his various holdings called Gulf Ports Terminal Railway.

After Henry died, nephew Elwood McLaughlin grabbed the throttle. Unable to stabilize the underlying firms, Elwood petitioned the

Interstate Commerce Commission in 1925 to abandon all the properties except for those in the immediate Pensacola area. The ICC gave its approval provided a buyer could be found for the unwanted entities. As the next chapter relates, part of the holdings were acquired by the Frisco Railroad (a formidable Midwest concern) so as to obtain a gulf port outlet.[3] The Frisco also acquired the Gulf, Florida & Alabama (G, F & A), whose predecessors included the aforementioned rail operation of Southern States Lumber. The G, F & A (nicknamed the Deep Water Route) operated two lines out of Cantonment into Alabama: one to Local, another to Gateswood.

Logging railroads once were a big fixture of the Panhandle, owing to the region's immense forestlands. Another firm of note was Bagdad Land & Lumber, whose rail line connected Bagdad with Whittey, Alabama, this by way of Milton, Cold Water, and Munson. Part of its 44-mile route had been constructed by Stearns & Culver Lumber; the remainder by the Bagdad firm in 1914. Connections with the L & N were made at Milton.

The Bagdad outfit called its rail operation the Florida & Alabama Railroad, but the railroad commission of Florida refused to grant it common carrier status because it had never been formally incorporated. Headquarters of the railway were situated at Munson, Florida, where a 19-mile branch departed for area turpentine camps. When the Bagdad mill folded in 1939, the rail line was sold for scrap.

East of Milton lay another L & N stopping point: Galliver. In the early 1900s, the Florida & Alabama Land Company opened a 25-mile line from Galliver to its logging mill in Falco, Alabama, calling it the Florida, Alabama & Gulf. When the parent firm went broke in 1912, McGowin-Foshee Lumber acquired the railroad and renamed it the Andalusia, Florida & Gulf. After area forestlands were denuded in the 1920s, the logging line out of Galliver started to vanish.[4]

Another Panhandle community served by the Louisville and Nashville Railroad was Crestview. In 1894, sawmill operator W. B. Wright opened the 26-mile Yellow River Railroad between Crestview and Florala, Alabama, via Auburn, Campton, and Laurel Hill. At Florala, spur tracks reached back into Florida to serve the lumber settings of Lakewood and Paxton.[5] Wright's outfit also installed a short branch from Laurel Hill to Wing, Alabama, where the firm connected with the afore-

Most of Florida's logging railroads connected with big firms to reach the outside world. Some, though, served just their lumber company owners. Steam-powered cranes often loaded the cut logs onto special rail cars. Author's collection.

mentioned Florida, Alabama & Gulf. The L & N supplied the Yellow River Railroad with freight cars and, in 1906, purchased the operation.

The town of Chipley was named for the L & N figurehead Colonel William Chipley (see chapter 5). In 1903, the Birmingham, Columbus & St. Andrews Railroad was empowered to build a line from Chipley down to pretty Southport, an arm on St. Andrews Bay. (The colonel was one of the line's early promoters.) Raising funds for the project proved tortuous, and only 15 miles of track were in service by 1907. Another five years passed before trains actually arrived in Greenhead and Southport. In fact, the Greenhead-Southport portion had to be constructed by the Southport Lumber Company, which had deeper pockets.

Once fully opened, the line out of Chipley actually prospered; logging trains were run at the drop of a hat. An interesting account of the railroad's salad days appeared in the October 1959 issue of *Railroad Magazine*. But after the region's lush timberlands played out, business declined and the lumber company later "went to the wall." In the 1920s, the rail line was sold to new owners, who reorganized everything as the Alabama & Western Florida. A decade later it, too, expired.

Fortunately not all Panhandle carriers were short-lived. A case in point is the Atlanta & St. Andrews Bay Railway, which exists to this day under a new name. A. B. Steele, who owned Enterprise Lumber in Dothan, Alabama, began building the logging railway in the early 1900s, between Dothan and the Florida state line. Common carrier status was granted in 1906, whereupon a twofold mission began to crystallize: linking Dothan with a gulf port, and becoming a conduit for traffic between Atlanta and the future Panama Canal. Steele's contractor advanced the "Bay Line" over the border to Campbellton and Cottondale, where a handy connection was made with the L & N. The project temporarily halted until a suitable southern terminus could be selected. A real estate syndicate convinced Steele that the ideal setting was Harrison, later renamed Panama City. Steele agreed, and construction resumed via Alford, Saunders, and Youngstown. The company's first passenger train arrived in Panama City on 29 June 1908.[6]

In order to complete the line to Panama City, Steele had to borrow $70,000 from Atlanta's Asa Candler of Coca-Cola fame. After Steele died, Candler got control of the Bay Line. In 1913, the railroad installed a branch over to Lynn Haven. In the following year, a local businessman, S. H. Drummond, constructed a spur off the Bay Line to a rival community called St. Andrews. Drummond's empire, the 2.6-mile St. Andrews Bay Terminal Railway, eventually faltered, and outright failed in 1926.

Interestingly, Steele's son eventually bought back his father's railway, who eventually sold it to Minor Keith, an executive of United Fruit. Keith wanted to establish a banana terminal at Panama City. The plan failed to materialize, and in 1931 Keith sold the Bay Line to the St. Andrews Bay Holding Company, a subsidiary of the International Paper Company. Shortly afterward, the big firm opened a mill at Panama City, and the Bay Line was awash in traffic.

Another firm having links to Panama City was German-American Lumber. In the early 1900s, Henry Bovis organized the St. Andrews Lumber Company. Bovis sold out to foreign investors in 1910, which previously had formed German-American Lumber in Pensacola.[7] (Members of German royalty were among the founders.) After acquiring the firm, the new owners constructed a mill in the Millville section of Panama City, together with a logging railroad. During the First World War, pro-German literature and guns were found at the mill inside a secret tunnel. American authorities confiscated and sold the operation. The mill and rail line reemerged as American Lumber.

Marbury Lumber Company, an Alabama firm, operated a logging railway between Ardilla, Alabama, and Malone, Florida, where the firm owned some 50,000 acres of virgin timber. In 1910, its rail line was incorporated as the Alabama, Florida & Southern. New owners later appeared on the scene and reorganized the logging line as the Alabama, Florida & Gulf. They also extended the track below Malone so as to reach Greenwood. But financial problem persisted, and before long a bank in Dothan, Alabama, was running the operation. Another sale took place, and the carrier surfaced as the Alabama & Florida Railroad. Most everything went to the scrap heap in the early 1940s.

The pride and joy of Calhoun County was the Marianna & Blountstown Railroad (M & B), whose many sobriquets included the "Meat & Bread" and "The Rich Uncle Railroad."[8] Chartered in 1909, the company not only had the right to build a railroad, but to buy and sell real estate, operate a mercantile business, broker timberlands, erect a hotel, and even operate a telephone company. The 29-mile pike opened for business in January 1910 between Marianna and Old Blountstown (McNeal). Connections with the L & N, which supplied its steel rails, were made at Marianna. Crossties, bridge timbers, and trestle-works were all milled from area forests.

At Old Blountstown, the M & B connected with steamboats plying the Apalachicola River. In 1912, the Blountstown Manufacturing Company, which controlled the M & B, built a 15-mile branch from Blountstown down to Scotts Ferry on the Chipola River. In 1925, the branch was extended to Myron, where a large sawmill stood. The M & B operated the branch, whose customers included the Marysville Naval Stores and the Chipola Turpentine Company. Logging trains of Neal Lumber and Manufacturing were also allowed to use the appendage, which paid eighty cents for every 1,000 feet of logs it conveyed.

In the 1930s, the "Many Bumps" (another sobriquet) thought about purchasing the aforementioned Alabama, Florida & Gulf and building a link between Marianna and Greenwood. The ICC approved the measure, but the plan withered. Traffic on the Blountstown–Scotts Ferry branch declined as area forests were stripped. Passenger trains vanished in 1929; in the late 1930s the once-busy branch was completely removed. Truckers then began to make serious inroads on the traffic north of Blountstown to Marianna.

New owners of the railroad came and went, and the M & B gradually slipped into decrepitude. According to the noted railroad historian and author Larry Goolsby, several wooden trestles upon the Marianna & Blountstown had to be steel-cabled to nearby trees so that they would only minimally sway under the weight of passing trains! Sadly, the pride and joy of Calhoun County died in 1972.

Another Panhandle firm that has withstood the test of time is the Apalachicola Northern. Incorporated in 1903, the company's founders wished to connect the port of "Old Apalach" with Chattahoochee, easternmost point of the Louisville and Nashville Railroad. Workers began building the 79-mile route in 1905 by way of Franklin, Sumatra, Elmira, and Greensboro.[9] The first train chugged into Apalachicola on 30 April 1907. Among the railroad's many customers were oyster, fish, and shrimp canneries, as well as naval stores and lumber operators.

In 1910, the Apalachicola Northern built a 20-mile extension from Franklin over to Port St. Joe that, in time, surpassed "Old Apalach" in railway importance. Special trains were immediately operated over the new line.

> The first excursion train left Apalachicola at 8 o'clock . . . the fare being fifty cents. Ladies of the Methodist Episcopal Church of Apalachicola took advantage of the opportunity and fed the hungry crowd on the beach at St. Joe, taking with them, on the 8 o'clock train, great quantities of edibles. After a run of fifty minutes the train reached Port St. Joe, discharged its passengers, and returned to Apalachicola for a second load. Previous to the arrival of the parties, tables had been set up under the trees. Church members served lemonade to the thirsty at 5 cents a cup. The ladies served a nice dinner for 25 cents, the menus consisting of baked beans, potato salad, pickles, baked ham, fried chicken, and roast beef. Cake was offered at 5 cents a slice, ice cream cones at 5 cents apiece, and fruit punch at 5 cents a cup. The receipts from the dinner amounted to $120.00 net. This money will be used for the organ fund.[10]

The first train of the Apalachicola Northern Railroad arrived in "Old Apalach" on 30 April 1907. Celebrants lined up on the flatcars like tin soldiers; some even sat atop the tender. State Archives of Florida.

Other area rail operations not to be easily forgotten was the rail line of Grand Ridge Manufacturing, near Sneads; the Caryville and Geneva Railroad, whose 20-mile route penetrated Washington County; the rail lines of Harbeson Lumber and Beach Rogero Lumber of DeFuniak Springs; and the little line of St. Joe Lumber & Export Company.

Furnishing railroad transportation between the capital and Carrabelle became the objective of the Augusta, Tallahassee & Gulf. By 1888, workers had completed the first 12 miles of track from the port of Carrabelle to the Sopchoppy River. Then financial problems set in. The company passed through a receivership and reappeared as the Carrabelle, Tallahassee & Georgia Railroad. William Clark, the famed thread maker, controlled the new firm. Construction bonds were floated—many were sold in Clark's distant homeland of Scotland—and proceeds financed the remaining construction to Tallahassee. The 50-mile line was opened throughout on New Year's Day, 1896. From Carrabelle, the company operated the steamboat *Crescent City* over to Apalachicola, a pleasant sea jaunt that took about three hours. The Clark Syndicate Companies, with offices in New York City, Chicago, and Glasgow, also owned the Georgia & Florida Investment Company, Gulf Terminal & Navigation, and the Scottish Land & Improvement Company. Clark even started a planned community near Carrabelle, called Lanark, which boasted 4 miles of waterfront and an inviting hotel.[11]

But not even millionaire Clark could resolve all the railroad's financial problems. In 1906, the firm was absorbed by the Georgia, Florida & Alabama Railway, which was based in Bainbridge, Georgia. In 1902, the latter had constructed a railroad between Bainbridge and Tallahassee by way of Jamieson and Havana.[12] Four years later, the company completed a branch from Havana to Quincy (via Freemont and Florence) to transport the region's large deposits of Fuller's earth, a mineral. In 1928, the G, F & A was leased to the Seaboard Air Line Railway. Because of declining traffic, the route between Tallahassee and Carrabelle was torn up in the early 1940s.

This brings us to a small pair of area lines called the Pelham & Havana and the Florida Central. The former, which connected Cairo, Georgia, with Havana, Florida, was operated by Massey-Felton Lumber in Cairo. Havana was reached around 1906, with the company renting space in the depot of the aforementioned Georgia, Florida & Alabama Railway. After area forests were stripped in the 1920s, the outfit vanished. The 81-mile Florida Central, owned by J. L. Phillips Lumber of Thomasville, Georgia, connected Thomasville with Fanlew, Florida, by way of Fincher, Capitola, El Destino, and Cody. Traffic consisted of logs, pulpwood, naval stores, and finished lumber. Profits, though, were razor-thin. A receivership had to take place in 1912, and that portion of the route between Fincher and Fanlew was sold to the Atlantic Coast Line Railroad in 1914. What remained disappeared in the early 1940s.

Without question a far more impressive area operation was the South Georgia Railway, which opened in 1901 between Heartpine, Georgia, and Greenville, Florida, via Lovett and Maysland. Three years later, a subsidiary, the West Coast Railway, extended the route south of Greenville to the lumbering epicenter of Perry, about the same time the South Georgia Railway moved its headquarters to Adel, Georgia.

In 1915, the aforementioned West Coast Railway acquired the 5-mile line of the Interstate Lumber Company, which ran between Perry and Hampton Springs. According to logging and short-line railroad expert Donald Hensley Jr., the owners of the South Georgia Railway (the Oglesby family) obtained rights to the mineral springs at Hampton, erected a bottling works and popular hotel, and eventually installed a golf course, swimming pool, spa, and recreation hall.[13] Amazingly, ten passenger and freight trains once daily serviced the resort, which is today but a memory. The South Georgia and West Coast entities merged in 1923. Later, in 1931, the South Georgia abandoned its Hampton Springs branch, a casualty of the Great Depression. The Brooks-Scanlon Corporation of Minneapolis eventually purchased what was left, later selling it to the Southern Railway.

Forest products, Sea Island cotton, and bright leaf tobacco were the traffic mainstays of the Valdosta Southern Railroad, which, at century's turn, operated between Valdosta, Georgia, and Madison, Florida, by way of Pinetta. In 1907, the 27-mile route was acquired by the Georgia & Florida Railroad. H. Roger Grant notes, in his recent *Rails through the Wiregrass: A History of the Georgia & Florida Railroad*, that the carrier was acquired by the Seaboard Air Line Railway in 1911, which, in turn, sold it to the Southern Railway in 1963.

A few miles south of Madison was situated the Weston sawmill of West Yellow Pine Company. The facility, as well as the company's logging camps, lacked rail service. This led to the creation of the Madison Southern Railway in 1906, which departed Madison southward to service the camp settings. (Dead Man's Bay, where West Yellow Pine envisioned a deepwater port, was not reached.) Rough and finished lumber were transported over the Madison Southern, along with an occasional passenger. In 1919, the railroad's assets included a single locomotive, one passenger coach, and five freight cars. Passenger revenues in 1921 amounted to thirty-seven dollars! Small wonder the feeble enterprise vanished.[14]

East of Madison was situated the bustling community of Ellaville, former head of navigation on the Suwannee River. One of the largest sawmill complexes in the state was located here, built by future Florida governor George Drew. North of town ran the Ellaville, Westlake & Jennings Railroad (owned by West Brothers Lumber), which served Grooven, West Lake, and Malloy Point. At West Lake, a branch forked northwest for Bellville. During its heyday, the little company owned two locomotives and thirty-eight freight cars. Traffic greatly declined before the First World War, prompting the line to be torn up and sold for scrap. The Suwannee River Railway, organized in the late 1880s by lumber mogul Charles Bucki, furnished rail service south of Ellaville to San Carlos, Flagler, Bald Hill, Hattysburg, and Frederica, where rails arrived in 1891. A branch departed Flagler for Hudson-on-Suwannee, which was renamed Dowling Park.

A labyrinth of lines once permeated the region south of Ellaville and Live Oak. Huge stands of timber existed here, and several railways competed to harvest, process, and transport the forest products. Two companies of note were the Florida Railway and the Live Oak, Perry & Gulf. The former, which surfaced in 1905 as a consolidation of the Live Oak & Gulf and the Suwannee & San Pedro Railroads, stretched between Live Oak and Perry; branches connected Wilmarth with Luraville, Mayo with Alton. The Live Oak, Perry & Gulf, which came alive about the same time, also serviced the Live Oak–Perry corridor, and additionally reached west of Perry to Hampton Springs, Waylonzo, Loughridge, Mandalay, and Flint Rock. A branch from Mayo serviced the big sawmill at Alton.

As noted, wealthy lumbermen figured into the lives of these railway firms. Traffic over their lines included pine logs, rough and finished lumber, wood pulp, naval stores, and, to a smaller extent, limestone, phosphate (mined in nearby Densler), bricks, citrus, vegetables, and bales of cotton.

The aforementioned Florida Railway slipped into receivership in 1915 and was abandoned four years later. Bonds of the Live Oak, Perry & Gulf were acquired by the Atlantic Coast Line Railroad beginning in 1905, leading to a purchase of the "Loping Gopher" (as the former was nicknamed) in 1918. A decade later, the Coast Line sold the logging railway to Brooks-Scanlon, which operated the impressive sawmill complex at Foley. As will be discussed later, the Georgia Southern & Florida (a Southern Railway subsidiary) purchased the Live Oak, Perry & Gulf in 1954 along with the South Georgia Railway, and allowed both to continue as independent firms. Years later, in 1972, Southern Railway folded the pair into a new subsidiary: the Live Oak, Perry & South Georgia Railway.

One day a book about Florida's fascinating logging and lumber railroads will be written. Literally dozens of operations existed in the Sunshine State. Most installed temporary spur tracks into forestlands from their respective main lines. After a specific region was cut over, the

Practically every logging railroad installed temporary spur tracks into forests. Once an area was cut over, the tracks would be disassembled and relaid elsewhere. By permission of the Collier County Museum, Naples, Florida.

portable spurs were disassembled and laid elsewhere. The felled logs were usually whisked off to a nearby millhouse, on special flatcars that quite often lacked brakes! (Fortunately the locomotives did not.) Many of the lines were hastily constructed with stiff grades, sharp curves, and rickety trestles, which caused logging trains to creak, screech, clank, and groan. Steam locomotives ran the gamut of design and reliability, and the "hoggers" (slang for engineers) who ran them were indeed a colorful lot. Some concerns occasionally transported passengers. Derailments on logging railroads were unfortunately quite common, and lucky was the firm whose trains never suffered a collision.

Another area carrier of note was the Florida & Georgia Railway, whose owner, R. J. Camp Lumber, wished to connect Macon, Georgia, with Lake City, Florida. But finding sufficient capital for the project proved elusive. In the end, standard gauge track was laid from Wellborn northward to White Springs, and on to Thaggard using narrow gauge rails. The Camp firm wasted little time in denuding area timberlands, and by 1914 both its rail lines were ripped asunder.

The Jacksonville Terminal Company (JTC), chartered in 1894, had the mission of building and maintaining a union station at the state's transportation gateway, along with the right "to switch, repair, and store trains, expedite the shipment of freight, and to provide comfort for travelers." The terminal building it erected in 1904 eventually proved inadequate, and in 1915 its joint owners (the Atlantic Coast Line, Seaboard Air Line, Florida East Coast, and the Southern railroads) began drawing up plans for a $3.5 million replacement.[15]

In the following year, all requisite land was acquired along West Bay and Lee Streets. A design competition ensued, with New York architect Kenneth Mackenzie Murchison (1871–1938), a graduate of Columbia University, winning the commission. Murchison's building, conceived in the Beaux-Arts style, measured 360 feet long, 90 feet high, and 78 feet wide. The waiting room, replete with a high-barreled ceiling, was 150 feet long. Separate ticket, restroom, and waiting facilities were incorporated for both white and black patrons. Built of reinforced concrete with a limestone veneer, the building's street-side colonnade was comprised of fourteen colossal Doric columns, each measuring 42 feet tall. The noble edifice, hailed as the finest in the South, opened on 18 November 1919. Nearly two hundred trains a day used the complex during the height of the 1920s land boom.[16]

In addition to furnishing and maintaining a union station, JTC was responsible for shuttling trains in and out of adjoining yards along with marshalling baggage, express, and mail cars. A fleet of locomotives handled the chores, and by the 1940s nearly two dozen train crews were on duty around the clock. (JTC was the city's second-largest employer, after King Edward Cigar.) Unfortunately, decreased passenger traffic and high maintenance costs prompted the building's closure in early 1974. A sensitive restoration took place, and the grand facility reopened in 1986 as the Prime Osborn III Convention Center.

Murchison, it should be noted, conceived many superb buildings in his lifetime, including the huge Delaware, Lackawanna & Western terminals in Hoboken and Buffalo; Cuba's Union Station in Havana; and the United States Marine Hospital on Staten Island. Interestingly, the

Jacksonville remains the railroad gateway to Florida. A union terminal building befitting its importance opened in 1919. Today, the colossal edifice is home to a popular convention center. Author's collection.

architect was also famous for his impersonations of President George Washington, to whom he bore a striking resemblance. Oddly enough, he died of a heart attack in 1938 near a subway booth under New York's Grand Central Terminal—which he did not design.[17]

Another carrier of the Jacksonville scene was the Jacksonville, Mayport and Pablo Railway and Navigation Company (J, M & P). Nicknamed the "Cash Road" because construction only advanced if cash was on hand, the 20-mile line opened between Arlington and Mayport in 1888, where its founders wished to develop a seaside resort at Burnside Beach. On opening day, the impossible happened: the locomotive hauling the inaugural train suddenly quit 6 miles from Arlington. Passengers had to detrain and walk home, an event not quickly forgotten. Before long the J, M & P received a sobriquet: "Jump, Men & Push."

Traffic on the Cash Road never met forecasts. New owners appeared on the scene in 1892, and the Arlington terminus was changed to the more convenient locale of South Jacksonville. Financial problems persisted, however, resulting in a receivership in 1895. Unable to meet the demands of creditors, the rails were taken up and sold along with the company's engines and cars. The roadbed was eventually acquired by Henry Flagler's Mayport Terminal Company.[18]

Two independent operations below Jacksonville were the St. Augustine & North Beach (whose track emanated from Baker) and the St. Augustine & South Beach Railway, which linked America's oldest city with Anastasia Island. Another regional pike was the Green Cove Springs & Melrose Railroad. Chartered in 1881, the narrow gauge logging line opened from Green Cove Springs, on the west bank of the St. Johns River, to Sharon in 1883. A reorganized entity, the Western Railway of Florida, advanced the project to Melrose, on Lake Santa Fe, in 1890. Forest products were principally transported over the 34-mile route. Additionally, the Western Railway operated a 10-mile lumber spur south of Sharon. Everything folded in 1899.[19]

The Gainesville & Gulf Railroad surfaced in 1895 to connect Sampson City with Gainesville and Micanopy. Like many undercapitalized firms, the so-called Grits & Gravy suffered its share of financial setbacks. In 1906, after passing through a receivership, the company emerged as the Tampa & Jacksonville, whose owners advanced the route beyond Micanopy to Emathla by way of Fairfield. In addition to passengers and freight, the "Tug & Jerk" also hauled phosphate along with produce and Fuller's earth.

Many farmers lived alongside the Tug & Jerk, and frequent short toots from a passing locomotive in winter months signaled that a frost was imminent! The Seaboard Air Line Railway acquired the outfit in the 1920s and reorganized it as the Jacksonville, Gainesville and Gulf Railroad. Passenger train service vanished in the 1930s. In the following decade, the line was sold for scrap except for a small portion of track around Gainesville that was acquired by the Atlantic Coast Line Railroad.

It was the carriage of vegetables, produce, and citrus that sustained the Tavares & Gulf Railroad, whose epithets were the "Tug & Grunt" and the "Taters & Grits." A predecessor firm, the Tavares, Apopka & Gulf (T, A & G), first installed rails near Tavares to Astatula, Monteverde, Minneola, and Clermont. The line opened in 1887 and connections with lake steamers were made at Clermont. The railroad's entrance into Tavares proper was made over the track of the Tavares, Orlando & Atlantic Railroad.

Tavares, seat of Lake County, was conceived by Alexander St. Clair Adams, first as a tourist community, then as a great industrial and railroad center, even the new capital of Florida! The Adams dream faltered, but not before Tavares became the western apex of the "Golden Triangle," a prosperous citrus-growing region with Mount Dora and Eustis as the other points.

The T, A & G later fell on hard times, creditors forced a foreclosure sale, and, in 1890, the firm became known as the Tavares & Gulf Railroad, with New York investor Henry H. Jackson at the helm. At that moment, the firm owned three wood-burning locomotives, a trio of passenger coaches, and about sixty freight cars. A year later, the company completed a branch below Monteverde to Oakland, which was advanced to Winter Garden in 1899, and to Ocoee in 1914.

Apparently little maintenance was performed on Jackson's firm, which prompted the Florida Railroad Commission to remark in its 1910 report that, "the Tavares & Gulf Railroad is probably in the worst condition of any line in the state." That same body also discovered that Jackson's company was charging the highest passenger fares of any state carrier: five cents a mile. Relations between the two parties remained rocky, but Jackson eventually performed needed repairs and improvements. In 1922, coal-burning locomotives arrived on the property. Seven years later, the company's first caboose was purchased. Then, in 1947, the first diesel-electric locomotive appeared.

The Seaboard Air Line Railway acquired the "Tug & Grunt" in 1926 and allowed the pint-size operation to exist as a separate subsidiary. According to Tavares & Gulf historian Phil Cross, the halcyon years of the company occurred in the 1940s, with record profits of $92,183 being announced in 1948.[20] Shortly afterward, the company claimed it originated more freight per mile of track than any other American railroad, a fact confirmed in the February 1949 issue of *Trains Magazine*. Profits in 1957 topped $120,000.

In time, the region's business patterns and markets shifted. Truckers made inroads on rail traffic; the stations at Astatula, Monteverde, and Ocoee closed around 1960; and the T & G track into Clermont was abandoned. Despite the setbacks, operations on the "Tug & Grunt" continued even after the Seaboard and the Atlantic Coast Line Railroads merged in 1967. Two years later, though, the last official train rumbled over the line.

Another area operator of note was lumberman J. M. Griffin, whose rail line helped harvest pine and red cypress in northeastern Orange and Osceola Counties. Peavey Wilson Company, a Louisiana-based firm, succeeded Griffin, who retained the latter's railroad connection with the Florida East Coast Railway at Holopaw. There was also the Apopka & Atlantic Railway, conceived in 1885, which connected Woodbridge with Forest City. Farther down the coast was the Fellsmere Company, which operated a 10-mile rail line from Sebastian, where connections were made with the Florida East Coast Railway to the inland setting of Fellsmere, where the company owned 118,000 acres of productive farmland and forests. Although the firm became the Trans-Florida Central Railroad in 1924, the traffic remained the same: agricultural products, cut logs, and lumber.

Hardly remembered today is the Jupiter & Lake Worth Railway, whose narrow gauge track ran across a strip of land between Jupiter and Juno. Operations commenced in 1889. For years, the line was known as the "Celestial Railroad" because of the localities it served: Jupiter, Neptune, Mars, and Venus. Henry Flagler, who used the portage line to help transport building supplies for his Royal Poinciana Hotel in Palm Beach, made overtures about buying the protoplasm, but its owners refused to sell. That was a mistake, for once Flagler's own rail line was put through to West Palm Beach, the Celestial foundered and eventually had to be abandoned.[21]

In 1909, the Seaboard Air Line Railway leased its branch (near Ocala) into Silver Springs to the Ocala Northern Railroad. E. P. Rentz, a wealthy lumberman, spearheaded the venture, and before long laborers advanced rails past the popular tourist attraction all the way to Palatka on the St. Johns River, by way of Daisy, Fort McCoy, Orange Springs, Kenwood, and Stokely. But the cost of creating the route, which opened in 1912, helped bankrupt Rentz. The line was then acquired by lumber mogul H. S. Cummings, who, in 1915, reorganized everything as the Ocklawaha Valley Railroad. Cummings purchased new engines for the pike along with new steel rails.

Legend has it that one of the Ocklawaha Valley's engineers, who lived in Fort McCoy, owned a playful goat. One day "Billy" chewed through his rope leash and wandered over to the depot in search of his master. Somehow the critter managed to board an outgoing train; another brought Billy back home. The romps continued, and thus unfolded a marvelous public relations story: "Billy, The Ocklawaha Valley Railroad Goat." Business declined as the years rolled by, and in the early 1920s the company was auctioned. The new owners, who specialized in distressed properties, finally sold the outfit for scrap.

The rail line of the Aripeka Sawmill Company, which opened in 1905 as the Brooksville & Hudson, connected Brooksville with Wiscom, where the route forked northwesterly to Tooke Lake and southwesterly to Weeki Wachee and Hudson. In 1911, the branch to Tooke Lake was sold to the Tampa Northern Railroad in 1911 (which itself was acquired by the Seaboard), while the branch to Hudson was operated by Aripeka for a few more years.

During the mid-1920s, Foshee Lumber constructed a logging line from Willow (southeast of Tampa) to its 11,000-acre timber tract in Manatee County, near Verna. The company's millhouse, which processed longleaf pine logs, was located at Willow. A few miles distant was situated the Palmetto Terminal Company, whose tiny 2.5-mile rail line connected the Hendrix Dock in Palmetto (foot of Central Street) with Memphis Hammock, where citrus and vegetables grew in abundance. An impressive civic ceremony launched the project in 1895, but when a Seaboard subsidiary arrived in Palmetto from Durant, the peanut-size firm fell on hard times and eventually rolled over.

As previous chapters have related, several railroads competed for the huge and profitable phosphate traffic of the Bone Valley, a 2,800-square-mile commercial district of the state located in Polk, Hillsborough, Manatee, Desoto, and Hardee Counties. After processing, the phosphate usually departs the region in special rail hopper cars bound for the transloading facilities on Tampa Bay, where the commodities are dumped into the holds of oceangoing ships.[22] One entity that chose to locate its phosphate terminal far outside the Tampa Bay area was the American Agricultural Chemicals Company. To reach its facility, the company built and owned a remarkable railroad operation that became known as the Charlotte Harbor & Northern (C H & N).

Initially, the C H & N transported pebble phosphate of the river variety that had been mined in and around the Peace River; in later years it would convey land pebble phosphate, which lay buried in a matrix of sand and clay.[23] River phosphate had been discovered near Fort Meade in 1881. Six years later, the Peace River Phosphate Company quietly purchased 43 miles of riverfront, announcing in 1887 that it would start mining and processing the mineral. Immediately, the Peace River region was abuzz with prospectors, land prices shot up, and seventeen other firms entered the fray.

Workers at first extracted the pebble river phosphate using picks and crowbars, whereupon the mineral was dumped into barges and brought to mechanical washers for processing. Later, steam-powered pumps with hoses, mounted on barges, were employed, which sucked the riverbed and adjoining banks. Moored alongside them were washer barges, whose apparatus removed tree roots, rocks, and stumps. The sand and clay fell back into the river, and the cleaned phosphate was sent to a facility where it was dried, screened, and readied for market. The product was then loaded into railroad hopper cars, brought to Arcadia, whereupon the cars were routed down to Punta Gorda. Here, the shipments were off-loaded into lighters and towed out to waiting ships in Charlotte Harbor—a most time-consuming process. Some 3,000 tons of pebble phosphate had been mined from the Peace River in 1888; within five years that figure jumped to 123,000 tons.

The phosphate boom created excess mining capacity that, in turn, gave way to consolidation. By 1894, one firm dominated all others: the Peace River Phosphate Mining Company, founded by Joseph Hull. Five years later, Hull sold out to American Agricultural Chemicals for $869,855.[24] The firm, which was founded by the Bradley Fertilizer Company of Massachusetts, was the second-largest fertilizer producer in the United States. (Phosphate is a key ingredient of fertilizer.) Peter Bradley's family had heavily invested in Hull's firm, and when the latter decided to sell out, the Bradleys were at the ready.

Among the assets conveyed to American Agricultural Chemicals was a narrow gauge railway that ran along the west bank of the Peace River from Hull (Fort Ogden) up to Arcadia, where hopper cars of phosphate were handed off to the Florida Southern Railroad. Mr. Hull also installed a 3.5-mile spur from Hull village down to the old Peace River hamlet of Liverpool, where he erected drying bins. Here, processed phosphate was dumped into lighters and brought down the river by tugs to Charlotte Harbor where, inside Boca Grande Pass, oceangoing ships awaited. (When the river was low, the railway connection via Arcadia and Punta Gorda had to be used.)

From the outset, Peter Bradley wanted to reduce his costs of transportation as much as possible. (The expense of transportation, technically called "transaction costs, adds to the expense of an item without adding to its intrinsic value.) That goal, Bradley felt, could best be achieved by having American Agricultural Chemicals build and operate a direct rail line between the phosphate deposits and a deepwater terminal—in this instance—on Gasparilla Island. Thus was born the Charlotte Harbor & Northern Railroad.

A few years before the Bradley family bought out Joseph Hull, two local events of note occurred: the legislature chartered the Alafia, Manatee & Gulf Coast Railway, and Albert Gilchrist of Punta Gorda, a future Florida governor, filed a plat in Lee County to create a community on Gasparilla Island called Boca Grande. The former had authority to construct a rail line from Plant City down to some objective point on Charlotte Harbor. Nothing yet had been built, and after American Agricultural Chemicals acquired Hull's company, Bradley's attorney got the railroad to sell its franchise in early 1905. The chemical concern then began acquiring the necessary rights-of-way for a railway upon Gasparilla Island, along with parcels for a deepwater phosphate terminal. By then, Bradley, who had become enamored of the Island's idyllic setting, formed Boca Grande Land Company. Among its officers was Albert Gilchrist! Soon the company began constructing a resort hotel at Boca Grande that became known as the Gasparilla Inn; it opened in 1911 and still functions today.

A large contingent of Irish, Italian, and Greek laborers constructed the Charlotte Harbor & Northern Railroad (C H & N). Parts of the old narrow gauge route between Hull and Arcadia were utilized for the project. Advancing the line from the mainland to Gasparilla Island itself required over 2 miles of trestleworks and two drawbridges, the remains of which are still visible. Company shops were established in Arcadia, the line's northern terminus, while a subsidiary firm, the Boca Grande Terminal Company, built and operated the "South Dock" phos-

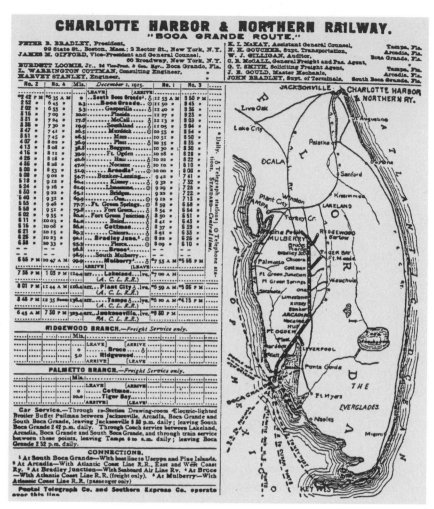

Phosphate was the lifeblood of the Charlotte Harbor & Northern. Passengers were also carried over the Boca Grande Route until 1959. What remains of the carrier today, north of Arcadia, is owned by CSX. Author's collection.

phate terminal at South Boca Grande. The railroad opened for freight and passenger traffic in 1907.[25]

Shortly after the C H & N was opened, workers began extending its track north of Arcadia to South Mulberry, in the very heart of the phosphate-rich Bone Valley, this by way of Garwood, Brewster, Bradley, and Achan. Previously, American Agricultural Chemicals had acquired considerable land holdings in the region and opened several mines and processing facilities. At Achan, connections were made with the Atlantic Coast Line Railroad, while at Bradley and South Mulberry the C H & N connected with the Seaboard Air Line Railway. Branches eventually stemmed from the C H & N main line so as to reach the mining communities of Tiger Bay and Ridgewood.

Employees of the railroad, terminal facility workers, locals, and winter visitors often traveled between Boca Grande and South Boca Grande in the railroad's unique battery-powered trolley car. At night, the latter was recharged at the terminal company's power house, which also supplied electricity for the island. In 1910, the C H & N built a splendid station in the Mediterranean Revival style at Park and Fourth Streets, replete with arcaded loggia and tiled roof. It was placed on the National Register of Historic Places in 1979 and still is commercially used.

By 1917, the Charlotte Harbor & Northern owned 11 steam locomotives, 217 freight cars, 15 passenger coaches, and 56 pieces of work equipment. Further, the company operated a creosote plant at Hull that chemically preserved railroad ties and bridge timbers, along with the Florida Townsite Company, a firm that sold land along the railroad route. At South Boca Grande, railroad passengers could board a private yacht for the thirty-minute jaunt over to Useppa Island.

Millions of tons of phosphate eventually came down the "Boca Grande Route" to Gasparilla Island. The railroad also conveyed countless passengers as well as express packages, mail, and untold numbers of winter tourists and visitors. Robert Bradley, Peter's brother, eventually ran the railroad, but his miserly cost-cutting ways greatly reduced worker morale, to the extent that employees gave the Charlotte Harbor & Northern a moniker: the "Cold, Hungry & Naked."

As noted in chapter 8, the Charlotte Harbor & Northern Railroad was acquired by the Seaboard in 1925. Passenger train service ceased to Boca Grande after the 1958–59 winter season. In 1967, the Seaboard Air Line and the Atlantic Coast Line Railroads merged. The Seaboard Coast Line Railroad continued to operate phosphate trains to South Boca Grande, but in time executives deemed the operation redundant. The last ship loaded with phosphate departed South Boca Grande in 1979, and two years later crews began dismantling the rails below Arcadia.[26] Today, the old rail route on Gasparilla Island helps form a popular rail-trail for walkers and bicyclists.

8

The Glorious 1920s

The United States paid Spain $5,000,000 for Florida on February 22, 1821—62 cents an acre. The King of Spain, Floridians say, spends much of his time now wishing his country had held on a little longer.

—*The Nations Business*, May 1925

One of the greatest migration and building episodes in American history took place in Florida throughout most of the 1920s. Record numbers of people arrived, lured by the inviting climate, agricultural possibilities, and real estate speculation. Countless new homes were built, along with hotels, apartments, office buildings, municipal projects, schools, churches, theaters, as well as other places of entertainment. Some twenty-four ready-made communities surfaced along Florida's extensive shoreline such as Boca Raton, Hollywood-by-the-Sea, Opa Locka, Coral Gables, and Venice, the latter having been conceived by America's oldest and largest union, the Brotherhood of Locomotive Engineers.[1]

Postwar prosperity had chiefly financed Florida's land boom. Many farmers in America had grown rich meeting wartime demands, factory workers accumulated substantial savings as a result of overtime, while countless business owners and manufacturers and industrialists made outright fortunes. All this put bankers and financiers in an expansive mood. Curiously, though, Florida itself did not materially benefit from the wartime economy.

Outside of lumber, turpentine, and building a few ships, the state profited little in the scheme of things. It had no great industrial cities furnishing munitions of war. And when the hostilities ended and the transformed plants converted back to corsets, clothing, typewriters, and automobiles, Florida folks sat tight.[2]

If anything, Floridians believed that the war had seriously interrupted the intake of newcomers, tourists, and vacationers. Prior to the hostilities, the state's largest railroad companies had been heavily advertising Florida's attractions in northern and midwestern publications, the results of which were just beginning to pay off when war was declared. After the Armistice was signed in 1918, Americans once again turned their thoughts to vacations, or where they might invest their recent savings. And for many, that meant only one destination: the "Empire in the Sun."

Before long, people from all parts of the nation began journeying to the Sunshine State. Many, of course, arrived in the family motorcar, often taking the 18-foot-wide Dixie Highway. And come they did! By 1924 the flow of flivers, tin lizzies, and limousines formed a dense struggling stream. Others came at the behest of builders and developers. "Immense buses bearing subdivision names rumbled down loaded with prospects from Mobile, Atlanta, Columbia, or from northern steamers discharging at Jacksonville."[3] Between 1923 and 1925, an estimated three hundred thousand persons permanently settled in Florida, where income and inheritance taxes were forbidden by the state constitution.

To the joy of Floridians, this tide of humanity began pouring serious money into the economy: "It is said that $445 million in northern money gladdened the hearts of the populace in 1924, and one billion will be surmounted in 1925—perhaps two billion."[4] Hotel, apartment, and lodge owners immediately benefited, along with store owners, restaurateurs, merchants, and wholesalers. Many folks liked what they saw and either purchased a home or bought land for a future abode. The demand for construction materials and supplies began to soar, service industries flourished, and before long the call went out across the country for all manner of trades people and laborers.

Of course, some folks decided to speculate in Florida real estate, buying something one season and selling it the next, often at a handsome profit. Others attempted to "turn" their investment the same season,

During the 1920s, Americans flocked to Florida as never before. At Christina, in Polk County, "A City for Colored People" arose. Prospects arrived by train; a stationlike building housed the real estate office. State Archives of Florida.

perhaps the following month, even the same day. Real estate success stories became rampant and were circulated "up North" to friends and neighbors who, in turn, came down for a slice of the American El Dorado. And in this way the frenzy began.

When the boom started, there existed thirty-two railroad companies in Florida that operated about 3,700 miles of track. Three players dominated the scene: the Atlantic Coast Line Railroad (with 1,791 miles), the Seaboard Air Line Railway (1,036 miles), and the Florida East Coast Railway (764 miles).[5] Together the Big Three controlled more than 80 percent of the state total. Not only were these three the principal beneficiaries of the boom, but they conveyed more passengers and freight than any other mode of transportation, including automobiles, buses, trucks, ships, or airplanes.

Prior to the frenzy, Florida's economy was progressing at a gradual rate. Increasing numbers of new people were coming into the state yearly, towns and winter resorts had been growing and improving, and new areas were being reclaimed and set out in citrus fruits and garden products. According to one industry publication, railroad traffic moved on a well-defined seasonal schedule, with much of the business passing through the state's transportation gateway of Jacksonville. Citrus fruit and vegetables began to move to market in October and continued until about the first of May. Heavy southbound passenger train business started in the fall and reached its height by late February, only to shift northward until the latter part of April. "Thus the busy season for the railroads serving Florida was from October to May, the remainder of the year being marked by light business of all kinds, with train service reduced to a minimum."[6]

The first abnormal activity was detected in 1920, when a considerable number of new people came into Florida, a growing interest in real estate began, and a large amount of building construction was begun or planned, particularly in the vicinities of Miami, West Palm Beach, and points north along the east coast. In succeeding years, these trends increased in intensity. Also, numerous municipal projects were undertaken, industry expanded, and a large amount of highway construction was begun. Gradually the fever spread to the west coast.

Then, in spring 1925, something odd happened: the normal lull in summer railroad traffic did not occur. Instead, people from every section of the country began pouring into Florida in record numbers, placing unprecedented demands on housing, hotels, apartments, and every kind of public utility. As *Railway Age* magazine remarked in its 19 November 1927 issue: "Enormous orders placed by merchants, the heavy movement of building and highway materials, coupled with one of the largest crops in the history of Florida, together placed an enormous burden upon the Big Three which became increasingly difficult to carry."

With no letup in sight and believing the boom would carry on for years, brokers and dealers now began ordering supplies far in excess of actual requirements. Trainloads of building materials, supplies, and merchandise often arrived in the state without any notice; or manifests were shipped to Florida without a specific destination, changing hands many times en route and often reaching a locale where no service tracks existed. This caused consignees (end customers) to literally leave freight in thousands of boxcars, occupying every available foot of track, tying up cars urgently needed elsewhere, and choking the movement of trains.

In addition to the above scenario, thousands of empty refrigerated cars started to appear that needed to be loaded with citrus and vegetables, the movement to northern markets being of paramount importance. Lastly, labor shortages arose, and delays were experienced caused by bad weather and flooding.[7]

To untangle the mess, traffic experts from around the country were rushed to Florida, where, on 31 October 1925, they decided to impose an embargo—the first in state railroad history. Immediately, all incoming and outgoing freight traffic was halted except for foodstuffs, agricultural products, livestock, petroleum, fertilizers, and a few other essential commodities. When the embargo was called, about four thousand freight cars were stranded in the Jacksonville yards, while another ten thousand were ordered held at outlying points such as Washington, D.C., Cincinnati, St. Louis, and New Orleans. In time, the congestion eased, and the embargo was lifted on 15 May 1926.[8] By then, though, the boom was running out of steam.

In retrospect, the so-called Big Three had been caught unprepared for the crush of boom traffic. Although each had initiated improvement and expansion measures before the First World War, practically every endeavor ground to a halt during federal ownership. When the companies were returned to stockholders in March 1920, all were in a worn condition. Wartime traffic had taken a toll upon the steel rails, many locomotives and cars needed replacing, labor shortages existed, rate increases were desperately needed, and final settlements had yet to be made with the U.S. Railroad Administration.

While these issues were being resolved, the boom was beginning to generate substantial amounts of freight and passenger traffic, compelling the Big Three to immediately undertake initiatives that would increase capacity, modernize physical plants, and furnish a competitive edge. Although more mileage was constructed in Florida in the historic 1880s, the Big Three spent infinitely more capital during the 1920s—by one estimate, over $100 million (2006 dollars: $1.12 billion). When the "era of effortless riches" finally ended, the railway map of Florida stood at its all-time greatest extent, some 5,700 miles when every track, yard, and leased company was factored. Further, the variety and frequency of railway service to, from, and within the Sunshine State was never again replicated.[9]

Florida East Coast Railway

No company was better located for boom traffic than the Florida East Coast Railway (FEC). Based in St. Augustine, its single-track main line descended the east coast of the state and penetrated every important community along what company literature often hailed as the "American Riviera." In addition to its 522-mile artery between Jacksonville and Key West, the FEC also operated eight branches that totaled an additional 233 miles.[10] In 1920, when the boom was surfacing, the railway had revenues of $13,701,191 and $1,826,169 in net operating income.

At the height of the land boom, in 1926, no less than one dozen passenger trains were dashing over the main line between Jacksonville and Miami. Some, such as the Havana Special, went beyond Miami to the island city of Key West, via the Key West Extension, where awaiting ships took excited passengers to the continental port of Havana. If one impediment plagued the FEC during the early 1920s, it was lack of capacity, owing to its single-track main line, but this was later remedied at great cost as the "era of effortless riches" unfolded.

William Beardsley, the former financial advisor and longtime private secretary to the FEC founder Henry Flagler, was president of the FEC when the boom began. After the war, Beardsley embarked upon a multiyear program of improvements that included the installation of heavier steel rail, building new stations, and improving the railway's yard facilities at South Jacksonville, New Smyrna, Fort Pierce, Buena Vista, and Key West. Further, questionable wooden bridges on the company's main line were reinforced with steel beams, new passing tracks were created, and orders were placed for many new engines and cars. Even a new headquarters building was begun in St. Augustine.

In 1924, Beardsley relinquished the presidency to William Rand Kenan Jr., another Flagler confidant and board member whose sister, Mary Lily Kenan, became Flagler's third wife in 1901. When Flagler died twelve years later, Mary stood to inherit her husband's $100 million–plus estate, provided she could outlive the trust fund. (Her brother, William, and Beardsley were two of the fund's trustees.)

Mary Flagler died in 1917. The bulk of her estate, which included the Flagler fortune in trust, then passed to her brother, William, and two other sisters—but not to Mary's next husband. Thus, the Kenan family

EAST COAST
of FLORIDA

*Where Spring is as constant
as the Skies are blue*

The Florida East Coast Railway issued
many promotional booklets during the
fabled land boom. This one glorified
every locale, attraction, and accommodation along what it called the "American
Riviera." Covers were printed in pastel
colors. Author's collection.

had both a proprietary and fiduciary interest in the Flagler System of
railroads, steamship lines, hotels, and land companies.[11]

As the boom years unfolded, Kenan made many strategic decisions
involving the FEC and its franchise. In 1923, the directors of the FEC
ordered a new double-track steel drawbridge for the St. Johns River
crossing in Jacksonville. Also, extensive renovations to the company's
shops in New Smyrna were approved, and that year the Interstate Commerce Commission approved the FEC extending its Okeechobee Branch
(Okeechobee down to Lemon City) and constructing a belt line around
Miami proper between Little River and Larkin (South Miami).

Kenan's board made a decision of far greater import the following year. Eager to possess its own route to Miami was the Atlantic Coast Line Railroad Company, which the FEC met, and exchanged traffic with, at Jacksonville. Kenan received a buyout overture from Henry Walters, the patrician chairman and principal stockholder of the Coast Line. Walters knew that the FEC was experiencing growing pains and that it lacked deep pockets. Kenan, who regarded Walters as both a mentor and father figure, ultimately concluded that he must keep the Flagler System intact, as its late founder and his sister would have wanted. Thus, instead of selling the railway, Kenan embarked upon a large and costly round of capacity and modernization projects.

The FEC engaged New York's Bankers Trust Company in 1924 to issue $1.8 million in trust equipment certificates, so that the railway could acquire twenty "Mountain-class" steam locomotives—they burned oil, not coal—along with five switching engines, three all-steel passenger cars, two hundred boxcars, one hundred ballast cars, and twenty cabooses. More importantly that year, the FEC issued $45 million of First & Refunding 5 Percent Mortgage Bonds, or "F&R 5s," the proceeds from which would fund a second main-line track from Jacksonville to Miami together with automatic block signals. J. P. Morgan & Company led the underwriting syndicate, which included First National Bank of New York and National City Bank. The issue was secured with yet another first mortgage lien upon all the present and future assets of the railway, just as the Key West Extension bonds had been years earlier. As Walter Campbell, Kenan's distinguished biographer, states: "By quadrupling the FEC's total bonded indebtedness, the F&R 5s set the stage for some of the longest and most grueling struggles of Kenan's life, struggles that emerged from the collapse of the Florida frenzy and the national depression that followed."[12]

Proceeds from the big bond issue also allowed the FEC to advance its Okeechobee Branch down to Pahokee, whose muck lands were producing fantastic yields of fruit, vegetables, and sugar cane. (Eventually the branch generated about half of all company revenues.) Other bond proceeds would help pay for the 18-mile belt line around Miami's north and west sides, the enlargement of Bowden Yard in Jacksonville, and the construction of several stations such as at Daytona and Hollywood.

Business results in 1925 were gratifying to say the least. Traffic soared as never before, just as several improvement and capacity projects came to fruition. The new 29-mile Moultrie Cutoff opened, which eliminated the long, westerly main-line swing through East Palatka; the massive $2.4 million drawbridge over the St. Johns River was completed; the busy Okeechobee Branch was pushed past Pahokee to Belle Glade; and the Miami Belt Line was completed between Hialeah and Larkin. Work also commenced on the new Miller Shops complex near St. Augustine, while in that same city a third addition was begun to the company's new headquarters building. If this were not enough, Kenan's board spent another $4 million on more locomotives and rolling stock.

Although the boom crested in 1926, that year the FEC enjoyed record revenues ($29,427,460) and net operating income ($5,167,479). The long-awaited second main-line track, which was equipped with a state-of-the-art signal system, fully opened between Jacksonville and Miami. Further, the impressive Miller Shops complex was completed, as was the aforementioned addition to the company's headquarters building. And, as in the previous year, orders were once again placed for additional engines and cars.

This euphoric state of affairs began to change in 1927. Real estate buyers vanished, the boom fizzled, and revenues started falling. In fact, that year the FEC experienced its first financial loss of the decade. In 1929, a mere $13.4 million was recorded in revenues, a far cry from the record set just three years earlier. The only bright spot that year was the opening of the Okeechobee Branch to Canal Point, which provided a handy connection with the Atlantic Coast Line Railroad.

Unfortunately, the bad news continued. Many Florida banks now failed, the stock market crashed, and the Mediterranean fruit fly ruined many valuable state crops. The boom was fast becoming a vanished dream. What did not vanish was the FEC's debt load and the obligation to service it. As the next chapter relates, the Florida East Coast Railway slipped into receivership in 1931, a scenario that quite likely founder Henry Flagler would not have tolerated.

Atlantic Coast Line Railroad

Florida's land boom furnished the Coast Line with much prosperity. Based in Wilmington, North Carolina, the company served six southeastern states with nearly 5,000 miles of track, a figure that soared to 13,333 miles when controlling interests in other railroads were factored. The company's main line—always impeccably maintained—stretched between Richmond, Virginia, and Jacksonville, Florida.[13] The Coast Line recorded revenues of $25,304,074 in 1920. Some 10 million passengers were transported over the system that year, along with 17.3 million tons of freight. Nearly twenty-five thousand workers were on the company's payroll.

Ever since obtaining the Plant System of Railroads in 1902, the Coast Line had undertaken annual expansion and improvement projects in Florida. When the boom started, the company was busily installing new steel rail in many locales, enlarging the freight yard at Lakeland, and erecting new stations such as at Lake Wales, Frostproof, Avon Park, and Richland. Improvements were also being carried out at the company's shops in High Springs and Sanford. Further, work had lately resumed on two taproots: the Haines City Branch and the Tampa Southern Railroad.

The Haines City Branch was completed between Haines City and Goodno (via Sebring and Lake Placid) just before the United States entered the First World War. Construction crews returned to the field after the hostilities, and by 1921 rails had reached the agricultural and timber setting of Immokalee, by way of Sears and Felda. Triweekly train service was then begun.

The Tampa Southern subsidiary opened between Uceta (East Tampa) and Bradenton in 1920. In the following year, the route was extended farther south to Palmetto. Also, a spur was installed off the Ellenton Belt Line to Senanky. Citrus and vegetable growers abounded in this region of the state, and there were several phosphate mines. The railroad reached Sarasota, which blossomed during the boom, in 1924.

When the 1920s commenced, the Coast Line was operating four separate passenger trains to Florida from New York: the ACL Express, the Havana Special, the Palmetto Limited, and the seasonal Florida Special. In the 1920–21 tourist season, the Everglades Limited was added as well as the all-Pullman Everglades. Later, the Florida West Coast Limited and the Florida East Coast Limited made their appearance. To meet additional demand, the company also revived its old West Indian Limited.

At the land boom's height, the Atlantic Coast Line Railroad operated nine daily Pullman trains to Florida. Among the most memorable were the West Indian Limited, the Florida Special, and the Havana Special. Author's collection.

At the height of the boom, no fewer than nine all-Pullman Coast Line trains were speeding between New York and Jacksonville. Five ran year-round, while four were put on just during the winter tourist season. Other carriers, in conjunction with the Coast Line, furnished service from Chicago and other key midwestern points. Some of the more famous trains were the Florida Seminole, Southland, St. Louis–Jacksonville Express, Floridan, Dixie Express, Dixie Flyer, Dixie Limited, and Flamingo.[14]

The territory below Fort Myers was without railway service when the boom began. Area businessmen, including millionaire Barron Collier, had been pushing for more rail transportation and obtained a charter for the Fort Myers Southern Railroad. The Coast Line acquired the paper company, and crews began advancing track below the "City of Palms" to Bonita Springs, where the iron horse arrived in 1925. After a right-of-way was secured, laborers began grading the route farther south to Naples.

That same year, another Coast Line contractor started grading the Moore Haven & Clewiston Railroad between its namesake settings so as to tap the vegetable and sugar cane traffic of the region. (The pint-size outfit connected with the Coast Line at Moore Haven.) Yet another Coast Line contractor resumed work on the Haines City Branch, south of Immokalee, to Deep Lake, where Barron Collier—who had made a fortune in streetcar advertising—owned extensive groves of grapefruit and many acres of fine timber.[15]

As part of its expansion program during the land boom, the Coast Line decided to extend its Tampa Southern subsidiary from Sarasota over to Southfort, near Fort Ogden. The Fort Ogden Extension essentially connected the taproot to the company's busy Lakeland–Fort Myers route. Also, the Coast Line broke ground on its Perry Cutoff between Perry and Monticello, which, when completed, gave the railroad an alternate route out of Tampa to Georgia that bypassed busy Jacksonville and shortened materially the rail route between the Sunshine State and the Midwest.[16]

Without question, the crush of boom traffic severely taxed the capacity of the Atlantic Coast Line Railroad. As Henry Walters stated to stockholders:

Your Company has watched the rapid growth of Florida and, as far as possible, has anticipated the transportation needs of the State by large and substantial improvement and development of your property. No one, however, could have foreseen the phenomenal growth and development that has taken place there in less than a year's time, thrusting suddenly upon the railroads such a volume of business that they were unable to give normal service and resulting in a congestion of traffic which could only be overcome by drastic measures.[17]

Record revenues of $97 million were recorded by the Coast Line in 1926. That same year, the company inaugurated train service between

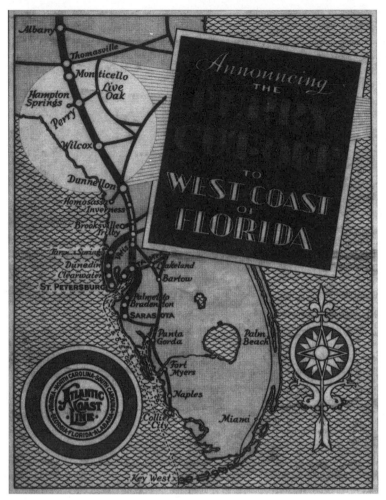

One of the most important projects completed in the boom by the Coast Line was its Perry Cutoff, which gave the company a direct route to the Midwest that bypassed the congested Jacksonville yards. Author's collection.

Bonita Springs and Naples and from Immokalee down to Deep Lake. Also, construction began on a huge new yard and shop complex at Uceta, in East Tampa, that the railroad claimed would eventually employ over one thousand workers. In the following year, freight trains began using the newly opened Perry Cutoff. Also, the Fort Ogden Extension of the Tampa Southern reached Southfort, while the Fort Myers Southern Railroad was opened to Collier City (Marco Island) in order to serve locals and a clam cannery.

Florida's land boom was essentially over by this time. Nevertheless, the Interstate Commerce Commission soon allowed the Coast Line to purchase Barron Collier's 14-mile industrial railway between Deep Lake and Everglades proper. Additionally, the Moore Haven & Clewiston Railroad was extended past Clewiston to Canal Point—it met the Florida East Coast Railway in the process—where another big plant of Southern Sugar Company existed.

In 1928, the Coast Line rebuilt Collier's flimsy Deep Lake Railroad, whereupon it inaugurated train service to Everglades. The setting, whose Spanish-style station now helps form a local restaurant, became the southernmost point of the entire Atlantic Coast Line Railroad system. Evidence, though, has yet to surface that the aging Henry Walters ever visited the remote and quaint locale.

Seaboard Air Line Railway

The Seaboard's response to the Florida land boom was both remarkable and astonishing. The company opened many new routes during the era, built numerous improvement projects, and took market share away from both the FEC and Coast Line railroads, both of whom regarded the Seaboard as an interloper. Orchestrating the company's aggressive tactics was Baltimore banker Solomon Davies Warfield, who was also the Seaboard's chairman and president. For years, Warfield had been enamored of Florida and its economic possibilities. His faith in the state was unshakable to say the least, and frequently at his side was Florida governor John Martin.

During the wee hours of the 1920s, Warfield was busily obtaining a just and final settlement with the U.S. Railroad Administration, the federal agency that controlled the nation's railroads during the First World War. Warfield felt that the Seaboard had been greatly shortchanged under the "Standard Return" compensation formula and that the agency had returned the company to stockholders in a far too worn condition.

After extracting what he thought to be a favorable settlement, the autocratic but charming chairman turned his attentions to the Florida land boom. Since before the war, Warfield had wished to connect both coasts of the state by rail. As he once remarked to stockholders: "The

Seaboard is not receiving its share of business originating in the territory for which it is justly entitled, and the development of Florida is retarded because of the lack of railroad facilities between the two coasts of the peninsula."[18]

To remedy matters, the Seaboard chartered a new subsidiary. The Florida, Western & Northern Railroad would connect the Seaboard mainline at Coleman (below Wildwood) with West Palm Beach, this by way of Auburndale, West Lake Wales, Avon Park, Sebring, Okeechobee, and Indiantown. To finance the line's construction, the Seaboard floated $7 million of bonds, whereupon Warfield gave the contract to Jefferson Construction Company of Charleston, South Carolina. The 204-mile route—much of it straight as a die—passed through the live oak hammocks of Sumter County to reach Polk City, whereupon rails pierced the beautiful "Ridge" country where countless citrus groves stood. Prairie lands were next encountered, after which surveyors located the route through seemingly endless parcels of longleaf pine. Warfield insisted that the contractor prosecute the work at breakneck speed. He did.

A considerable amount of mechanized equipment was brought in for the big project, as well as an army of laborers. As always, the contributions of African American workers proved indispensable:

> A considerable portion of grading the roadbed was performed by that famous institution of our southern country—the station man. Given a shovel, a wheelbarrow, and a board to run it on, and provided with rations and a contract for one, this fellow will build his little thatch hut and live, eat, and sleep on the job. He works in the cool hours of the day and on moonlit nights until his contract is completed, then moves on to another. Hundreds of these faithful workers were employed, and they took great pride in the fact that they were doing their part to have the grading all ready when the track gang came along.[19]

Dragline tractors helped overcome the swamp and muck lands, while steam shovels were utilized for the tall embankments situated in the Ridge country. In Sebring, some twenty-five homes had to be relocated for the right-of-way. Numerous trestles were built, and the American Bridge Company fabricated drawbridges for the Kissimmee River and the St. Lucie drainage canal. In all, the new extension consumed

700,000 crossties. The Bethlehem Steel Works furnished the 100-pound-to-the-yard steel rail. Harvey & Clarke, an architectural firm in West Palm Beach, designed practically every station along the new line, including the splendid edifice at West Palm Beach (still in use), with its Spanish Baroque details.[20]

The last spike was driven home on 21 January 1925. Four days later, four separate sections of the newly christened Orange Blossom Special made their way over the extension to West Palm Beach amidst public ovations. Warfield and Governor John Martin were on board, together with five hundred guests and dignitaries. Afterward, the luxury train began furnishing all-Pullman service between New York and Florida during the winter tourist season.[21]

Shortly after the extension to West Palm Beach opened, two other Seaboard projects of importance were completed: the Valrico Cutoff and the Gross-Callahan Cutoff. The former branched from the Seaboard mainline at Valrico (east of Tampa) and proceeded in a southeasterly direction for Welcome Junction, where Seaboard rails existed to Mulberry, Bartow, and West Lake Wales. At West Lake Wales, the new extension to West Palm Beach was intercepted. This allowed the Seaboard to immediately offer train service from Tampa to West Palm Beach, in essence creating a cross-state route. The other shortcut, which linked Callahan with Gross, gave Seaboard trains a quick exit out of Florida, one that completely bypassed the congested yards at Jacksonville. Another project of note was completed in 1926, when a 19 mile gap between Brooksville and Inverness was closed.

Warfield's initiatives naturally attracted press attention. Among those who became enamored of the bachelor chairman was Clarence W. Barron, owner of the *Wall Street Journal*. In fact, Barron wrote a series of favorable articles about the Seaboard entitled "Florida by the Air Line."[22] Interestingly, the stories led many people to think that Warfield was actually creating an airline company, an industry whose stocks were then in vogue. Quite unexpectedly, Seaboard stock began to rise!

Revenues on the Seaboard jumped to $62,864,711 in 1925, a healthy increase over the previous year thanks to Florida's land boom. Warfield then announced his biggest expansion measure to date: the Seaboard All-Florida Railway project. In brief, the new subsidiary would extend the recently opened West Palm Beach line southward to Miami and beyond. The new entity also would furnish a much-wanted presence in southwest Florida—from Fort Ogden down to Fort Myers and Naples. After obtaining permission from the Interstate Commerce Commission, the Seaboard floated a $25 million bond issue for the two new extensions (and other purposes), whereupon Warfield hired the nation's largest railroad contractor—Foley Brothers of St. Paul, Minnesota—to complete the work.

The 66-mile route from West Palm Beach down to Miami (via Fort Lauderdale, Pompano, Boca Raton and Opa Locka) was completed in December 1926, along with a short branch at Miami to the Seaboard's new yard at Hialeah. Another 28-mile extension, south of Hialeah to Homestead, was finished in April 1927. The extension below West Palm Beach pierced the sacrosanct territory of the Florida East Coast Railway, which annoyed the latter to no end.

Groundbreaking ceremonies for the extension to Naples took place in Fort Myers on 8 February 1926. The 69-mile taproot commenced at Hull (Fort Ogden), a way station on the Charlotte Harbor & Northern Railroad, which the Seaboard had acquired in the previous year. At Estero, some 15 miles below Fort Myers, another Seaboard subsidiary (the Naples, Seaboard & Gulf) advanced the project to Bonita Springs and Naples, which Warfield regarded as "a most attractive place with beautiful beaches, the latitude approximately that of Miami, and one of the best situated winter resorts on the west coast." Warfield actually envisioned a deepwater port at Naples, though it was never built. Land for the extension project was secretly acquired, and when the Seaboard formally announced its plans the Atlantic Coast Line Railroad, which already served southwest Florida, was taken aback.

Many streams had to be bridged on the extension to Miami, like the New River in Fort Lauderdale. But the greatest engineering challenge occurred on the west coast; specifically, bridging the wide Caloosahatchee River at Fort Myers, where a long, low-slung drawbridge was installed. Harvey & Clarke, the architectural firm, designed a stunning $75,000 passenger station for the "City of Palms," where also a commodious freight facility was built along with a fourteen-track switching yard complete with water tank and electric coaling tower. Another splendid station in the Mediterranean Revival style arose in downtown Naples.[23]

Laying Rails   Seaboard Ry
Passing Gordon River Grove
December 1926

Naples was agog when the Seaboard Railway arrived in 1926. Here, two nattily dressed spectators watch the action at Gordon River Grove. One stands near the surveyor's stake line. Courtesy of the Collier County Museum, Naples, Florida.

Two branches ultimately stemmed from the Seaboard's Fort Ogden–Fort Myers–Naples extension: a 30-mile appendage from Fort Myers to LaBelle via Alva, Buckingham, and Floweree; and a 9-mile branch from South Fort Myers that was to connect with the old cattle dock at Punta Rassa—where today's causeway to Sanibel Island begins. But the latter was only completed to Truckland, in the Iona district, where truck farmers and potato growers were beginning to flourish.

North of Fort Myers, at Tamiami City, the new extension intersected the rail operation of McWilliams Lumber Company. In 1929, the latter was succeeded by Dowling-Camp, whose logging trains ran over the Seaboard to Fort Myers, then headed east over the LaBelle Branch to the timberlands near Alva. At Hickey Creek, portable logging spurs penetrated area forestlands. Lumber company workers actually resided at the remote setting in modified boxcars! (Hickey Creek today has become an inviting Lee County park.)

After the east and west coast extensions were completed, Warfield staged a triumphant grand opening. Over seven hundred guests from ninety cities and eighteen states were invited to the party, most of them

Seaboard chairman S. Davies Warfield (*right*) and Florida governor John Martin (*left*) opened the company's extensions to Naples and Miami. At Opa-Locka, actors in Arabian garb boarded the train and performed a skit. State Archives of Florida.

being important Seaboard shippers and investors. For several days beginning on 5 January 1927, Warfield pampered the entourage aboard five completely separate sections of the Orange Blossom Special. Stops were made at most every community, where the Warfield entourage was greeted by cheering crowds, flag wavers, and, sometimes, band music. Florida governor John Martin rode the lead train with Warfield and addressed the well-wishers. Nearly five thousand persons greeted the delegation at Miami's Royal Palm Park.[24]

Not only did the Seaboard construct new lines during the boom, but it also acquired other railroads as well, such as the Charlotte Harbor & Northern; East & West Coast Railway; Tampa Northern; Tavares & Gulf; Gainesville & Gulf; Tampa & Gulf Coast; and Georgia, Florida & Alabama. Other projects included the laying of a second main-line track at several busy choke points, and installing miles of automatic block signals. Further, several engine and yard terminals were enlarged, and orders were placed for many new locomotives and cars.

Naturally these expansion and improvement measures came at a price. In 1926, the Seaboard enjoyed record revenues ($67,024,854) and net income ($17,771,852). But in the following year, after the boom crested, profits plummeted to a mere $31,576. That same year, the company's revered chairman passed to his reward. But even upon his hospital deathbed, Warfield's faith in the Sunshine State remained unshakable; he always believed that the company's huge investments in Florida would one day pay off. As the chairman once penned:

> FLORIDA! with its tropical sunshine, its endless mileage of bathing beaches on the Ocean and on the Gulf—the gentle breezes crossing innumerable Central Florida lakes laden with the aroma of the orange blossom—yachting and motor boating in waters mirroring the colors of the tropics—polo—golf—tennis—racing at Hialeah, Pompano and other courses—all amid scenes of unsurpassed and beautiful surroundings, is without equal in this or any country.[25]

The Frisco

Our journey through Florida's land boom has thus far focused on its three principal beneficiaries: the Atlantic Coast Line, Seaboard Air Line, and Florida East Coast railroads. However, no account of this remarkable era would be complete without mentioning another carrier that arrived on the scene that decade.

The St. Louis–San Francisco Railway, better known as the Frisco, was a big and profitable carrier that served the midwestern section of the nation with over 5,600 miles of track. Although the firm serviced many river ports within its territory, it lacked an ocean port where products and commodities could be placed in ships and sent around the globe. The impediment nagged at Frisco management, especially after the company obtained an entrance into the great coal, iron, and steel belt of Birmingham, Alabama. Fortunately, a window of opportunity opened during the Florida land boom.

Pensacola possessed the greatest deepwater port on the Gulf of Mexico. For decades, the Louisville and Nashville Railroad practically monopolized the setting. But it was not the only carrier. Among the independent firms was the Gulf, Florida & Alabama (G, F & A) whose underlying companies included the rail lines of Southern States Lumber and Gulf Ports Terminal.

The G, F & A main line stretched between Pensacola and Kimbrough, Alabama, by way of Cantonment and Muscogee. It also owned a valuable dock at the Pensacola waterfront. Owing to poor finances and a weak management, though, the G, F & A went bust, later emerging as the Muscle Shoals, Birmingham & Pensacola Railroad. Despite a new name and new owners, business remained sluggish, and, in 1925, the Frisco managed to purchase the entity for $305,000.

Connecting Kimbrough, Alabama, with the Frisco system at Aberdeen, Mississippi (by way of Demopolis, Alabama) now became the order of the day. Frisco engineers tackled the project with gusto, and within two years a 152-mile connector linked the two firms. The company additionally rebuilt the existing route into Pensacola. New crossties and rails were installed, as well as fresh ballast. New station and freight platforms also appeared, and every suspect trestle and bridge was outright replaced.

The Frisco opened its new route into Pensacola on 27 June 1928. A special train loaded with dignitaries arrived from the railroad's headquarters in St. Louis. The City of Pensacola declared a city holiday that day. Storefronts were gaily decorated, and grand opening festivities included a parade, a boat regatta on Escambia Bay, along with a sumptuous banquet. Although the Frisco did not figure into the land boom of the 1920s per se, this big and prosperous carrier definitely became part of Florida railroad history that decade.[26]

9

Pursuing Traffic

CSX was the code name we selected for the incorporation of the new company for purposes of the Interstate Commerce Commission application. The letters simply stood for Chessie (C), Seaboard (S) and everything else and the growth we expected to result from the merger (X).

—Watkins, *Just Call Me Hays*

The 1930s was a painful era for the United States, American business in general, and certainly for the nation's railroad industry. Not only did the Great Depression impact revenues and profits, but many rail carriers lost much traffic to automobiles, trucks, and airplanes. In response, railroad executives had no choice but to slash expenses, reduce payrolls, and defer maintenance. In fact, many companies could not endure the downward pressures, and either became wards of the court or completely failed.

The Atlantic Coast Line Railroad, the biggest carrier serving Florida, avoided insolvency by also reducing unneeded services and tabling expensive projects. Henry Walters, its revered chairman, died in 1931 and was succeeded by his nephew, Lyman Delano. When financial problems worsened, Delano suspended stock dividends and even reduced the salaries of management. Interestingly, the company's premier passenger train, the luxurious Florida Special, was hardly affected by the adverse times. Not only did patronage on it remain steady, but the flyer managed to establish a new speed record between New York and Jacksonville: 29 hours and 40 minutes.

Business upon the Coast Line eventually improved, which prompted Delano to order new rolling stock and twelve of the biggest steam locomotives the company ever owned.[1] In 1939, the rival Seaboard Air Line Railway inaugurated a lightweight streamlined train in the New York to Florida market called the Silver Meteor, which was powered by a fast and efficient diesel-electric locomotive. Champion Davis, a respected Coast Line executive, told Delano that if the company did not own one, it would lose more market share. When Delano learned that the Florida East Coast Railway was about to order one as well, the Coast Line got into the act.

Two streamlined, diesel-powered train sets, each comprised of seven stainless steel cars, were subsequently ordered from Budd Manufacturing in Philadelphia. They cost $70,000 each, while each diesel-electric locomotive, built by Electro Motive in Illinois, ran $175,000 apiece. A nationwide contest was held to name the flashy trains, and over one hundred thousand people submitted suggestions for the $300 prize.

Amidst considerable fanfare, the newly named Champion made its inaugural run from New York's Pennsylvania Station in December 1939. At Jacksonville, the train was handed over to the Florida East Coast Railway for operation to Miami. In a masterful publicity stunt at Fort Lauderdale, the Champion was joined by the Henry M. Flagler, the new streamliner of the Florida East Coast Railway. The two flyers then descended the twin-track main line of the FEC side by side, at times reaching speeds of 75 miles per hour. Overhead, biplanes chased the duo and discharged smoke trails.

S. Davies Warfield, the aggressive chairman of the Seaboard Air Line Railway, died in 1927. That year, the company's finances were already in a weakened state, largely because Warfield had spent so much money on improvements and new routes in Florida. Even before the 1929 stock market crash, Warfield's successors were busy instituting cost-cutting measures. Despite their best efforts, though, the company failed to meet its fixed charges in 1930, whereupon it entered into a receivership. When debt issues could not be reconciled with bondholders and creditors, the Seaboard became the first railroad casualty of the Great Depression. The receivers assigned to the property were ordered by the court not to pay certain bond interest coupons and rental monies until solvency was restored. Amazingly, the company would not emerge from court protection until 1946.

Once the receivership was established, the Seaboard began pruning away many unprofitable or little-used lines. Among those getting the axe in Florida were the branches to Silver Springs and to Tooke Lake; along with trackage between Alcoma and Nalaca, from Gainesville to Sampson City, Archer to Cedar Key, Wannee to Bell, and the feeder leading to Covington. The Florida Central & Gulf (Hernando to Port Inglis) also vanished, as did the East & West Coast Railway between Arcadia and Manatee.   ·

Like any company in receivership, the Seaboard was temporarily relieved from servicing its long-term debt. This, in turn, freed up funds for many projects that otherwise were not possible to undertake, such as building a new power plant at the company's South Boca Grande phosphate facility; installing warning signals at many dangerous Florida highway crossings; and purchasing air-conditioned cars for its famed Orange Blossom Special passenger train. The temporary reprieve also allowed for many new stations to be built—such as the one at Tavares—together with repairs to the company's big shops in West Jacksonville. Also, a new bridge over the Nassau River near Yulee was constructed, as well as a new engine house at Wildwood, and the railway's shops at Hialeah were expanded.[2]

Air-conditioned cars with reclining seats, along with lower passenger train fares, went far in luring customers back to the Seaboard. So did the Silver Meteor, the company's first streamlined train. The latter's 2,000-horsepower diesel-electric locomotives were even painted in an eye-catching citrus color scheme of yellow, orange, dark green, with silver wheel trucks. The popular flyer, which became an instant success, began operating between New York and Miami in February 1939. The dining cars featured low-cost dinners of baked bluefish, fricassee of chicken, and beef pot pie. At Wildwood, the streamliner split into two sections, so as to also offer service to the sunny shores of St. Petersburg. During the 1930s, the Seaboard also purchased air-conditioned "rail buses" for use between Jacksonville and Tampa, and from Jacksonville to River Junction (Chattahoochee), which were far more economical to operate than steam-hauled passenger trains.

An up-tick in Seaboard freight revenues occurred in the late 1930s, thanks to new services and lower rates. One could even ship an automo-

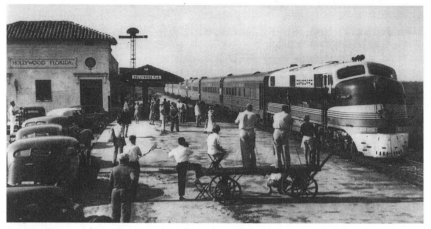

The Seaboard unveiled its first streamlined passenger train in February 1939. Here, "moving-picture" folks and photographers capture its arrival at Hollywood en route from New York City. Author's collection.

bile to Florida in a boxcar—a concept also offered by the Atlantic Coast Line and the Illinois Central railroads. Further, the 1938 longshoremen's strike generated unexpected revenue streams, as did the new pulp and box mills at Jacksonville and Fernandina. To accommodate shippers of citrus, vegetable, and beef, the Seaboard erected several refrigerated buildings at its Jacksonville complex.

Like its competitors, the Florida East Coast Railway also experienced a terrific drop in revenues and profits during the Great Depression. Train service was reduced on both main-line and branch tracks, while much obsolete equipment was retired to lower taxes and insurance costs. In 1931, the FEC entered into a receivership and remained under court protection for many years.

The receivership itself had been precipitated by the company's inability to pay interest on its First and Refunding Mortgage Bonds, a $45 million issue floated during the 1920s land boom (see chapter 8). At first, the testamentary trust that owned the railway's stock advanced millions of dollars to cure the defaults. But when they continued, the handouts ceased, whereupon the company became a ward of the court. Later, in 1941, the receivership became a bankruptcy proceeding.[3]

While the receivers attempted to sort out the claims of bondholders and creditors, the quest for cutting costs intensified. Trains on the Orange City Branch were replaced with buses and trucks; two years later, the branch was completely taken up. The Mayport Branch, between Spring Glen and Mayport, vanished about the same time, as did the spurs to Ormond Beach, Palm Beach, and from East Palatka to Palatka proper. Wages of workers were trimmed as well. Also, passenger train fares were reduced (to lure customers back), and the FEC began delivering many small freight shipments door to door using a fleet of trucks. Revenues in 1934 amounted to a paltry $7.6 million, a far cry from the $29.4 million enjoyed in 1926.

If financial problems were not enough, the hand of nature dealt a serious blow. On Labor Day weekend in 1935, a powerful tropical hurricane struck the Florida Keys. Hundreds of persons perished, including many World War I veterans who had come to the region to build highway bridges. An FEC rescue train was dispatched from Miami to Lower Matecumbe, where many of the workers were huddled. But while the train struggled at Islamorada, the storm's tidal wave came ashore, which engulfed and overturned the cars. Within minutes, over 40 miles of the railway's fabled Key West Extension were ripped asunder.[4]

The cost of rebuilding the extension could not be justified, and the receivers ultimately sold it to several government and municipal agencies. What had cost nearly $30 million to create netted a mere $640,000. The rail route later helped form the 127-mile Overseas Highway, which opened in 1939.

Fortunately, both freight and passenger business perked up on the FEC as the 1930s ended. Among those trains enjoying an up tick in patronage was the Florida Special, which was jointly operated with the Atlantic Coast Line Railroad. In fact, on 29 February 1937, no fewer than seven completely separate sections of the famed flyer departed New York City for Miami in convoy style, one after the other. A year later, the famous train celebrated its fiftieth year of operation.

As noted, the FEC purchased two streamlined train sets from Budd Manufacturing and two diesel locomotives from Electro Motive. The Henry M. Flagler serviced the Jacksonville-Miami corridor, while the other operated in the New York–Florida market with the pair owned by the Coast Line. The seating arrangements, car interiors, and air-conditioning apparatus differed from those cars built by Budd for the Seaboard's Silver Meteor.

At least one ownership change occurred in Florida during the Great Depression. In 1933, the Apalachicola Northern Railroad, located in the Panhandle, was acquired by millionaire Alfred du Pont. (Edward Ball, his brother-in-law and business confidant, arranged the transaction.) The purchase also included the town of Port St. Joe, 240,000 acres of area timberlands, a sawmill, and the St. Joe Telephone & Telegraph Company, all this in preparation of du Pont building St. Joe Paper Company. Even though its finances were rickety, du Pont believed that the Apalachicola Northern could ably transport pine logs and chemicals to his new mill and carry away finished paper products to the outside world.[5] He was correct.

The 1940s

The Second World War furnished America's railroads with an unprecedented amount of traffic. Revenues and profits soared, as each carrier did everything in its power to expedite the movement of soldiers, munitions, and wartime supplies. Numerous military installations were established in Florida, including air training bases, ammunition storage facilities, and flexible gunnery schools. Many of these settings had their own private railroad spur. During the war Florida's railroads transported endless carloads of phosphate, petroleum, citrus, sugar, and bananas, largely because the submarine menace on the Atlantic seaboard had halted practically all coastal shipping.

One of the first companies to experience the wartime surge in traffic was the Atlantic Coast Line Railroad. Shortly after the hostilities began, shipments of phosphate and fertilizer doubled while the movement of construction materials tripled. Citrus car loadings also dramatically rose, as did those for sugar and gasoline. In 1941, revenues of the firm amounted to $67.4 million. A year later, they reached $115.1 million; by 1943, they stood at $155.9 million![6]

The Coast Line would convey substantial amounts of forest products, especially what which was harvested on its Immokalee Branch in southwest Florida. Deep within Collier County there existed huge stands of virgin bald cypress. Intensive harvesting in the Big Cypress Swamp and the Fakahatchee Strand was conducted by Lee Tidewater Cypress Company in Copeland, where connections were made with the

Coast Line. The big logging outfit quickly became the world's largest supplier of cypress lumber. The federal government became the company's sole customer during the war, purchasing about 1 million board feet of cypress each month. Later, in the 1950s, operations here reached their zenith hour.[7]

Only a small amount of Coast Line trackage was abandoned in Florida during the 1940s. That which connected Fincher and Fanlew was taken up for lack of business, as well as the little-used line south of Bonita Springs to Naples and Collier City (Marco Island). Although the Coast Line sacrificed its own track into Naples, the company opted to purchase and operate what the Seaboard had constructed between Bonita Springs and Naples, in the process obtaining a far better entrance into Naples proper and a beautiful Mediterranean Revival station, which is now a museum. Another land boom project that got the axe was the Fort Ogden Extension, which connected East Sarasota with Southfort, near Fort Ogden.

In 1946, after a four-year hiatus, the Coast Line's Florida Special resumed winter operations. To combat lost traffic to automobiles, the railroad began offering more passenger train service, better dining cars, comfortable sleeping accommodations, and streamlined coaches. No market was ignored, even those against whom all southern carriers discriminated against:

> One of the more stable classes of rail travel, particularly in the South, is colored passengers. In recognition of this, as well as in the hope of retaining and increasing the traffic, posters were placed in colored waiting rooms and in colored coaches expressing appreciation of the patronage your Company is receiving from colored passengers. A replica of the poster, against a suitable background, has also been used as an advertisement in newspapers for colored people.[8]

Like the Coast Line, the Seaboard's finances rapidly improved in the 1940s, which allowed the company to undertake many improvements. Revenues amounted to $64.6 million in 1941, while a year later they skyrocketed to $110.2 million. New shop facilities were built at Tampa and Hialeah, along with an automobile-loading platform at Miami. Extra cars were acquired for the ever-popular Silver Meteor, which was eventually hauled (along certain portions of its route) by multiple diesel-electric locomotives. During the war itself, the Seaboard installed spur tracks to several military bases, such as Opa Locka, Camp Blanding, and the huge flexible gunnery school at Buckingham, near Fort Myers. A new connecting track was placed into service, too, at Fort Lauderdale so the railway could serve Port Everglades.

As part of cost-cutting measures that decade, the Seaboard's receivers abandoned many unprofitable or little-used lines in Florida. For example, rails between Turkey Creek and Durant were taken up, as were those connecting Tallahassee with Carabelle, Havana with Quincy, between San Carlos and Truckland, Alva and LaBelle, South Fort Myers to Naples, Lake Villa and Tarpon Springs, Elfers and New Port Richey, and the once-popular branch leading to Indian Rocks Beach.

On a more upbeat note, the receivers funded a new yard at Tallahassee and thoroughly rehabilitated the existing ones at Baldwin, Wildwood, Pierce, and Tampa. Also, icing facilities were added to the Hialeah yard, and a new turntable was installed at the Seaboard's West Jacksonville complex. A Centralized Traffic Control system (one dispatcher controlling signals and switches from a remote location) was also purchased and integrated along several busy stretches of track in Florida. Many localities received radio communications. Tabulating machines, which used IBM punch cards, were also acquired, which greatly aided freight accounting and the preparation of payrolls.

A historic event took place on 1 August 1946, when the Seaboard Air Line Railroad emerged from receivership. At that moment, the company employed nineteen thousand workers and operated some 3,800 miles of track. Phosphate was the single-biggest freight item it transported in Florida. In July 1949, the Gulf Wind passenger train (operated jointly with the Louisville and Nashville Railroad) began operating between Jacksonville and New Orleans. About this time, the Dade County Port Authority got the Seaboard to relocate its shops and yard at Hialeah to another nearby location, allowing that agency to expand what became Miami International Airport.[9]

The Florida East Coast Railway, which was already in receivership, entered bankruptcy in 1941 because its receivers had failed to craft an acceptable reorganization plan. Litigation then ensued as to who really owned the railway: the so-called Bingham Trust (which owned the rail-

Few persons in Florida history have wielded the power that Ed Ball once possessed. Loved and hated, his greatest career challenge was wresting control of the Florida East Coast Railway. State Archives of Florida.

way's stock) or the owners of the First & Refunding 5 Percent Mortgage Bonds? Among those parties with a growing interest in the matter was the aforementioned Edward Ball, who represented the testamentary trust of Alfred I. du Pont. When the railway declared a profit in excess of $5 million in 1942, the ownership questions took on an even more serious dimension.

The bonds cited above, which were also known as the "F&R 5s," were held by many institutions and individuals. The largest owners banded together and submitted a reorganization plan for the court to consider. Ed Ball also submitted a plan on behalf of the du Pont trust that, at first, was rejected. About this same time, the Interstate Commerce Commission became involved in the matter, declaring that whoever owned a majority of the F&R 5s was also the de facto owner of the railway, and *not* the stockholders. Since no party owned a majority of the bonds, Ball began striking alliances with minority owners, including the wealthy Miami investor S. A. Lynch and the Atlantic Coast Line Railroad.

But Ball underestimated both parties. Before long, the Coast Line began pursuing its own interests by enlisting a powerful political voice—Florida U.S. senator Claude Pepper. At this time, Pepper and Ball greatly disliked one another, a relationship that has been ably chronicled by historian Tracy Danese.[10] The senator attacked Ball from every angle, but in the end the latter won the day for he had obtained a majority of the bonds (at very depressed prices) and submitted a re-organization plan that was supposedly more in the public interest. The Coast Line, though, refused to give up, and a new round of appeals and hearings got under way. Later, in 1947, the Interstate Commerce Commission reversed itself and sided with the Coast Line! Ball vigorously challenged the verdict in several venues and again won, although the case was not finally settled in his favor until the late 1950s.

America's railroads performed yeomen's service in the Second World War, and the FEC Railway was no exception. During the hostilities its receivers operated the property in a most economical manner. In 1944, the company abandoned a huge portion of its Okeechobee Branch—from Maytown down to a remote location below Okeechobee, a total of 136 miles. Then the firm constructed a new 29-mile cutoff to what remained from Fort Pierce. According to the 26 April 1947 issue of *Railway Age* magazine, the project commenced in 1945, but owing to the war and unavailability of certain supplies, it was not opened for traffic until March 1947. Sugar cane and cane by-products (like molasses) were the traffic mainstays on the branch, as were citrus and vegetable shipments.

Mention was previously made of the Apalachicola Northern Railroad, which was now controlled by Ed Ball and St. Joe Paper. After the war, Ball had the carrier completely rebuilt and dieselized; new steel rails were installed; and its drawbridge over the Apalachicola River was completely rehabilitated. Pulpwood and chemicals remained the largest inbound traffic items on the railroad, while Kraft paper, produced at the Port St. Joe mill, dominated outbound shipments.[11]

Another Panhandle carrier playing a strategic wartime role was the Atlanta & St. Andrews Bay Railway. To a large extent, its business uptick was linked to the Wainright Shipyard in Panama City—Liberty ships were built here—and to events occurring at Tyndall Air Field and the wartime needs of several nearby Coast Guard and naval installations. In response to the traffic increases, the Bay Line had to erect a new freight warehouse at Panama City. The company's passenger train business soared too, as a result of gasoline rationing, and a successful bus company was operated that served such points as Pensacola; Cottondale; Mariana; Dothan, Alabama; and Columbus, Georgia.

During the war years, the Bay Line conveyed countless carloads of petroleum products—from the docks at Panama City to northern destinations. Wartime profits allowed the firm to install new steel rails along with treated crossties and slag ballast. A new freight yard at Panama City was also constructed, and the company became the first American railroad to completely dieselize its locomotive fleet—this on 19 June 1947. Four years later, the company even managed to retire all of its long-term debt![12]

The 1950s

Florida's railroads prospered in the 1950s, but not as greatly as in the previous decade. The postwar economy attracted an influx of newcomers to Florida—air-conditioning and mosquito control helped too—and many new businesses opened and industries arose. Although freight and passenger traffic did not match wartime figures, they nevertheless remained at respectable levels.

As always, the Atlantic Coast Line Railroad continued to be meticulously maintained. Also, the last of the company's steam locomotives were retired. Further, many lightweight passenger coaches and sleeping cars were acquired for such trains as the East Coast Champion, the West Coast Champion, the Vacationer, and the Florida Special. Passenger traffic from the Midwest increased, especially on such connecting trains as the Dixie Flagler, South Wind, and the City of Miami.

One goal that evaded Coast Line directors was obtaining financial control of the Florida East Coast Railway. In 1954, the U.S. Supreme Court ruled that the Interstate Commerce Commission had exceeded its authority by forcing an involuntary merger of the two firms, whereupon the case was remanded to the federal district court in Jacksonville. Four years later, the ICC once again reversed itself by approving a takeover proposed by Ed Ball and St. Joe Paper. Only then, after years of expensive dueling, did the Coast Line relinquish the fight.[13]

W. Thomas Rice, a highly experienced railroader and decorated military veteran, became president of the Coast Line in 1957. Rice, unlike his predecessor, took a keen interest in the railroad's marketing and public relations activities. He also promulgated the idea of moving the company's headquarters in North Carolina to Jacksonville, alongside the St. Johns River. During the late 1950s, the Coast Line inaugurated "piggyback" train service (truck trailers on railway flat cars) between Virginia and Jacksonville. Another signal event occurred in 1959, when the ICC approved Rice's plan to merge the Coast Line with rival Seaboard Air Line Railway, though the actual marriage would not be consummated until 1967.

The Seaboard, too, retired the last of its steam locomotives in the 1950s. The company's new yard at Hialeah also opened that decade, while Centralized Traffic Control was activated between Yulee and Baldwin. Teletype services also came of age, which connected key points in Florida with the entire Seaboard system. Also, the City of Orlando gave the Seaboard property for a new yard and facilities in exchange for the railway's parcels in the downtown district—a plan that greatly relieved vehicular congestion and provided much-needed parking. City fathers in St. Petersburg did likewise, and in January 1959 a new passenger station opened in the popular winter setting.

The Seaboard abandoned one significant stretch of track in Florida that decade. What remained of its old Fort Myers Line (Fort Ogden to Fort Myers), which had been built during the 1920s land boom, was removed in 1952, including the branches that led eastward out of Fort Myers to Alva and west of South Fort Myers to San Carlos, some 65 miles total. Potato and gladioli growers greatly opposed the abandonment, but the ICC concluded that southwest Florida did not need the services of two trunk line carriers. Thus, service in the region resorted back to the Atlantic Coast Line Railroad.

Locating new industries and shippers along Seaboard tracks in Florida was the mission of the company's industrial development department. Among the many firms that ultimately relocated to or expanded in Florida at this time were producers of cement, beer, glass, grocery wholesalers, chemical concerns, concrete pipe manufacturers, gypsum board producers, and bag and paper mills.

Revenues on the Florida East Coast Railway stood at $26.8 million in 1950, rising to a decade high of $38.9 million in 1957. Still though, the cost of doing business and servicing debt was expensive, to the extent that losses were reported every year except for 1955. Management tried to cut expenses by running fewer trains and reducing the payroll, but the measures did not completely stem the flow of red ink. As the decade closed, the problems fell upon the railway's new owner: Ed Ball and St. Joe Paper. The last of the company's steam locomotives vanished in 1959, about the same time that the railway began vigorously pursuing a new and growing profit unit: piggyback traffic.

One of the more interesting events of the 1950s took place in the Panhandle, when an out-of-state railroad was literally disassembled and moved to Florida. In 1949, the government-owned line connecting Camps Polk and Claiborne in Louisiana became surplus property. This aroused the interest of Florida's Eglin Air Force Base, which ended up contracting an Alabama firm to dismantle and move the outfit lock, stock, and barrel.

Eglin's railroad, which had cost just $600,000, linked the base with Mossy Head, where connections were made with the Louisville and Nashville Railroad. A "silver spike" ceremony took place on 1 February 1952, and operations commenced the following month with a single steam locomotive named the Eglin Queen. Everything from fresh meat to armored tanks came to be transported over the line. Two diesel engines appeared in 1959, and in 1967 a derelict steam engine was even acquired for target purposes! Shortly afterward the military railway ceased operations.

The 1960s

The Atlantic Coast Line Railroad opened its new corporate headquarters in Jacksonville during the 1960s, together with a new passenger and freight facility in Lakeland. In Fort Myers, the company vacated its downtown freight yard and built a new 40-acre switching facility south of the city—now used by Seminole Gulf Railway, a short line.

The Coast Line's passenger department aggressively sought customers throughout the decade by cosponsoring theater train tours, Champion train vacations, educational excursions, trips to athletic events, and holiday Santa Claus trains. In 1961, a new passenger reservation bureau opened in Jacksonville. Three years later, the company began transporting Floridians to the New York World's Fair. Business started to improve on the Florida Special, especially after candlelight dinners were instituted along with fashion shows, movies, games, song fests, and train hostesses.

The Coast Line became an early adaptor of computer technology, at the behest of President Tom Rice, as well as high-horsepower diesel-electric locomotives. The biggest event of the decade took place on 1 July 1967, when the Coast Line officially merged with its rival, the Seaboard. The resulting entity became known as the Seaboard Coast Line Railroad.[14]

Like the Coast Line, the Seaboard enjoyed good growth in the 1960s. Piggyback traffic increased, which prompted the company to build new loading platforms in Orlando, Auburndale, and Hialeah. In 1961, a major TOFC (trailer on flat car) terminal opened in Tampa. Also that year, the Seaboard transported approximately eleven thousand piggyback shipments. A new yard and engine facility was completed at Hialeah in 1966, while Centralized Traffic Control was activated between Baldwin and Tallahassee.

The Florida East Coast Railway emerged as a new entity in 1961, ending a receivership/bankruptcy stigma of some thirty years. Chairman Ed Ball and his able management team immediately addressed two unsettling issues: depressed revenues and profits, and the unrealistic wage demands of many unions. Although the FEC had bargained in good faith and made numerous offers during negotiations, its proposals were severely limited by high operating costs. However, none of this mattered to union workers, who went on strike in January 1963. Picket lines were formed; traffic on the railway ground to a halt. (Connecting passenger trains of the Atlantic Coast Line Railroad were then rerouted to Miami via the Seaboard Air Line Railway.)

Ball and his managers countered by allowing supervisory personnel to operate the trains. Although traffic began to roll again, the action sparked more ill-will. Some disgruntled workers began committing

The state ordered the Florida East Coast Railway to operate passenger trains during its 1965 strike. Here, a three-car consist eases over the St. Johns River drawbridge in Jacksonville en route to Miami. Photograph by David W. Salter.

crimes against the railroad, such as firing guns at passing trains, removing rails, tampering with switches, and causing wrecks. On 9 February 1964, two trains were dynamited. President Lyndon Johnson, who happened to be attending a labor convention in Miami, flew over the wreckage and quickly involved federal authorities, who, within weeks, arrested the perpetrators. Even though the acts of violence subsided, the strike continued.

Pursuant to a state order, passenger train service resumed on the FEC, albeit on a very limited basis, in August 1965. Three years later, the money-losing operation ceased. In the meantime, Ball's management team was busily integrating many innovative ideas, such as reducing the size of train crews; compensating train crew members on an eight-hour-day basis; running shorter, more frequent trains without cabooses; and installing welded rail atop concrete crossties.

Finally, in 1970, one of the striking unions accepted the company's terms, and its members returned to work. But not until the mid-1970s did the last of the union holdouts reach a settlement with the railway, thus ending a disturbing chapter in American labor history.[15]

Between 1967 and 1980, the railroad landscape of Florida was dominated by a single player: the Seaboard Coast Line (SCL). When formed in 1967, the SCL became the eighth-largest railroad in the nation with nearly twenty-three thousand employees, 9,600 route miles, 62,000 cars, and over 1,000 locomotives. John W. Smith, former president of the Seaboard, was named chairman of the SCL, while W. Thomas Rice, former head of the Coast Line, became its president. Management expected a full five years to pass before all the financial benefits of the merger would manifest. In the meantime, the company began the job of eliminating redundant track and facilities, retiring little-used or unprofitable routes, pooling locomotives and cars, and consolidating stations, yards, and terminal facilities.

During its first year of operation, Seaboard Coast Line generated $417.3 million in revenues. A great variety of commodities were hauled over the system, such as foodstuffs, pulp, paper, phosphate, fertilizer, farm products, coal, minerals, forest products, and piggyback trailers. Phosphate continued to be the biggest and most lucrative traffic item transported in Florida, which prompted the SCL to build a state-of-the-art loading terminal at Rockport, below Tampa, which opened in July 1970.

The 1970s and 1980s

For several years, the Seaboard Coast Line operated passenger trains in Florida, and aggressively marketed its New York to Florida service. In 1970, Congress passed the Rail Passenger Service Act, which created a quasi-public entity called the National Railroad Passenger Corporation, or Amtrak. Railroads that chose to join the entity paid an entrance fee and were relieved of operating passenger trains unless Amtrak contracted them. SCL made a one-time payment of $22.1 million to the new organization, and on 30 April 1971 the railroad operated its last passenger train. The following day Amtrak became operational, but with SCL operating its Florida service.

Another passenger operation that surfaced in 1971 was the Auto Train Corporation, which transported automobiles and their owner between Lorton, Virginia, and Sanford, Florida. The two terminals, along with the train's locomotives and cars, were owned by the privately held

Countless trains of the Seaboard Coast Line Railroad serviced the phosphate-rich Bone Valley of central Florida. This impressive scene was composed by Fred Clark Jr. at the big Agrico plant in Pierce.

firm, while the SCL furnished the tracks along with the train crews. Financial problems, though, plagued the firm, and operations ceased a decade later. Amtrak successfully resurrected the scheme in 1983.

During the 1970s, the Seaboard Coast Line rehabilitated its big yard at Baldwin. It also began advertising its various railroad entities as the "Family Lines System." Phosphate continued to be the biggest commodity transported in Florida. Other important revenue generators included coal, piggyback trailers, automobiles, paper, and chemicals.[16]

In 1978, Seaboard Coast Line announced it was in merger discussions with the Chessie System of railroads, which included the Baltimore & Ohio, Chesapeake & Ohio, and Western Maryland firms. Stockholders ratified the merger on 13 February 1979, and within twenty months the ICC sanctioned the marriage. The resulting entity, known as CSX Corporation, came alive on 1 November 1980 as the largest railroad company in the United States with seventy thousand employees and 27,000 miles of track. First-year revenues of CSX amounted to $4.8 billion. Prior to CSX being formed, the U.S. Congress had approved the famed Staggers Rail Act, which erased many archaic government regulations and made railroad megamergers far easier to consummate.[17]

After the merger, CSX began eliminating redundant facilities, reducing its workforce, and offering new services to freight customers. In 1981, its outdated phosphate terminal at South Boca Grande, on Gasparilla Island, began to be dismantled. In the following year, the company's various railroad operations were folded into CSX Transportation. A centralized train dispatching center for the new division opened in West Jacksonville. In 1986, a $19 million intermodal terminal was completed in Jacksonville to expedite the movement of piggyback trailers.

Revenues on CSX topped $7.5 billion in 1988. Again, management sought ways to reduce the size of the company and its workforce. Buyouts and furloughs became the order of the day, and many little-used or unprofitable lines were either abandoned or were sold or leased to smaller railroads known as short lines. Unquestionably, a new era was beginning to unfold in Florida railroad history: the *era of megamergers and short lines*.

10

Today's Players

Establishing commuter rail will ease congestion, which will improve the quality of life of people both on and off the road. Improving the existing railways will enhance the safety and mobility of both goods and people, which will generate new economic opportunity for millions of Floridians.

—Governor Jeb Bush, announcing plans to bring commuter rail service to central Florida, 2 August 2006

There exist today about 2,900 miles of railroad lines in Florida, down from nearly 6,000 when the high-tide mark was reached in the Roaring Twenties. More than a dozen freight railroads currently serve the state—mostly short lines—along with two passenger train entities. All are subject to the regulations of the Surface Transportation Board, the Federal Railroad Administration, the Florida Department of Transportation, along with certain environmental and/or securities laws.

The Surface Transportation Board, an economic agency created by Congress that is affiliated with the U.S. Department of Transportation, was established under the Interstate Commerce Commission Termination Act of 1995. Its three-member panel oversees certain freight rates, the extension or abandonment of rail lines, as well as the acquisition, consolidation, and merger of carriers.

One of many agencies within the U.S. Department of Transportation, the Federal Railroad Administration (FRA) has as its primary mission to promote and enforce railroad safety. Specifically, the FRA establishes equipment standards for the industry, as well as track maintenance procedures, rules for hazardous shipments, inspection and repair criteria for locomotives and rail cars, operating practices, and determines the qualifications of train crew employees such as locomotive engineers.

Headquartered in Tallahassee is the Rail Office of the Florida Department of Transportation (FDOT). The Rail Office (www.dot.state.fl.us/rail) has a long history of establishing rail policies, performing safety inspections, overseeing rail-highway crossings, rendering project assistance, and it periodically updates the so-called Florida Rail Plan. The FDOT is strongly committed to efficient railway transportation, believing it "reduces highway congestion, improves safety, and protects environmental quality by hauling thousands of tons of freight daily that would otherwise move on Florida's highways."[1]

According to the 2007 edition of *Business Florida* magazine, the FDOT is currently funding several rail projects "that are essential to keeping Florida's economy, people, and products moving." Both the Bay Line and the Florida Northern railroads have received monies to upgrade portions of their track; Norfolk Southern has obtained $2.5 million to build a siding extension in Jacksonville to increase yard capacity, while the South Central Florida Express is to receive $10.5 million to enhance its route between Sebring and Moore Haven. Further, the 2006 Florida Rail Plan notes that investments are pending to improve track capacity on CSX Transportation between Jacksonville and central Florida (by way of Ocala) and along its corridor between Jacksonville and Pensacola that parallels Interstate 10. Other projects include double-tracking portions of the Florida East Coast Railway between Jacksonville and Miami; acquiring CSX lines in the Orlando area for future commuter train operations; and funding roadway improvements near the proposed CSX Integrated Logistics Center in Winter Haven.

In 2004, Florida's freight railroads conveyed about 1.2 million carloads of freight and 805,260 intermodal loads (truck trailers and containers), "effectively removing six million heavy trucks from the state's roadways."[2] (Nearly half of all this traffic remained in Florida and went no farther.) The largest commodity groups include phosphate shipments to the Port of Tampa and the transportation of aggregates (crushed stone or sand) that are used in statewide construction projects.

Recent editions of the Florida Rail Plan note that seven different industry groups rely upon railroad freight service, industries that account for 34 percent of Florida's entire gross state product and 28 percent of state employment. The groups include: the phosphate and fertilizer industry, distribution and retail, food and agriculture, paper and fiber, automobile distribution, auto carriers, and energy.[3]

The 2004 Florida Rail Plan notes that every day CSX Transportation shuttles thousands of rail cars between the phosphate-rich Bone Valley of central Florida (Hillsborough, Polk, and Hardee Counties) to the Port of Tampa, creating for that facility 40 percent of its volume. The phosphate rock is then off-loaded into the holds of oceangoing vessels that are frequently bound for China, India, Australia, and Brazil.

Merchandise and food items, another important industry group, are often sent to Florida by rail from huge distribution hubs located in Chicago, Atlanta, and Dallas–Fort Worth, and from distant gateways like Los Angeles–Long Beach, where consumer items arrive from Asia. One of the more popular agriculture and food items conveyed by rail is orange juice. The Tropicana juice plants in Bradenton and Fort Pierce send a considerable portion of their output to the northeastern states, the Midwest, and California via the so-called Tropicana Juice Trains, whose refrigerated cars—each are equivalent to four separate truck trailers—are painted bright orange.

Railroads also play a key role in processing paper and fiber. The industry requires endless carloads of chemicals to complete the manufacturing process, and then uses rail cars to transport a variety of finished products to marketplace. Likewise, efficient rail transportation is integral to the automobile industry. New cars produced in America are often sent to Florida by rail from assembly plants located in the Southeast and Midwest. In 2003 alone, some "30,000 carloads of automobiles arrived by rail from Kentucky, 22,000 from Michigan, 15,000 from Ohio, and 10,000 from Illinois."[4] Also, many imported vehicles arrive by ship at the deepwater seaports of Jacksonville and Tampa along with an endless stream of parts, whereupon trains convey these products to a variety of destinations.

Because Florida is home to several fossil fuel utility plants, dedicated coal trains can often be seen threading their way about the state. Some 12 million tons of coal were shipped to Florida in 2003, accounting for 12 percent of all freight that the state's carriers transported. Equally dependent on rail transportation is the construction industry. The variety of items hauled by trains is extensive, and includes such commodities as metals, lumber, cement, and aggregate rock.

The Rail Office of the FDOT has identified three important issues currently facing the state's freight railroads: the more than five thousand at-grade road-rail crossings, which often create safety problems and traffic delays; the need to upgrade track and bridges so routes can accommodate the 286,000-pound rail car—an industry standard; and certain capacity and safety issues that may arise from intercity and commuter passenger trains sharing freight routes. Additionally, the Rail Office has documented the current concerns of shippers and railroad executives, such as main-line and yard-capacity issues, labor and car shortages, service problems on out-of-state railroads that affect Florida traffic, and the lack of recurring public funds for rail projects within the state.[5]

According to the Association of American Railroads (AAR), 560 railroad companies exist in America today that operate 140,249 miles of track. The AAR classifies the nation's freight carriers into three categories. The seven "Class I" railroads have annual revenues of $319.3 million or more and own about 70 percent of the national network of tracks. The thirty "Regional" railroads of the country operate at least 350 miles of road and/or have revenues between $40 million and the Class I revenue threshold. "Local" railroads and "Switching & Terminal" railroads (523 firms) have revenues less than the Regional criteria. (Local railroads are frequently referred to as short-line railroads.) Regional and Local railroads operate about 44,500 miles of the national total and provide "feeder traffic" to the big Class I carriers.[6]

Presently, two Class I railroads serve Florida: CSX Transportation and Norfolk Southern. Both service the eastern United States and connect Florida to the national railroad network. CSX has a commanding presence in the Sunshine State; Norfolk Southern a minimal one. Just one Regional railroad exists in Florida: the Florida East Coast Railway. All other operators are Local or Switching & Terminal railroads. Florida is additionally served by two passenger train entities: Amtrak and Tri-Rail.

CSX Transportation

Headquartered in Jacksonville, the CSX Corporation enjoyed revenues of $9.56 billion in 2006 and net earnings of $1.31 billion. The company's

Michael J. Ward, a career railroader and graduate of the University of Maryland and Harvard Business School, currently guides the fortunes of CSX as chairman, president, and CEO. By permission of the CSX Corporation.

principal operating component is CSX Transportation (www.csxt.com), which is the largest railroad in the eastern United States, with 21,000 route miles in twenty-three states, the District of Columbia, and two Canadian provinces. Approximately thirty-two thousand workers are employed systemwide. The railroad unit owns or leases 3,700 locomotives and 105,000 freight cars. About 49 percent of the railroad's revenues are generated by merchandise traffic.[7]

CSX Transportation owns approximately 1,750 miles of track in Florida—about 65 percent of the state total. Each year the company transports about 508,000 carloads of freight in the state. Major traffic items include phosphate, fertilizers, chemicals, truck trailers, automobiles, coal, orange juice, sugar, feed, limestone, and aggregates. CSX employs some six thousand Floridians, over four thousand just in the Jacksonville area.

CSX is today the biggest railroad carrier in Florida. In this scene, local freight train 0701 advances through Largo with many cars of merchandise. Photo courtesy of Mike Woodruff.

Each day about 1,200 trains move about the CSX system nationwide, and practically all are dispatched from the railroad's Dufford Transportation Center in West Jacksonville. Major rail yards are situated at Jacksonville, Baldwin, and Tampa, while locomotive servicing facilities can be found at Hialeah, Jacksonville, Lakeland, Orlando, Pensacola, Tallahassee, and Tampa, where car repair shops also are situated. Intermodal terminals, where truck trailers are loaded and off-loaded, are maintained at Jacksonville, Miami, Orlando, West Palm Beach, and Tampa.

CSX also operates in Florida rail-to-truck metals distribution facilities at Fort Lauderdale and Tampa; rail-to-truck transloading facilities in Fort Lauderdale, Jacksonville, Sanford, and Tampa; and finished automobile distribution centers at Blount Island, Jacksonville, Ocala, Orlando, Tampa, and Palm Center. One of the railroad's most profitable activities is moving processed phosphate from the Bone Valley of central Florida to the company's Rockport transloading facility below Tampa, a 24/7 operation that is frequently featured in trade publications.[8]

Norfolk Southern Corporation

Though its presence in Florida is minimal, Norfolk Southern Railway Company is nonetheless an impressive Class I carrier. Headquartered in Norfolk, Virginia, Norfolk Southern Corporation (www.nscorp.com) posted revenues of $9.40 billion in 2006 and net income of $1.49 billion. Its railway unit, which operates about 21,000 miles of track in twenty eastern states, the District of Columbia, and Ontario, employs thirty-one thousand workers. Norfolk Southern Corporation itself was formed in 1980. Two years later, it acquired the Norfolk & Western Railway and the Southern Railway, complete ownership of both having been consummated in 2005.[9]

Norfolk Southern operates two rail lines into Florida for less than 150 miles. Both depart Valdosta, Georgia: one route proceeds to Simpson Yard in Jacksonville, by way of Sargent, Crawford, and Duval, while another heads in a more southeasterly direction to Lake City and Navair via Jennings and Jasper. (Both lines were previously owned by Southern Railway.) Additionally, Norfolk Southern has trackage rights over CSX from Jacksonville to Palatka—site of a large paper mill—as well as a haulage agreement with the Florida East Coast Railway between Jacksonville and Miami.

Each day about twelve Norfolk Southern trains depart or arrive Simpson Yard that transport merchandise, finished automobiles, lumber, paper products, and steel. The company also operates three auto mobile distribution centers in the state (Jacksonville, Titusville, and Miami) as well as an intermodal facility in Jacksonville that receives port traffic from the Talleyrand Terminal Railroad.[10] Connections with CSX and the Florida East Coast Railway are made at Jacksonville. Norfolk Southern employs about 140 Floridians, and their annual payroll is about $4.2 million.

Florida East Coast Railway

In recent years, this Regional carrier has undergone phenomenal growth owing to market conditions, strong demographics, and an aggressive management team—formerly headed by Robert Anestis and now by CEO/Chairman Adolfo Henriques. In 2006, Florida East Coast

Industries (FECI) (www.feci.com) posted record revenues of $458.2 million and $90.4 million in operating profit. The rail unit of FECI, the Florida East Coast Railway, furnished $264 million toward that revenue figure and $78.4 million in profits. The rest came chiefly from FECI's lucrative real estate unit.[11]

After businessman Ed Ball obtained control of the Florida East Coast Railway in the late 1950s, the Alfred I. du Pont Testamentary Trust eventually owned 68 percent of the railway's first mortgage bonds and 5 percent of all company stock. The trust also owned 83 percent of St. Joe Paper Company which, in turn, owned 52 percent of the railway's stock and 10 percent of its bonds.[12] This interlocking relationship changed in 1983, when Florida East Coast Industries, a wholly owned subsidiary, was formed to handle ownership of the railway and its burgeoning real estate division called Flagler Development Group. Until October 2000, St. Joe Paper Company owned 54 percent of Florida East Coast Industries. It then spun off its interest to shareholders by distributing FECI Class B common shares, a dual stock classification that ceased in 2003 when both stock issues again became one.

With the support of the Florida Department of Transportation, the Florida East Coast Railway is installing 12 miles of double track between Titusville and Cocoa to increase capacity. The railway itself has lately taken delivery of several new, state-of-the-art diesel-electric locomotives; opened a new yard for aggregates at Medley in Miami-Dade County; and received a coveted Harriman Gold Medal for railroad safety. In April 2007, the national trade publication *Railway Age* gave the company its "Regional Railway of the Year" award.

Intermodal shipments (truck trailers and containers) furnish about 59 percent of all company revenues, the railway's top customers being Wal-Mart, UPS, Pepsi, and the shipping lines of Crowley Maritime, Tropical and Seaboard Marine. About 27 percent of its revenues are derived from aggregate shipments (crushed rock, sand, etc.). One of the company's more important shippers is Tropicana Products, which operates a large juice-processing facility in Fort Pierce. The Florida East Coast Railway also exclusively serves the ports of Miami, Port Everglades (Fort Lauderdale), and Palm Beach as well as the Kennedy Space Center. Interestingly, about 60 percent of all rail traffic both originates and terminates on the system.

The FEC Railway employs about 800 workers, 560 of whom are represented by unions. Its 351-mile main-line track, which connects Jacksonville with Miami, is meticulously maintained, and consists of continuous welded rail supported on concrete crossties. The railway also owns 268 miles of branch, switching, and secondary track, along with 167 miles of yard track. In March 1998, FEC signed a trackage agreement with South Central Florida Express Railroad that allows that firm to operate and maintain 56 miles of an old FEC branch between Fort Pierce and Lake Harbor. Some eighty diesel locomotives are either owned or leased by FEC Railway, along with 6,262 freight cars.[13]

On 8 May 2007, Florida East Coast Industries publicly announced that it would be acquired by funds of the Fortress Investment Group of New York, in an all-cash transaction valued at $3.5 billion. The merger agreement, which its board has approved but is subject to customary closing conditions and regulatory approvals, is scheduled to take effect in late 2007. Upon completion, Florida East Coast Industries will then become a private-held company, and its common stock will no longer be publicly traded.

Alabama and Gulf Coast Railroad

Based in Monroeville, Alabama, the Alabama and Gulf Coast is one of many Local (or short-line) railroads that currently serve Florida. Readers will recall that during the late 1920s, the Frisco Railroad acquired a route into Pensacola, Florida, in order to obtain a gulf port outlet. In 1980, the Frisco was absorbed by the Burlington Northern Railroad, which merged in 1995 with the Santa Fe to form the Burlington Northern Santa Fe Railroad (BNSF). Two years later, the BNSF sold its lightly used line into Pensacola to States Rail of Dallas, Texas, which owned a group of short-line companies. In 2002, States Rail sold the Pensacola appendage to RailAmerica; headquartered in Boca Raton, it was then the world's largest short-line holding company (www.railamerica. com).

Each year about sixteen thousand carloads of forest products, paper, chemicals, and merchandise are handled by the Alabama and Gulf Coast Railway. Connections with CSX are made at Cantonment. The primary customers in Florida include paper mills and the Pensacola Marine

Shipyard complex. Formed in 1992, RailAmerica, Inc. had revenues of $423.6 million in 2005 and a net income of $30.8 million. That year the publicly owned corporation owned forty-two Regional and short-line railroads that operated 7,800 route miles and employed two thousand workers.[14] In February 2007, RailAmerica was sold and merged into an affiliate of the Fortress Investment Group in New York (www.fortress inv.com).

AN Railway, Bay Line Railroad, Talleyrand Terminal, First Coast Railroad

This quartet of firms helps form Genesee & Wyoming Inc. (G & W), one of the nation's premier operators of short-line and Regional freight railroads (www.gwrr.com). Based in Greenwich, Connecticut, the parent firm has interests in forty-eight separate carriers, which operate 6,800 miles of track. Revenues in 2006 totaled $478.8 million, and $134.0 million was recorded in net income. Assets of the highly successful company, which went public in 1996, now stand at $1.14 billion.[15]

In 2005, G & W acquired substantially all of the rail operations of Rail Management Corporation of Panama City, Florida. In doing so, G & W obtained control of two historic Florida firms: the Apalachicola Northern Railroad and the Atlanta & St. Andrews Bay Railway. Beginning in September 2002, St. Joe Paper had allowed Rail Management Corporation to operate its Apalachicola Northern Railroad, which it renamed the AN Railway. Two months later, St. Joe Paper began dismantling its big paper mill at Port St. Joe (built by du Pont interests in 1933), a project that furnished AN Railway with many carloads of scrap metal. Other traffic the firm currently transports includes chemicals, forest products, as well as commodities from the barge-rail transload facility at Port St. Joe. G & W controls the property by lease.

The Bay Line Railroad was purchased by the Rail Management Corporation from Stone Container in 1994. In 1929, the Southern Kraft Division of International Paper announced it would build a mill at Panama City, which opened two years later. A subsidiary of International Paper, the St. Andrews Bay Holding Company, acquired the Atlanta & St. Andrews Bay Railway as part of the project. In 1977, International

Paper sold its Panama City mill and railway to Southwest Forest Industries. Stone Container, in turn, purchased the latter operation a decade later. Today, the 81-mile Bay Line Railroad, which the G & W now owns outright, transports coated pipe, wood chips, paper products, chemicals, aggregates, petroleum, agricultural commodities, pulp board, and truck trailers.

Talleyrand Terminal Railroad, which is really owned by the Jacksonville Port Authority, operates about 10 miles of track and performs switching chores between Jaxport and the Jacksonville rail yards, where connections are made with CSX and Norfolk Southern. Genesee & Wyoming has leased the Switching & Terminal outfit since 1996.

First Coast Railroad began operations in April 2005, after the company signed a twenty-year agreement with CSX Transportation to lease 32 miles of its track between Fernandina, Florida, and Seals, Georgia. The firm employs about twenty persons. Approximately fifteen thousand annual carloads are moved over First Coast that consist of paper, pulp, chemicals and agricultural products.[16]

The AN and Bay Line Railroads help form Genesee & Wyoming's Southern Region, while the First Coast and Talleyrand firms help comprise the company's Rail Link subsidiary.

Georgia and Florida Railway

OmniTRAX, a subsidiary of the Broe Companies in Denver, Colorado, owns this Florida short line along with several others in the United States. In April 2005, OmniTRAX (www.omnitrax.com) purchased the 297-mile Georgia & Florida RailNet, whose clutch of lines radiated from Albany, Georgia.[17] One extends into the Panhandle from Adel so as to reach Perry and Foley, by way of Greenville. During the early 1990s, the line was owned by Norfolk Southern Corporation. In 1995, the latter sold its Live Oak, Perry & South Georgia subsidiary to the Gulf & Ohio Railway. Four years later, the G & O sold it to the Georgia & Florida RailNet. Wood, pulp, paper, and chemicals are chiefly conveyed over the line.

Seminole Gulf

In 1987, CSX Transportation leased two rail lines in southwest Florida to what became Seminole Gulf Railway (www.semgulf.com). The firm acquired several used locomotives, and operations soon commenced on two unconnected track segments: the company's 78-mile Fort Myers Division (Arcadia south to Fort Myers and North Naples) and its 30-mile Sarasota Division from Oneco southward to Sarasota and Venice. Connections with CSX are made at Arcadia and Oneco.[18]

The Fort Myers–based short line transported 14,500 carloads of traffic in 1988, about 10 percent more than CSX had conveyed in the previous year. Among the commodities the railway currently hauls are building materials, plastics, liquefied petroleum gas, forest products, aggregates, foodstuffs, and newsprint.[19]

In the early 1990s, Seminole Gulf acquired several passenger and dining cars so it could inaugurate dinner and excursion trains, both of which have proven popular with locals and tourists. The company additionally owns and operates a state-of-the-art warehouse and food distribution center located in North Fort Myers, called Florida Freezer.

Seminole Gulf Railway is among several short-line companies that operate in Florida. The train above has halted at South Punta Gorda to perform switching chores. Courtesy of Michael Mulligan.

South Central Florida Express

CSX sold that portion of its railroad between Sebring and Lake Harbor (by way of Lake Placid and Moore Haven) to a subsidiary of Lukens Steel called Brandywine Valley Railroad in June 1990. The latter organized a new company to operate the acquisition: South Central Florida Railroad. Headquarters were established in Clewiston. In September 1994, Lukens sold the short line to the United States Sugar Corporation, also of Clewiston, which it renamed South Central Florida Express (www.ussugar.com/sugar/sugar_railroad.html).

Among the commodities the railroad conveys are sugar cane, bulk raw and refined sugar, fertilizers, molasses, liquefied petroleum gas, pulpwood logs, paper, and farm equipment. In 1998, the firm signed an agreement with the Florida East Coast Railway, allowing it to operate and maintain the latter's branch between Lake Harbor and Fort Pierce. About seventy-two thousand carloads of freight were conveyed on the SCFX in 1999. Today, the company operates about 171 miles of track and owns approximately fourteen locomotives and one thousand special-purpose cane cars.[20]

Florida Central, Florida Midland, Florida Northern

This trio of short lines is owned by the Pinsly railroad group that was formed in 1938 by New Englander Samuel Pinsly. Although the holding company is based in Westfield, Massachusetts, local offices of the firm are maintained in Plymouth, Florida.

Pinsly's properties in Florida (www.pinsly.com) were formerly operated by CSX. Its Florida Central unit, which began operations in 1986, extends from the CSX connection at Orlando to Umatilla by way of Toronto, Plymouth, Tavares, and Eustis. Branches stem from the main line in order to reach Sorrento, Forest City, and Winter Garden.

The Florida Midland started up the following year with two unconnected segments of track between West Lake Wales and Frostproof; another from Winter Haven to Gordonville. Connections with CSX are made at West Lake Wales and Winter Haven. (Pinsly's trains also have trackage rights over approximately 10 miles of CSX that connect the two branch lines.)

Service on the 24-mile Florida Northern commenced in 1988 from Lowell southward to Ocala and Candler. (CSX is met at Ocala.) The company's West Coast Subdivision recently acquired 76 miles of CSX track between High Springs and Red Level, over which mostly coal trains operate.

A variety of commodities are handled over the Pinsly lines such as limestone products, fertilizer, coal, foodstuffs, chemicals, lumber, crushed stone, scrap metal, fly ash, pumice, furniture, and citrus juices.[21]

Florida West Coast Railroad

This short line began operations in 1987 by leasing 44 miles of track from CSX. Communities then served included Newberry, Trenton (company headquarters), Fanning Springs, and Chiefland. Cattle feed and fertilizers were the principal commodities transported, and connections with CSX were made at Newberry.

In 2004, the Surface Transportation Board allowed Florida West Coast Railroad to abandon service. However, the deadline to accomplish this has now been delayed to January 2008. All or perhaps a substantial portion of the Trenton-Newberry section may become a state rail-trail.

Amtrak

Amtrak (www.amtrak.com) was incorporated in 1971 pursuant to the Rail Passenger Service Act of the previous year. Its mission is to operate a nationwide system of passenger rail transportation. Like many worldwide passenger train system operators, Amtrak has a long history of recurring losses. It is also dependent on subsidies from federal and state governments to function. (Its federal subsidy is received through an annual appropriation by Congress.) Revenues amounted to $2.04 billion in 2006, expenses of $3 billion were incurred, and a comprehensive net loss of $962.8 million was recorded.[22]

Amtrak serves forty-six American states and operates over 21,000 miles of routes, 70 percent of which are owned by other railroad companies. About 24.3 million passengers were transported nationwide

Amtrak's Auto Train has the distinction of being the longest passenger train in the world. Here it is pounding past the DeLand depot en route to Sanford, where the southbound journey from Lorton, Virginia, terminates. Courtesy of Bob Pickering.

in 2005. That year the company owned 1,437 passenger cars, 436 locomotives, 80 automobile carriers, and 74 baggage cars. Nationwide, the company employs some nineteen thousand workers, 90 percent of whom are covered by labor agreements.

Over the decades, Amtrak has furnished Florida with a variety of services, the amount and frequency directly related to funding appropriations and ridership. In 2006, three trains served the state: Auto Train transports cars and their owners between Lorton, Virginia, and Sanford, Florida; the Silver Meteor offers daily passenger train service with meals and sleeping accommodations between New York City (Pennsylvania Station) and Miami by way of Jacksonville and Orlando; while the Silver Star covers almost the same route as the Meteor but also stops in Tampa. Currently in suspension is the Sunset Limited, which once operated between Los Angeles and Orlando. Discussions continue about future Amtrak service along the state's east coast using tracks owned by the Florida East Coast Railway.

Amtrak transported 841,240 passengers in Florida during 2005. The three busiest stations are Sanford, Orlando, and Tampa. Approximately 940 Floridians work for the company, and the annual payroll amounts to some $45 million. Maintenance facilities are located at Sanford and

Tri-Rail is currently the state's only commuter train operator. This scene was snapped at the attractive station at Boca Raton. Photo provided by the South Florida Regional Transportation Authority/Ari Justin Rothenburg.

Hialeah. Additional state and national facts can be viewed on the Amtrak Web site.

Tri-Rail

The Florida Department of Transportation purchased 81 miles of railway track from CSX Transportation, between West Palm Beach and Miami in May 1988 for $264 million, thereafter calling it the South Florida Rail Corridor. About this time, Interstate 95 in that area was being widened, and state transportation planners envisioned a temporary commuter rail operation to help ease congestion as construction of the highway progressed. Tri-County Commuter Train Authority was formed, which instituted push-pull train operations in January 1989 using a contract operator—Herzog Transit Services. The response to the service exceeded expectations, and before long the operation became a permanent fixture of Broward, Miami-Dade, and Palm Beach Counties.[23]

By 2003, some 2.7 million passengers were utilizing Tri-Rail (www. tri-rail.com), which is today one of top fifteen commuter railroads in

America. That same year the Pompano Beach–based carrier officially became part of the South Florida Regional Transportation Authority.

Over the years, the South Florida Regional Transportation Authority (parent of Tri-Rail) has undertaken an impressive array of expansion and improvement measures, such as double-tracking its route with new signals, adding more trains, erecting new stations, refurbishing locomotives, and opening—on 13 April 2007—a $78 million double-track bridge over the New River near Fort Lauderdale. (The old single-track drawbridge will still be used by trains of CSX Transportation.)

In the near future, the 72-mile commuter rail operation, which offers service between Mangonia Park in West Palm Beach southward to Miami Airport, will dispatch its own trains—a service currently supplied by CSX. Because of Tri-Rail's popularity, transportation planners are now considering expanding service north of Palm Beach into Martin County and Jupiter, south into Kendall in Miami-Dade County, as well as east-west expansions along the Dolphin Expressway and Interstate 595. Tri-Rail authorities estimate that it will experience 27,900 daily boardings by the year 2015.

High-Speed Rail

According to the 2004 Florida Rail Plan, the state has been evaluating high-speed rail service since the mid 1970s, when "the Florida Transit Corridor Study analyzed 150-mph trains operating between Daytona Beach and St. Petersburg."[24] In November 2000, Florida voters approved a constitutional amendment mandating the development of high-speed passenger train system that would link the state's five largest urban areas. The trains themselves were to exceed 120 mph and operate on brand-new tracks or guideways.

All the foregoing led to the enactment of the Florida High-Speed Rail Authority Act. The agency, formed in March 2001 with nine members, eventually called for proposals to design, build, operate, maintain, and finance an "an initial high-speed rail service between Tampa and Orlando," a project estimated to cost $2.4 billion (www.floridahigh speedrail.org). Many Floridians found the cost unreasonable, and in November 2004 the mandate was overturned. Currently, the agency is completing the study begun for the Tampa-Orlando section. "Beyond that, the future of high-speed rail service in Florida is unclear."[25]

Central Florida Commuter Rail

Highway traffic has grown at a staggering rate in central Florida. In 2006, in partnership with CSX Transportation, the state agreed in principle to invest $491 million to improve infrastructure and expand capacity on two existing rail lines, one of which will be used for commuter rail service through four Florida counties between DeLand, Orlando, and Kissimmee.

The first phase of latter project, covering about 31 miles with ten stations between DeBary/Saxon Boulevard and Orlando Amtrak/Orlando Regional Medical Center, is projected to open in 2009, just as the FDOT begins a major Interstate 4 highway-rebuilding project. Special diesel-powered, double-decker commuter train sets would be purchased for the service. Further details about the landmark project, including the historic agreement between FDOT and CSX Transportation, can be viewed on the Central Florida Commuter Rail Web site (www.cfrail.com).

Preservation

For years, organizations have existed in Florida that are dedicated to preserving some aspect of railroading or re-creating what train travel once was like. Most all are not-for-profit groups that rely upon the efforts and contributions of many dedicated volunteers and a supportive public.

Perhaps the state's most famous attraction is the Gold Coast Railroad Museum in Miami (www.goldcoast-railroad.org), which features restored railway cars and equipment along with both standard-gauge and miniature train rides. Another popular destination is the Florida Railroad Museum in Parrish (www.frrm.org), whose inventory of restored cars and locomotives help form the very trains that visitors ride on. Excursion and dinner trains that utilize vintage equipment can also be found on the Inland Lakes Railway in Mount Dora (www.inland lakesrailway.com). Several exhibits of note can be enjoyed at the West

Many Florida stations have undergone sensitive restorations, such as the former Seaboard edifice at Venice, built 1927. Local citizen Rollins Coakley spearheaded the effort;
Sarasota County government furnished most of the funds. Photo by Michael Mulligan.

Florida Railroad Museum in Milton (www.wfrm.org) and at the Pioneer
Florida Museum and Village in Dade City (www.pioneerfloridamuseum.
org). Another success story is the Railroad Museum of South Florida
(www.trainweb.org/lprr), which maintains an inviting steam locomotive exhibit at Lakes Park in South Fort Myers and operates a popular
miniature train ride.

Literally hundreds of railroad depots once dotted Florida, and today
many have been restored for museum purposes. Among them are Winter Garden, home to the Central Florida Railroad Museum (www.cfcnrhs.
org); Deerfield Beach, home to the South Florida Railway Museum
(www.sfrm.org); Fort Myers, headquarters of the Southwest Florida
Museum of History (www.cityftmyers.com/museum/index/aspx); and
Palatka, which houses the Palatka Railroad Preservation Society (www.
railsofpalatka.org).

Other noteworthy depot restorations have occurred in such Florida
communities as Archer (www.afn.org/~archer/), Arcadia, Avon Park,
Barberville, Bowling Green, DeLand, Dunedin (www.dunedinmuseum.
org/), Fort Lauderdale, Fort Meade, Frostproof, Hollywood, Lady Lake,
Lake Placid (www.lpfla.com/visit/museum/html), Lake Wales (www.
cityoflakewales.com/depot/), Largo, Mulberry, Naples, Ocala, Orlando,
Pompano Beach, Punta Gorda, San Antonio, Sebring, Trenton, Umatilla, West Palm Beach, and Zephyr Hills (www.zephyrhills.net/depot

museum.html). State, county, and city grants, along with the generous support of civic-minded citizens, have made many of these preservation projects possible.

Our journey into Florida railroad history comes now to a close. Much has happened since that first train departed St. Joseph (near Port St. Joe) in 1836. For years, Florida's slender population and lack of big industry retarded railway development. The state lent a helping hand in the 1850s by giving qualified firms a generous land grant and guarantying the interest on their construction bonds. That helped, but much of the erstwhile construction that followed was decimated during the Civil War.

Little railroad activity occurred during the painful years of Reconstruction, except for an outrageous carpetbag fraud. Fortunately the clouds began to lift in the 1880s, when several spectacular developers arrived on the scene. Railroad fever then raged throughout Florida, until the power and influence of the industry reached an imperial proportion. Then, several big out-of-state systems established a presence in the state. But not until the late 1920s did the railway map of Florida reach its all-time greatest extent.

Although the railway map of Florida has shrunk in recent decades, the need for railroad transportation ever continues. In certain ways, railroads themselves are living organisms, expanding and contracting in size as market conditions dictate. Even the actual players and owners come and go. But one concept that does not vacillate is how efficient the flanged railroad wheel rolls on steel track with so little friction and demand for energy.

Today, most of Florida's railroads convey freight. But there is a growing public demand for more passenger train service. Why? Everyone knows that that the expensive outlays for highways have not completely solved the traffic congestion problem, the air pollution problem, the greenhouse gas problem, perhaps even the next-election problem. State transportation planners are certainly sensitive to these demands, but the issues of funding, a sustainable ridership, gubernatorial support, getting motorists to leave their cars, and so on often make solutions a daunting challenge. Nevertheless, the quest for a balanced transportation system in Florida continues.

Notes

Introduction

1. Gerstner, *Early American Railroads*, 635.
2. A. D. Chandler Jr., *The Visible Hand*, 86.
3. Proctor, *Napoleon Bonaparte Broward*, 152.
4. Stover, *American Railroads*, 13.
5. Haney, *A Congressional History*, 285.
6. Turner, *A Short History of Florida Railroads*, 8. *Poor's Manual of Railroads* first appeared in 1868.
7. Stover, *The Railroads of the South*, 94.
8. Ibid., 193.
9. Turner, *Florida Railroads in the 1920s*, 7–8.
10. Stover, *American Railroads*, 245–47.
11. Jensen, *Railroads in America*, 7.

Chapter 1. A Railway Primer

1. Cleveland and Powell, *Railroad Promotion*, 188–90.
2. *New York American*, 20 June 1836. The article states that "a group of gentlemen from Boston and Georgia have obtained a liberal charter from the Legislative Council of Florida for a Rail-road between St. Marks, across the isthmus of Florida, to come out upon the Atlantic at Brunswick in Georgia—the distance being 180 miles. Books of subscription for the capital stock of two million dollars are about to be opened, and the work of the Railroad may commence this ensuing fall and winter from Brunswick to the Georgia line, after the handful of Indians are removed from Florida, and then proceed to St. Marks."
3. Turner, *A Short History of Florida Railroads*, 75.
4. When the Seaboard Air Line Railway opened its so-called West Coast Extension on 7 January 1927, the *Fort Myers Tropical News* gave the event front-page coverage and furnished readers with a special supplement.
5. Cleveland and Powell, *Railroad Promotion*, 156.
6. Dodd, "Railroad Projects," 14.
7. Turner, *A Short History of Florida Railroads*, 16.

8. A. D. Chandler Jr., *The Visible Hand*, 91. Foreign investors first acquired bonds of the U.S. government, and then those of individual states.

9. Veenendaal, *Slow Train*, 11–15, 76–78, 116–18.

10. Ulmer, *Capital in Transportation*, 169.

11. Ripley, *Railroads*, 143–45.

12. Prominent Floridians were also appointed receivers or trustees. For example, former governor John Martin became a bankruptcy trustee of the Florida East Coast Railway.

13. Danese, *Claude Pepper and Ed Ball*, 156–84; Campbell, *Across Fortune's Tracks*, 249–53; Altman, "In the Public Interest?" 32–47. Ball bought a majority of the company's First & Refunding Bonds early on but did not obtain control of the FEC Railway until 1958.

14. Flint, *The Railroads*, 19.

15. *Pensacola and Georgia Railroad Company, Annual Report of 1855*, 5.

16. Turner, *A Short History of Florida Railroads*, 36–37; Black, *The Railroads of the Confederacy*, 208–13.

17. *Pensacola and Georgia Railroad Company, Annual Report of 1855*, 4.

18. Gonzalez, "Pensacola," 7.

19. Turner, *Railroads of Southwest Florida*, 44.

20. A. D. Chandler Jr., *The Visible Hand*, 93.

21. Shofner, *Nor Is It Over Yet*, 115–16.

22. Stover, *American Railroads*, 21.

23. Ibid., 145.

24. Pettengill, *The Story of the Florida Railroads*, 39.

25. Taylor and Neu, *The American Railroad Network*, 79. Southern railway officials ultimately agreed not upon the exact standard gauge measurement of northern states but something very close: 4 feet, 9 inches.

26. D. S. Johnson, "The Railroads of Florida," 6–11.

27. Stover, *American Railroads*, 44; Jensen, *Railroads in America*, 45–49. American steam locomotives devoured some 5 million cords of wood in 1856. The fuel was harvested and cut to size by locals, whereupon it was stacked alongside the track at strategic intervals. Locomotives requiring fuel halted at these points, whereupon the firewood would be tossed into the locomotive tender. After "wooden up" was completed, the journey resumed. Often an intake of boiler water was simultaneously made.

28. Further information can be found in the magisterial works of John H. White Jr., such as the *History of the American Locomotive*, *The American Railroad Passenger Car*, and *The American Railroad Freight Car*.

29. Scudder, *Recollections*, 275–76.

30. Pettengill, *The Story of the Florida Railroads*, 35.

31. Gerstner, *Early American Railroads*, 738.

32. Joubert, "A History," 73.

33. For an inside look at the industry, consult John H. Armstrong's, *The Railroad: What It Is, What It Does*.

34. A. D. Chandler Jr., *The Visible Hand*, 89.

Chapter 2. Panhandle Pioneers

1. Morrison, *The Oxford History*, 161.
2. Gerstner, *Early American Railroads*, 737.
3. Morris and Morris, *The Florida Handbook*, 291–95.
4. Phillips, *History of Transportation*, 3–4.
5. Abbey, *Florida*, 153.
6. Ibid., 221.
7. The history of this wonderful region is superbly recounted in Clifton Paisley's *The Red Hills of Florida, 1528–1865.*
8. *Tallahassee Floridian and Advocate*, 20 January 1831.
9. Ibid.
10. "An Act to Incorporate the Leon Rail Way Company," *Laws of Florida Territory, 9th Session, 1831.*
11. Dodd, "Railroad Projects," 27.
12. "An Act to Incorporate the Tallahassee Rail Road Company," *Laws of the Legislative Council*, 1834, chap. 793, no. 54.
13. Doherty, *Richard Keith Call*, 88. Call's estate ("The Grove") was located east of the capital on the edge of Tallahassee. By 1840, he owned some 6,000 acres of prime land, sixty-six slaves, and numerous lots. An ardent Unionist, Call greatly opposed the Civil War, convinced such a conflict would open "The Gates of Hell."
14. Cullum, *Biographical Register*, 328.
15. "Memorial of the Tallahassee Railroad Company," 1834.
16. Articles of Agreement, 1835.
17. Doherty, *Richard Keith Call*, 89.
18. Gerstner, *Early American Railroads*, 731–45.
19. Ibid., 737–38.
20. Ibid., 730.
21. Ibid.
22. Ibid., 739.
23. Ibid.
24. Castelnau, "Essay," 199.
25. *Railway Age*, 10 October 1931.
26. Federal Writers' Project, *Florida*, 491.
27. Porter, *The Lives of St. Joseph*, 21.
28. Dodd, "Railroad Projects," 18, 36.
29. Gerstner, *Early American Railroads*, 740. The company's real estate along the coastline had cost $8,879.
30. Porter, *The Lives of St. Joseph*, 23; Dodd, "Railroad Projects," 20.
31. Porter, *The Lives of St. Joseph*, 32. In order to traverse the 8-mile route in eight minutes, the locomotive would have needed to travel at 60 miles per hour, likely an impossibility owing to the primitive track structure.
32. Gerstner, *Early American Railroads*, 741.
33. Ibid.

34. Ibid.

35. Dodd, "Railroad Projects," 23. Gerstner claims the amount to be $325,000.

36. Gerstner, *Early American Railroads*, 742.

37. Ibid.

38. Dodd, "Railroad Projects," 24.

39. Ibid., 25–26; Gerstner, *Early American Railroads*, 742–43.

40. Porter, *The Lives of St. Joseph*, 96–97.

41. Dodd, "Railroad Projects," 30.

42. *Pensacola Gazette*, 1 August 1840.

43. Gerstner, *Early American Railroads*, 743.

44. Dodd, "Railroad Projects," 45.

45. *Charters of the Bank of Pensacola and the Alabama, Florida and Georgia Rail Road Company*, 18.

46. Dodd, "Railroad Projects," 47.

47. McGrane, *Foreign Bondholders*, 223.

48. Ibid, 224. For every mile the railroad completed, the bank could issue $10,000 worth of bonds.

49. Ibid. The author renders a thorough account of the "Faith bonds" in chapter 11. The Union Bank of Tallahassee and the Southern Life Insurance and Trust Company in St. Augustine were also empowered to issue such securities.

50. Ibid., 226.

51. Ibid. 224.

52. *U.S. Statutes at Large*, 23rd Cong., 2nd sess., chap. 45 (1835): 778.

53. Dodd, "Railroad Projects," 50.

54. *Pensacola Gazette*, 9 April 1836.

55. Gerstner, *Early American Railroads*, 744.

56. *Pensacola Gazette*, 10 January 1835.

57. Dodd, "Railroad Projects," 57.

Chapter 3. Government Lends a Hand

1. Gannon, *Florida*, 40.

2. *New York Times*, 16 December 1852.

3. *Report of the Internal Improvement Board of Florida*, 1855, 3.

4. The report was prepared for the Hon. J. D. Andrews, who had been appointed by the U.S. secretary of the treasury "to collect information and make a report on the Improvements, Commerce and Resources of the different States of the Union."

5. *Florida Senate Journal, 1852*, 1–3.

6. Ibid., 14–15.

7. Rerick, *Memoirs of Florida*, 175. A campaign broadside of Broward, in which he deplores the land grant scheme to railroads, can be found at Special Collections, Carpenter Library, University of North Florida. According to Cabell's 1852 report, the federal government owned at this time about "eleven-twelfths" of Florida. A U.S. General Land Office statement, appended to the report, discloses that Florida contained 37,931,520 acres of land. If Cabell's statistic was correct, then the federal government still owned roughly 92 percent of the state, or 34,896,998 acres.

8. Abbey, *Florida*, 249.

9. *Report of the Internal Improvement Board of Florida*, 1855, 16.

10. Ibid., 8–13.

11. Ibid., 1.

12. McCullough, "Legislative Regulation," 24; Brevard, *A History of Florida*, 2: 22. In 1963, the Internal Improvement Fund took control of the State Land Office from the commissioner of agriculture. Six years later, the IIF received a new name: the Board of Trustees of the Internal Improvement Trust Fund. The latter was transferred to the Department of Natural Resources in 1975, then to the Division of State Lands in 1979. In 1993, the board was transferred intact to the Department of Environmental Protection, which now also operates the State Land Office.

13. *Laws of the State of Florida, 1854–55*, chap. 610, 1–26.

14. Ibid., 13.

15. Ibid., 19.

16. Ibid.

17. McCullough, "Legislative Regulation," 40.

18. *Report of the Trustees*, 1856, 44.

19. Ibid., 44–45.

20. Smyth, *The Life of Henry Bradley Plant*, 47.

21. *Florida Senate Journal, 1852*, 20.

22. Fenlon, "The Florida, Atlantic and Gulf Central," 71–80.

23. Canter Brown Jr., "The Florida, Atlantic and Gulf Central Railroad," 411–429; Turner, *A Short History of Florida Railroads*, 23.

24. *Minutes of Proceedings of the Stockholders*, 5–23.

25. Ibid., 6.

26. Ibid., 7.

27. Davis, *History of Jacksonville*, 342.

28. Ibid.

29. *Minutes of Proceedings of the Stockholders*, 17.

30. Turner, *A Short History of Florida Railroads*, 25.

31. *Minutes of Proceedings of the Directors*, 1855, 18.

32. Ibid., 26.

33. *Laws of Florida, 1855*, chap. 735, no. 125, 26–27. In addition to allowing the trustees to alter certain construction specifications, the amendment reduced the so-called 20-mile rule to 10 miles; the duties of the state engineer could now be performed by any civil engineer acceptable to the trustees. Another project worthy of IIF aid was a line of railway connecting Pensacola with Montgomery, Alabama.

34. *Minutes of Proceedings of the Directors, 1855*, 37.

35. Ibid.

36. Ibid., 41–42.

37. Paisley, *The Red Hills*, 157; *Tallahassee Floridian*, 21 May 1853, 11 February 1854.

38. *Tallahassee Floridian*, 20 December 1856.

39. Ibid., 19 December 1857.

40. Paisley, *The Red Hills*, 163.

41. Pettengill, *The Story*, 24–26.

42. It has not been learned what attracted Cabell to St. Louis. During the Civil War, he served in the Confederate Army as a lieutenant colonel, after which he practiced in New York City and returned to St. Louis, where he was elected to the state Senate. He died 28 February 1896 and was buried in Bellefontaine Cemetery in St. Louis. Cabell's papers are at the University of Virginia.

43. *Tallahassee Floridian*, 1 and 14 January 1859; 25 February 1860. At Baldwin station, the Florida, Atlantic and Gulf Central connected with the Florida Railroad to Fernandina. But the agreement prohibited using this routing, which allowed the Central to receive a bigger revenue haul.

44. *Laws of Florida, 1852–53*, chap. 483, 38.

45. *Report of the President, 1856*; *Pensacola Gazette*, 27 December 1856.

46. Hildreth, "Railroads Out of Pensacola," 407; Bowden, *Iron Horse in the Pine-lands*, 11.

47. Hildreth, "Railroads Out of Pensacola," 408.

48. Pettengill, *The Story of the Florida Railroads*, 115; Cline, *Alabama Railroads*, 30; Black, *The Railroads of the Confederacy*, 51.

49. Bathe, *The St. Johns Railroad*, 2.

50. Ibid., 9.

51. Dodd, "Railroad Projects," 59–60.

52. Lord, "David Levy Yulee," 123.

53. *St. Augustine News*, 13 July 1844.

54. Hanna and Hanna, *Florida's Golden Sands*, 129–32.

55. *Florida Senate Journal, 1858*, "Evidence and Documents Reported by the Joint Select Committee," 54.

56. *Report to the Directors, 1855*, 9. Yulee notes that the transit from New York to New Orleans via his railroad would take just six days as opposed to the all-water route, which took twenty.

57. Ibid., 4.

58. Ibid.

59. *Florida Senate Journal, 1858*, 54. Gilliland was killed by Indians near Charles Ferry on the Suwannee River; Bird eventually returned to his native Georgia.

60. Ibid., 56.

61. Ibid.

62. *St. Augustine Examiner*, 30 June 1860.

63. *Laws of Florida, 1855*.

64. *Articles of Agreement of Contract, 1855*.

65. Ibid. General MacRae possessed an extensive railroad background and was highly regarded in the Carolinas. George W. Call, a Florida state senator who was also secretary and treasurer of the Florida Railroad Company, later testified that he opposed director Joseph Finegan taking the contract. Of the contract itself, he said: "I do not believe that any other man in the United States of any responsibility whatever would have made such a contract. Finegan & Company took it when no one else would." As noted, Yulee himself had drawn up the document (*Florida Senate Journal, 1858*, 148).

66. Ibid., *Articles of Agreement*, sec. 8.

67. *Florida Senate Journal, 1858*, 33.

68. Lord, "David Levy Yulee," 130.

69. Ibid., 131–32.

70. Knetsch, "Madison Starke Perry," 13–23; Lord, "David Levy Yulee," 131.

71. *Journal of the Florida Legislature*, House, 1858, 356–58. Dancy resigned as the state engineer before the report was actually issued and was appointed as the state land surveyor of Florida by President James Buchanan.

72. Hanna and Hanna, *Florida's Golden Sands*, 134–36.

73. Pettengill, *The Story of the Florida Railroads*, 22.

74. David Levy Yulee Papers, 1861.

Chapter 4. The Agonies of War, Reconstruction, and Fraud

1. Morrison, *The Oxford History*, 2: 389.

2. Davis, *The Civil War*, 38.

3. Morrison, *The Oxford History*, 381. David Yulee gave up his senatorial seat on a January 1861. In the previous month, he had written Florida Railroad directors Finegan and Call about seizing the Pensacola forts and naval yard, a communication later viewed as treasonous.

4. Gannon, *Florida*, 42.

5. Morrison, *The Oxford History*, 402.

6. P. Johnson, *A History of the American People*, 476, 479.

7. Black, *The Railroads*, 3.

8. Morrison, *The Oxford History*, 459.

9. Davis, *The Civil War*, 152; Turner, *A Short History of Florida Railroads*, 34.

10. *New York Times*, 15 March 1862. Whether the train actually advanced over the drawbridge to the mainland, as most sources claim, is a matter of conjecture, for the same article further states that a party of "twenty Negroes" went to the bridge and hauled back the locomotive "pulling it all the way with ropes." On 17 March, that newspaper published a letter of fleet commander Commodore DuPont to a U.S. senator in Washington, D.C., that the victory at Fernandina was "most complete in results" and that *Ottawa* had pursued the train for a mile and a half. After shelling the train, the passengers "rushed out into the woods, one of your late members among them, Mr. Yulee! He passed the night under a bush and I hope he had a blanket, as it was the coolest of the season."

11. Ibid.

12. Turner, *A Short History of Florida Railroads*, 35; Clarke, "The Florida Railroad," 183.

13. Clarke, "The Florida Railroad," 182.

14. Ibid., 184.

15. Ibid., 185; *New York Times*, 25 June 1866.

16. Davis, *The Civil War*, 157.

17. Bathe, *The St. Johns Railroad*, 35.

18. Turner, *A Short History of Florida Railroads*, 35–36; Black, *The Railroads of the Confederacy*, 201–2; Shofner, *Nor Is It Over Yet*, 255; Bowden, *Iron Horse in the Pinelands*, 13.

19. Shofner and Rogers, "Confederate Railroad Construction," 218.

20. Black, *The Railroads of the Confederacy*, 208.

21. Shofner and Rogers, "Confederate Railroad Construction," 219.

22. Black, *The Railroads of the Confederacy*, 211; D. S. Johnson, "The Railroads of Florida," 34–37.

23. Black, *The Railroads of the Confederacy*, 212; Davis, *The Civil War*, 193–96.

24. Black, *The Railroads of the Confederacy*, 212–13. The Atlantic and Gulf Railroad, which built the Georgia side of the Live Oak Branch, linked Savannah with Bainbridge via Jesup, Lawton, and Thomasville. In 1879, said company was acquired by Henry Plant, it being his first railway purchase.

25. Davis, *The Civil War*, 276–93.

26. Ibid., 324.

27. Boyer, *The Oxford Companion to United States History*, 653.

28. Fish, *The Restoration of the Southern Railroads*, 3–6.

29. *New York Times*, 1 August 1865.

30. D. S. Johnson, "The Florida Railroad," 294.

31. Davis, *The Civil War*, 335. Provisional Florida governor Marvin wrote to President Johnson for Yulee's pardon: "He is President of a railroad company whose interests are suffering for want of his supervision and care." Davis claims that if embittered northern politicians had gotten their way, Yulee and his colleagues would have been tried and executed for treason. Yulee was released from prison in early 1866.

32. *Gainesville New Era*, 9 March 1867.

33. D. S. Johnson, "The Florida Railroad," 295.

34. Vose was a partner of Vose, Livingston & Company, a New York firm that imported iron rail from abroad and that supplied most of the rail for Yulee's Florida Railroad. Yulee's board compensated Vose with promissory notes (worth $130,000) and 195 company bonds ($195,000). Unable to redeem either, Vose sued for the notes in New York on 25 October 1867; and he brought suit for the bonds in federal court, in the Northern District of Florida, on 3 November 1870. Vose accused the IIF trustees of committing "waste, fraud and misappropriation." The courts lent a sympathetic ear to Vose and issued an injunction, whereupon the IIF was immediately placed into the hands of Receiver Aristides Doggett, who froze the fund's assets. Not until 1881 was the IIF able to resume business, a prerequisite being a full settlement with the Vose heirs.

35. *The Florida Railroad* pamphlet, n.d., n.p., 13–14. Copy in Dodd Room, Florida State Library. See also the *Commercial and Financial Chronicle*, 25 January 1873.

36. Veenendaal, *Slow Train*, 117–18; D. S. Johnson, "The Florida Railroad," 296.

37. Hallock, *Camp Life in Florida*, 118.

38. J. King, *The Great South*, 387–88.

39. Hildredth, "Railroads Out of Pensacola," 410; *Pensacola Commercial*, 26 February 1868.

40. Bowden, *Iron Horse in the Pinelands*, 13.

41. Shofner, *Nor Is It Over Yet*, 255. The Pensacola Railroad absorbed the rights and privileges of the Pensacola and Louisville Railroad. Martin Sullivan was cofounder of

the Alger-Sullivan Lumber Company in Century, Florida. As is discussed in chapter 5, the Sullivans sold their line to the Louisville and Nashville Railroad.

42. Pettengill, *The Story of the Florida Railroads*, 40.

43. *Commercial and Financial Chronicle*, 23 December 1865.

44. D. S. Johnson, "The Railroads of Florida," 41.

45. Herbert, *Why the Solid South?* 79.

46. *Jacksonville Florida Union*, 2 May 1868.

47. *Reports of the President*, 4–19; *Jacksonville Florida Union*, 15 July 1869; Shofner, *Nor Is It Over Yet*, 112–13; Bailey, "Alabama and West Florida Annexation," 219–32.

48. Ibid, 113.

49. The Western Division of the Western North Carolina Railroad had been empowered to construct lines between Asheville and Paint Rock, and from Asheville to Ducktown on the Tennessee border.

50. C. K. Brown, "The Florida Investments," 275.

51. Fenlon, "The Notorious Swepson-Littlefield Fraud," 242.

52. Wallace, *Carpetbag Rule*, 102.

53. Daniels, *Prince of Carpetbaggers*, 240; Fenlon, "The Notorious Swepson-Littlefield Fraud," 245–46.

54. C. K. Brown, "The Florida Investments," 278; Davis, *The Civil War*, 660. The Jacksonville, Pensacola and Mobile Railroad operated the Florida Central Railroad from June 1870 to October 1871. The latter was still under a ninety-nine-year lease to the Pensacola and Georgia Railroad, which became the Tallahassee Railroad in June 1869.

55. Davis, *The Civil War*, 663.

56. C. K. Brown, "The Florida Investments," 282.

57. Davis, *The Civil War*, 662; Daniels, *Prince of Carpetbaggers*, 244.

58. Veenendaal, *Slow Train*, 116–18. This superb work not only recounts the sordid tale from the Dutch perspective but provides valuable insights into many Dutch investment houses. Readers will recall that Dutch investors were first scammed by the Bank of Pensacola during territorial days.

59. *Tallahassee Sentinel*, 17 January 1872.

Chapter 5. An Extraordinary Quartet

1. Rerick, *Memoirs of Florida*, 348–52.

2. Ibid., 349.

3. Dovell, "The Railroads and the Public Lands," 237.

4. Iatarola and Gephart, *Tacony*, 14; Silcox, *A Place to Live*, 27–35. The Disston Saw Works, which employed some six thousand workers in its heyday, was located in Tacony village.

5. Dovell, "The Railroads and the Public Lands," 238; Bramson, "A Tale of Three Henrys," 117–19. Sanford, who came from an old and wealthy Connecticut family, was Lincoln's minister to Belgium.

6. Abbey, *Florida*, 351.

7. Dovell, "The Railroads and the Public Lands," 245.

8. "English Purchase in Florida," *New York Times*, 21 December 1881. The Reed and Wertheim syndicate formed the Florida Land and Mortgage Company with offices in Jacksonville and London with the aim of disposing their holdings to English and Dutch immigrants. The article reveals that Sir Edward was competing against Disston for the same 4 million acre purchase and actually was in Florida while the negotiations with Disston were unfolding. Possibly Bloxham leveraged this fact to motivate Disston. The investment groups represented by Reed and Wertheim were already invested in Florida railroads.

9. Williamson, "William D. Chipley," 333; Bowden, *Iron Horse in the Pinelands*, 17–21.

10. *Annual Report, Louisville and Nashville Railroad, 1879–80*, 17–19. The L & N officially absorbed Sullivan's road in October 1880. See also the *Commercial and Financial Chronicle*, 18 September 1880. During 1881–82, the Pensacola Railroad Division of the L & N had gross earnings of $180,834 and expenses of $145,490. Of the first amount, $120,418 had been created by freight traffic, $53,608 from passengers, while the difference came from mail and express.

11. Hildreth, "Railroads Out of Pensacola," 413. Pettengill claims 2,202,623 acres were ultimately conveyed to the Pensacola & Atlantic Railroad (*The Story of the Florida Railroads*, 45). Florida was not the only state to gift land to railroads. Railroad companies got one-fourth of the states of Minnesota and Washington; one-fifth of Wisconsin, Iowa, Kansas, North Dakota, and Montana; one-seventh of Nebraska; one-eighth of California; and one-ninth of Louisiana. The biggest corporate recipient was James Jerome Hill's Northern Pacific Railroad, with 44 million acres. In all, the United States deeded some 242,000 square miles to railroads in the nineteenth century, a territory larger than Germany or France (P. Johnson, *A History of the American People*, 532–36).

12. *Commercial and Financial Chronicle*, 20 August 1881.

13. Shofner, *Jackson County*, 344.

14. J. D. Smith, "The Construction of the P & A," 22.

15. Pettengill, *The Story of Florida Railroads*, 118–19.

16. Turner, *A Short History*, 85–86. The L & N's route from Pollard, Alabama, into Pensacola became known as the company's Pensacola Division.

17. Klein, *History of the Louisville & Nashville Railroad*, 284–85. Export Coal Company was succeeded by Gulf Transit Company in 1895, a wholly owned subsidiary of the L & N. The latter acquired Pensacola Trading Company, a British concern, which operated two steel screw steamers: *August Belmont* and the *E. O. Saltmarsh*. The facilities at Pensacola were enlarged to accommodate nineteen vessels. Its Tarragona Street Wharf in Pensacola, which boasted a 500,000-bushel grain elevator, sat aside the Commandancia Street Wharf, which had a long two-story warehouse. In 1915, the L & N disposed of the trading company and its remaining vessels.

18. Bowden, *Iron Horse in the Pinelands*, 31–36.

19. A slender folder about Sir Edward, containing the secret telegraphic code and some real estate correspondence, can be found at the Florida Bureau of Archives and Record Management. Reed's code name was *Carnage*.

20. *Oxford Dictionary of National Biography*, 173.

21. Ibid.; *Times* (London), 1 December 1906.

22. *The Corporate History*, 59.

23. *New York Times*, 28 December 1881.

24. *The Corporate History*, 67–68; Prince, *Seaboard Air Line Railway*, 74–76; Veenendaal, *Slow Train*, 89–90.

25. Stover, *The Railroads of the South*, 141; *New York Times*, 2 March 1884.

26. Turner, *A Short History of Florida Railroads*, 53.

27. Veenendaal, *Slow Train*, 76, 89–90.

28. Smyth, *The Life of Henry Bradley Plant*, 1.

29. Turner and Bramson, *The Plant System*, 16.

30. Reynolds, *Henry Plant*, 89–90.

31. Bramson, "A Tale of Three Henrys," 117–19.

32. Plant Investment Company Papers.

33. Turner and Bramson, *The Plant System*, 27–29; Hoffman, *Building a Great Railroad*, 57–58.

34. Turner, *A Short History of Florida Railroads*, 58.

35. Turner and Bramson, *The Plant System*, 31–32; Webber, *The Eden of the South*, 5.

36. The Live Oak and Rowland's Bluff Railroad carried the Plant project from the Georgia state line down to New Boston, while the Live Oak, Tampa & Charlotte Harbor advanced it beyond to Newnansville and Gainesville.

37. *Florida Times Union*, 22 March 1886.

38. For a superb account of how the railroad changed the Peace River valley, consult chap. 17 of Canter Brown Jr.'s *Florida's Peace River Frontier*. Equally informative are the following two works by Vernon E. Peeples: "Charlotte Harbor Division," 291–302; and "Trabue, Alias Punta Gorda," 141–47.

39. Reynolds, *Henry Plant*, 147–57.

40. Turner and Bramson, *The Plant System*, 61–70.

41. For a full account of Demens, consult Albert Parry's *Full Steam Ahead*!

42. Stover, *The Railroads of the South*, 268–70.

43. Holbrook, *The Age of the Moguls*, 65–67.

44. Cherow, *Titan*, 112.

45. Braden, *The Architecture of Leisure*, 135–200; Graham, "Henry M. Flagler's Hotel Ponce de Leon," 97–111.

46. Bramson, *Speedway to Sunshine*, 17–30.

47. Ibid.

48. Akin, *Flagler*, 136.

49. Turner and Bramson, *The Plant System*, 67–69.

50. Braden, *The Architecture of Leisure*, 208–29. This work recounts in wonderful detail the Florida hotels of both Flagler and Henry Plant.

51. Papers of James Edmundson Ingraham, 1850–1924.

52. Bramson, *Speedway to Sunshine*, 57.

53. Cherow, *Titan*, 344–46.

54. Standiford, *Last Train to Paradise*; see also Gallagher's, *Florida's Great Ocean Railway*; and Zeiller's, *The Florida Keys Overseas Railway*.

55. The Great Southern Railway had the backing of many dignitaries and persons of wealth who were keen to build a rail line from Millen, Georgia (junction of the Central of Georgia Railroad), through Florida to Turtle Bay, thence to Key West. Chartered in Florida in February 1870, the railway had a capitalization of $10 million, and the incorporators included Florida governor Harrison Reed. A hardbound book describing the project at length was eventually released (*Great Southern Railway: A Trunk Line between the North and the Tropics* [New York: Wm. Hickok, 1878]). Construction was attempted in a few places, but the undertaking eventually failed.

56. Hoffman, *Building a Great Railroad*, 143; Turner, *A Short History of Florida Railroads*, 75.

57. Patterson, "The Florida East Coast Extension," 1036–43; Willing, "Florida's Overseas Railroad," 287–302.

58. Ibid.

59. "Big Morgan Loan to Flagler Road," *New York Times*, 22 June 1909. Two other New York banks aided Morgan's firm with the underwriting: First National and the National City. Flagler himself took $2 million of the so-called Firsts, while the Morgan syndicate sold almost half to their largest customers, including New York Life, Equitable, Prudential, and the Mutual Life insurance companies. As noted in the text, the issue was secured with a lien upon all existing and future lines the railway owned. In the mid-1920s, the FEC would issue First & Refunding 5 Percent Bonds ("F&R 5s"), which were also secured with a first lien. As later discussed, which bondholder class had the superior claim on assets would give rise to court rulings, endless litigation, and an eventual takeover.

60. "Over-Sea R.R. Opening," *New York Times*, 23 January 1912.

Chapter 6. Regulation, System Builders, and Federal Control

1. A. D. Chandler Jr., *The Visible Hand*, 171.

2. Rerick, *Memoirs of Florida*, 362.

3. *Laws of Florida, 1887*, 118–26.

4. Ferguson, *State Regulation of Railroads*, 154.

5. A. D. Chandler Jr., *The Visible Hand*, 142.

6. Long, "Florida's First Railroad Commission," 249.

7. *Florida Times-Union*, 19 May and 6 June 1891.

8. Akin, *Flagler*, 194–95; Danese, "Railroads, Farmers and Senatorial Politics," 146.

9. Ferguson, *State Regulation of Railroads*, 157.

10. Proctor, *Napoleon Bonaparte Broward*, 78. The two companies within Florida that Broward cited were the Florida Central and Peninsular and the Jacksonville, Tampa & Key West railroads; the two outside the state were the Savannah, Florida & Western and the East Tennessee, Virginia and Georgia railroads. The corporations naturally denied the charges. In 1894, Broward also stated: "I don't blame the railroads for taking all they can get, and making the long haul every time, if the people will stand heedlessly by, with their mouths open, and be treated this way. I believe that nothing short of just and proper legislation will do us any good" (Proctor, Napoleon Broward, 152).

11. *Laws of Florida, 1897,* 82–96. William Bloxham had returned to the governorship by this time and, for whatever reason, allowed the new commission act to become law without his signature (*New York Times,* 10 May 1897).

12. *Railway Age,* 4 May 1897.

13. Ferguson, *State Regulation of Railroads,* 182.

14. *First Annual Report of the Florida Central and Peninsular Ry. Co., 1890,* 8–9.

15. Ibid., 11.

16. Murdock, *Outline History,* 8–9. Chartered in 1881, the Tavares, Orlando and Atlantic had been empowered to construct a line east of Tavares to Titusville, on the east coast. The 32 miles between Tavares and Orlando opened for traffic in 1884. A majority of company bonds were owned by the F C & P, and failure to pay bond interest prompted a foreclosure sale. The East Florida and Atlantic Railroad, chartered 1891, was a consolidation of the 6-mile Orlando and Winter Park Railway (chartered 1886; opened 1889) and the 10-mile Osceola and Lake Jesup Railway (chartered 1889; opened 1890). When opened, the Osceola and Lake Jesup was leased to the Orlando and Winter Park Railway.

17. To extend its presence beyond Savannah to Columbia, South Carolina, the Florida Central & Peninsular leased the South Bound Railroad for ninety-nine years in October 1893.

18. Surpassing the Flying Cracker in elegance was the company's jointly operated New York & Florida Limited, which ran between New York and St. Augustine in the winter season. The Pennsylvania Railroad hauled the latter between New York and Washington, D.C.; the Southern Railway handled it to Columbia, South Carolina; the Florida Central & Peninsular did the honors to Jacksonville; while the Florida East Coast Railway brought the famed consist into historic St. Augustine. Advertised as the "Finest Train in the World," it was comprised of Pullman compartment and drawing-room cars, a library and observation car, an elegant diner, as well as sleeping cars. The southbound edition left New York in the late morning and arrived in St. Augustine early the following afternoon.

19. *Sixth Annual Report, Florida Central and Peninsular Railroad, 1895,* 5.

20. Grismer, *The Story of Sarasota,* 135. The Sarasota-Bradenton corridor had previously been served by the Arcadia, Gulf Coast & Lakeland Railroad, a comical operation nicknamed the "Slow & Wobbly" owing to its poor track. Opened in 1892, the railroad was reorganized the following year, though the Florida, Peninsular & Gulf fared no better. It later flickered out of existence. See Turner, *Railroads of Southwest Florida;* and Sulzer, *Ghost Railroads of Sarasota County.*

21. Tedder, "Seaboard's Covington Subdivision," 14–25.

22. Sulzer, *Ghost Railroads,* 22–24.

23. Prince, *Seaboard Air Line Railway,* 92–96; R. W. Johnson, *Through the Heart of the South,* 51–52.

24. Hoffman, *Building a Great Railroad,* 1–11; Dozier, *A History of the Atlantic Coast Line,* 1–9.

25. For a superb account of the father and son, consult William R. Johnston's *William and Henry Walters, The Reticent Collectors.*

26. *Annual Reports of the Atlantic Coast Line Railroad, 1903–1919*; Hoffman, *Building a Great Railroad*, 136–40.

27. Turner and Bramson, *The Plant System*, 122–23. Erwin, an 1874 graduate of Connecticut's Trinity College, was greatly admired by Henry Walters. After the Plant System purchase, Walters named Erwin president of the Atlantic Coast Line Railroad, while Henry Plant's son, Morton Freeman Plant, became just a director. Erwin died at his game farm at Fenwick, Connecticut, in 1905, at age fifty-two.

28. Hoffman, *Building a Great Railroad*, 166–68.

29. Turner, *Railroads of Southwest Florida*, 33–34.

30. *Glades County, Florida History*, 43.

31. Dixon and Parmelee, *War Administrations*, 198.

Chapter 7. Vignettes

1. Florida Railroad Commission, *The Railroads of Florida*, 2–4.

2. Lawson, *Logging Railroads of Alabama*, 137–40. The company was incorporated on 7 June 1900 by General Russell Alger of Grand Rapids, Michigan, and Martin Sullivan of Pensacola. (Alger contributed $1 million in cash and Sullivan a like amount in standing timber and other assets.) At its peak, the mill at Century manufactured 125,000 board feet of dimensional lumber in a ten-hour day.

3. Turner, *Florida Railroads in the 1920s*, 81–82.

4. Lawson, *Logging Railroads of Alabama*, 163–64.

5. Paxton, Florida, was also served by the Central of Georgia Railroad.

6. T. Smith, *The History of Bay County*, 2, 13, 59; Sistrunk, "The Atlanta & St. Andrews Bay," 40–47.

7. Records of German-American Lumber are located at Strozier Library, Special Collections, Florida State University Libraries.

8. Clark, "Rich Uncle Railroad," 6, 8.

9. Porter, *The Lives of St. Joseph*, 125, 129, 133.

10. *Apalachicola Times*, 7 May 1910. In the early 1960s, the former main line between Franklin and Apalachicola was abandoned for lack of business.

11. An 1896 booklet describing the Clark Syndicate Companies can be found in the Dodd Room of the Florida State Library.

12. The route was also eventually pushed north of Bainbridge to Richland.

13. Hensley's outstanding Web site (www.taplines.net) furnishes much valuable information about the logging and short-line railways of Florida. Greenville, Florida, was also home to the Greenville Southern Railway, incorporated in 1907 and owned by Greenville Yellow Pine Company. Supplies for its lumber camps at Fowler and Myrick were carried over the 10-mile line along with pine logs. Sawmill employees actually ran the railroad! The operation lasted until the First World War.

14. Records of West Yellow Pine Lumber Company and Madison Southern Railway are located at Special Collections, Florida State University Libraries.

15. "Jacksonville Terminal, Mr. Wilkes, and Me," *Trains Magazine*, June 1978.

16. *Railway Age*, 2 January 1920. In all, some $3.5 million was spent on building the terminal station, yards, and adjoining facilities.

17. *New York Times*, 16 December 1938.

18. Pettengill, *The Story of the Florida Railroads*, 126–27.

19. Hilton, *American Narrow Gauge Railroads*, 371.

20. Cross, "The Tavares and Gulf Railroad," 39.

21. Shappee, "The Celestial Railroad," 122.

22. For an introductory overview of the famed Bone Valley, see Jerry Pinkepank's, "Wet Rock, Dry Rock, and the Seaboard," *Trains Magazine*, October 1984.

23. Blakey, *The Florida Phosphate Industry*, 23.

24. Ibid. Another source claims $1,750,000 (Gibson, *Boca Grande*, 119). Hull then exited the Peace River scene and began mining for pebble phosphate, of the land variety, near Mulberry, naming his prospect camp "Prairie." Within a decade, he was the biggest phosphate producer in Florida, shipping over 500,000 tons annually. In 1899, Hull sold out to the International Agricultural Corporation for $8 million.

25. Turner, *Railroads of Southwest Florida*, 43–54; Hoeckel and VanItallie, *Boca Grande*, 27–50; Fischer, *Boca Grande, Once a Railroad Town*, 73.

26. Schwieterman, *When the Railroad Leaves Town*, 21–24.

Chapter 8. The Glorious 1920s

1. Turner, *Venice in the 1920s*, 19–38.

2. Powell, "Simply Staggering! Says Florida," 18.

3. Shelby, "Florida Frenzy," 177–78.

4. Powell, "Simply Staggering! Says Florida," 19.

5. Mileage figures are extracted from the 1920 report of the Florida Railroad Commission, 248–49. Aside from the Big Three, the carriers included the Andalusia, Florida & Gulf (20 miles); Apalachicola Northern (99); Atlanta & St. Andrews Bay Railway (68); Birmingham, Columbus & St. Andrews (38); Charlotte Harbor & Northern (112); East and West Coast (50); the Fellsmere Railroad (11); Florida Central & Gulf (20); Georgia & Florida (18); Georgia, Florida & Alabama (84); Georgia, Southern & Florida (162); Gulf, Florida & Alabama (45); Jacksonville Terminal Company, (4); Live Oak, Perry & Gulf (83); Louisville and Nashville (246); Madison Southern (7); Marianna & Blountstown (44); Ocala Southwestern (23); Ocklawaha Valley (54); Pelham & Havana (6); Pensacola, Mobile & New Orleans (31); Port St. Joe Dock & Terminal (2); South Georgia (44); St. Johns River Terminal Company (10); Tampa & Gulf Coast (86); Tampa & Jacksonville (56); Tampa Northern (62); Tampa Union Station (2); and Tavares & Gulf Railroad (37).

6. *Railway Age*, 19 November 1927.

7. Ibid.

8. *Railway Age*, 28 November 1925.

9. Turner, *Florida Railroads in the 1920s*, 7–8.

10. Factual material for this chapter segment has been extracted from the annual reports of the Florida East Coast Railway, 1920–31. See also Bramson, *Speedway to Sunshine*, 99–108. The specific branches ran between South Jacksonville and Mayport (24 miles); East Palatka to the west end of the Palatka Bridge over the St. Johns River (1.8); San Mateo Junction to San Manteo proper (2.8); Ormond to the Ormond Hotel

(1.7); New Smyrna to Orange City Junction (27); Titusville to Enterprise Junction (35); and West Palm Beach to Palm Beach (1.5). The longest, however, was the 139-mile Okeechobee Branch, which descended New Smyrna for Okeechobee.

11. The H. M. Flagler Trust was to terminate five years after Henry Flagler's passing. However, the trustees could extend the time frame an additional five years if necessary, which they did. William Rand Kenan Jr., an industrialist by reputation who codiscovered calcium carbide, came to Flagler's attention at a young age and eventually carried out special assignments for the Flagler System. In 1916, Mary Kenan Flagler married Judge Robert Bingham of Louisville, Kentucky. Before the wedding, Bingham signed a prenuptial agreement renouncing his half interest in Mary's huge estate, which one day he might be entitled to receive under Kentucky law. Shortly after Mary died, accusations surfaced that she had been murdered with drugs. Her body was exhumed and an autopsy performed, but the pathology report was never made pubic, and no criminal prosecution resulted. The H. M. Flagler Trust finally expired in June 1923, whereupon its assets were transferred to the twenty-one-year trust established under Mary's will for the maintenance of the Florida East Coast Railway and hotel properties.

12. Campbell, *Across Fortune's Tracks*, 210–11. Dr. Campbell's absorbing biography was the source for some of the information in the previous note.

13. In 1922, the Coast Line began double-tracking its 661-mile main line (Richmond to Jacksonville), which it completed in December 1925. Automatic block signals were also installed as well as 100-pound-to-the-yard steel rail.

14. Hoffman, *Building a Great Railroad*, 210–11. Readers desiring comprehensive information about the myriad trains that serviced Florida from the Midwest should consult R. Lyle Key Jr.'s *Midwest Florida Sunliners*.

15. Turner, *Railroads of Southwest Florida*, 55–88; Turner, *A Short History of Florida Railroads*, 77–90.

16. "The Perry Cutoff: ACL's West Coast Gateway to Florida" is an informative, fact-filled account of the Perry Cutoff by railroad historian Russell Tedder. The cutoff itself, 166 miles in length, stretched northward from Dunnellon, Florida, to Thomasville, Georgia. To perfect the route, the Coast Line had to construct 35 miles of new track between Perry and Monticello along with 18 miles from Thonotosassa to Richland (Vitis Junction). The remaining portion of the route existed.

17. *Ninety-second Annual Report*, 19.

18. *Annual Report of the Seaboard Air Line Railway Company for the Fiscal Year Ending December 31, 1924*, 6–7. Other factual information for this chapter segment was condensed from the company's 1925–30 annual reports.

19. "Seaboard Air Line R. R. Builds Florida Extension," *Railway Review Magazine*, 1 August 1925.

20. Ibid., 168; "These Stations Fit into the Scenery," *Railway Review Magazine*, 5 December 1925.

21. Shrady, *Orange Blossom Special*, 14. The train had been christened in Winter Haven by several "fair damsels" who poured orange blossom perfume over the pilot of the lead locomotive.

22. *Wall Street Journal*, 26 February 1925. In railway parlance, an "air line" route meant the shortest, most direct path between the beginning and ending terminals.

23. Turner, "The Seaboard's Fort Myers–Naples Extension," 14–29.

24. Turner, *A Milestone Celebration*, 17–178.

25. Ibid., 33.

26. Turner, *Florida Railroads in the 1920s*, 81–88.

Chapter 9. Pursuing Traffic

1. The so-called Northern-class type locomotives, which had a 4–8–4 wheel arrangement, arrived in 1938. Built by Baldwin, they boasted 80-inch-tall driving wheels, weighed 460,270 pounds, and cost nearly $159,000 apiece. Despite their prodigious appetites for coal and water, the behemoths could wheel twenty heavyweight Pullman cars between New York and Jacksonville at over 60 mph.

2. Factual information for this chapter segment was extracted from the annual reports of the Seaboard Air Line Railway for the years 1929–39.

3. Campbell, *Across Fortune's Tracks*, 238–39, 242, 249–54; Danese, *Claude Pepper and Ed Ball*, 157–60. Most of the railway's stock was held in the Bingham Trust, which had been established for Mary Lily Flagler Bingham, the third wife of FEC founder Henry Flagler. Mary's brother, William Kenan Jr., along with another trustee, controlled the trust, whose assets included practically all the railway's stock. (Kenan was also chairman and president of the railway.) William Kenan allowed a friendly suit to be brought against the railway by Standard Oil of Kentucky, paving the way for the receivership. Kenan and the railway's general counsel, Scott Loftin, were then named receivers and retained control. When news of the action broke, the large owners of the First & Refunding 5 Percent Bonds brought foreclosure proceedings for nonpayment of interest; however, they were unable to appoint receivers of their own choosing.

4. Standiford, *Last Train to Paradise*, 225–54; Bramson, *Speedway to Sunshine*, 118–19. See also "The Florida Hurricane," *Railway Age*, 7 March 1936.

5. Gunning, "The Port St. Joe Route," 57. Du Pont died in 1935, and Ball became trustee of the du Pont estate. St. Joe Paper was formed in 1936, the mill was begun the following year, and the first run of paper was produced in 1938. St. Joe Lumber & Export Company was formed to harvest area timberlands and perform switching chores at the docks.

6. Hoffman, *Building A Great Railroad*, 243–49.

7. Turner, *Railroads of Southwest Florida*, 91. The cypress logs were processed at the company's millhouse in Perry, Florida, some 400 miles from the self-contained company town of Copeland. An interesting article on the company's operations in Collier County appeared in the 29 May 1954 *Saturday Evening Post*.

8. *One Hundred and Sixteenth Annual Report*, 14.

9. Factual material for this chapter segment was extracted from annual reports of the Seaboard for the years 1940–49.

10. See also Stoesen, "Road from Receivership," 132–56.

11. *Railway Age*, 25 December 1948.

12. Factual information for this period was extracted from the annual reports of

the Atlanta & St. Andrews Bay Railway for the years 1940–51. For additional information about the bus subsidiary, see "Short Line Blazes Service Trails," *Railway Age*, 26
April 1941. For the postwar rebuilding program, see "Progressive Short Line Rejuve-
nated," *Railway Age*, 2 August 1947. Passenger train service lasted until 15 July 1956.
Piggyback service on the Bay Line began in 1962. In 1971, the Bay Line opened a 7-mile
branch between Campbellton and Graceville to serve a peanut processor and lumber
facility.

13. Hoffman, *Building A Great Railroad*, 265–68, 279.

14. Ibid., 281–82.

15. Bramson, *Speedway to Sunshine*, 149–53; Danese, *Claude Pepper and Ed Ball*,
230–39; Altman, "In the Public Interest?" 32–47.

16. Griffin, *Seaboard Coast Line & Family Lines Railroad*, 1–13. See also "Seaboard
Coast Line: Anatomy of a Merger," *Railway Age*, 24 July 1967; "ACL + SAL = SCL,"
Trains Magazine, October 1964; along with Warren and Clark's, *Seaboard Coast Line in
Florida*.

17. H. T. Watkins, *Just Call Me Hays*, 178–93.

Chapter 10. Today's Players

1. *Florida Rail Plan*, ES–1.

2. Of the 117 million tons moved, 43 million tons were inbound (interstate traffic
terminating in Florida); 15 million were outbound tons (interstate traffic originating
in Florida); while local tonnage (intrastate traffic) amounted to 57 million. Also transported were 2 million tons of through traffic, that is, traffic that neither originated
nor terminated in Florida but merely passed through the state (*Florida Rail Plan*,
2004, ES–4).

3. Ibid., ES–10 to ES–13.

4. A single, trilevel auto carrier rail car of today can accommodate roughly ten to
fifteen new vehicles.

5. *Florida Rail Plan*, ES–15 to ES–16.

6. *Railroad Facts*, 3. The Surface Transportation Board (STB) adjusts the revenue
thresholds annually for inflation. Further, the STB calls Regional railroads Class II
carriers, while Local railroads are referred to as Class III operators.

7. *CSX Corporation 2006 Annual Report*, 1–9.

8. Of special note is Scott Hartley's "Big Business in the Bone Valley," *Trains Magazine*, June 2005.

9. *Norfolk Southern Corporation Annual Report 2006*, pt. 1 of 10–K.

10. *Florida Rail Plan*, 3–14.

11. Florida East Coast Industries 2006 Annual Report, 10–K statement, 33.

12. According to the FECI 10–K statement for 2004, the Alfred I. du Pont Testamentary Trust owned 11,469,273 shares, or 31.2 percent, of all FECI common stock
outstanding.

13. Ibid., 33–36.

14. *Rail America Annual Report 2005*, 1–14.

15. *Genesee & Wyoming Annual Report 2006*, 1–10. Mortimer B. Fuller III acquired a
controlling interest in the G & W in 1977. Fuller's great-grandfather founded the Gen-

esee & Wyoming Railroad Company in 1899, a 14-mile line serving the salt industry in upstate New York. Today, the company has railroad interests in the United States, Canada, Mexico, Australia, and Bolivia.

16. L. King, "First Coast's First Days," 34–39. First Coast and the Talleyrand help form the G & W's Rail Link Region, while the Apalachicola Northern and Bay Line Railroads are part of its Southern Region.

17. *Trains Magazine*, July 2005, 19. Georgia and Florida RailNet was owned by North American RailNet based in Bedford, Texas.

18. Dressler, "The Seminole Gulf Railway," 38–45.

19. *Fort Myers News-Press*, 3 January 1988; Turner, *Railroads of Southwest Florida*, 112.

20. Turner, *A Short History of Florida Railroads*, 151; Turner, *Railroads of Southwest Florida*, 112.

21. Oates, "Ghosts of the Past," 4–11, 21–26.

22. *National Railroad Passenger Corporation, Consolidated Financial Statements,* 2006, 3.

23. Orenstein, "Miami Tri-Rail," 54–59.

24. *Florida Rail Plan, 2004*, Passenger Rail Component, ES–11.

25. Ibid.

Bibliography

Abbey, Kathryn Trimmer. *Florida, Land of Change*. Chapel Hill: University of North Carolina Press, 1941.

Akin, Edward N. *Flagler, Rockefeller Partner and Florida Baron*. Gainesville: University Press of Florida, 1991.

Altman, Burton. "In the Public Interest? Ed Ball and the FEC Railway War." *Florida Historical Quarterly*, 64, no. 1 (July 1985): 32–47.

Annual Report of the President and Directors of the Louisville and Nashville Railroad Company for the Fiscal Year Commencing July 1, 1879 and Ending June 30, 1880. Louisville: Courier Journal, 1880.

Annual Report of the Seaboard Air Line Railway Company for the Fiscal Year Ending December 31, 1924. Portsmouth, Va.: Seaboard Air Line Railway Company, 1924.

Annual Reports of the Atlantic Coast Line Railroad, 1903–1919. Wilmington: Atlantic Coast Line Railroad Company.

Armstrong, John H. *The Railroad: What It Is, What It Does*. Omaha: Simmons-Boardman Books, 1990.

Articles of Agreement between the Tallahassee Rail Road Company and John D. and William Gray, May 16, 1835. Copy in Dodd Room, Florida State Library.

Articles of Agreement of Contract Entered June 11, 1855 between David L. Yulee, President of the Florida Railroad Company, and Joseph Finnegan & Company of the State of Florida. Box 146, Florida Railroad Company Papers, Special Collections, Florida State University Libraries.

Bailey, Hugh C. "Alabama and West Florida Annexation." *Florida Historical Quarterly* 35 (July 1956–April 1957): 219–32.

Bathe, Greville. *The St. Johns Railroad, 1858 to 1895*. Philadelphia: Allen, Lane and Scott, 1958.

Black, Robert C., III. *The Railroads of the Confederacy*. Chapel Hill: University of North Carolina Press, 1952.

Blakey, Arch Frederic. *The Florida Phosphate Industry*. Cambridge: Harvard University Press, 1973.

Bowden, Jesse Earle. *Iron Horse in the Pinelands*. Pensacola: Pensacola Historical Society, 1982.

Boyer, Paul S., senior editor. *The Oxford Companion to United States History*. New York: Oxford University Press, 2001.

Braden, Susan R. *The Architecture of Leisure, The Florida Resort Hotels of Henry Flagler and Henry Plant*. Gainesville: University Press of Florida, 2002.

Bramson, Seth H. *Florida East Coast Railway*. Charleston: Arcadia, 2006.

———. *Speedway to Sunshine, The Story of the Florida East Coast Railway*. Erin, Ontario: Boston Mills Press, 1984.

———. "A Tale of Three Henrys." In special "Florida Theme" issue, *Journal of Decorative and Propaganda Arts*, no. 23. Wolfsonian–Florida International University, 1998.

Brevard, Caroline Mays. *A History of Florida*, 2 vols. Deland: State Historical Association, 1924.

Brown, C. K. "The Florida Investments of George W. Swepson." *North Carolina Historical Review* 5, no. 3 (July 1928): 275–88.

Brown, Canter, Jr. "The Florida, Atlantic and Gulf Central Railroad, 1851–1868." *Florida Historical Quarterly* 69, no. 4 (April 1991): 412–30.

———. *Florida's Peace River Frontier*. Orlando: University of Central Florida Press, 1991. (In chapter 7, Dr. Brown renders a superb account of how railroading affected the Peace River valley.)

Campbell, Walter E. *Across Fortune's Tracks: A Biography of William Rand Kenan, Jr.* Chapel Hill: University of North Carolina Press, 1996.

Castelnau, Comte de. "Essay on Middle Florida, 1837–1838." Translated by Arthur Seymour. *Florida Historical Quarterly* 26, no. 3 (January 1948): 119–217.

Chandler, Alfred D., Jr. *The Visible Hand: The Managerial Revolution in American Business*. Cambridge: Harvard University Press, 1977.

Chandler, David Leon. *Henry Flagler, The Astonishing Life and Times of the Visionary Robber Baron Who Founded Florida*. New York: Macmillan, 1986.

Charters of the Bank of Pensacola and the Alabama, Florida and Georgia Rail Road Company. Philadelphia: John Clark, 1838.

Cherow, Ron. *Titan, The Life of John D. Rockefeller, Sr*. New York: Vintage, 2004.

Clark, Roy G. "Rich Uncle Railroad." *Railroad Magazine* 52, no. 3 (August 1950): 6–8.

Clarke, Robert L. "The Florida Railroad Company in the Civil War." *Journal of Southern History* 19, no. 2 (May 1953): 180–92.

Cleveland, Frederick A., and Fred Wilbur Powell. *Railroad Promotion and Capitalization in the United States*. New York: Longmans, Green, 1909.

Cline, Wayne. *Alabama Railroads*. Tuscaloosa: University of Alabama Press, 1997.

The Corporate History of the Seaboard Air Line Railway Company. Norfolk: Burke and Gregory, 1922.

Cross, Phil. "The Tavares and Gulf Railroad: A History." *National Railway Bulletin* 42, no. 4 (1977): 28–47.

CSX Corporation 2006 Annual Report. Jacksonville: CSX Corporation, 2006.

Cullum, George W. *Biographical Register of the Officers and Graduates of the United States Military Academy at West Point, from March 16, 1802 to January 1, 1850*. New York: J. F. Trow, 1850.

Danese, Tracey E. *Claude Pepper and Ed Ball: Politics, Purpose, and Power*. Gainesville: University Press of Florida, 2000.

———. "Railroads, Farmers and Senatorial Politics: The Florida Railroad Commission in the 1890s." *Florida Historical Quarterly* 75, no. 2 (fall 1996): 146–66.

Daniels, Jonathan. *Prince of Carpetbaggers*. Philadelphia: Lippincott, 1958.

Davis, T. Frederick. *The Civil War and Reconstruction in Florida*. Gainesville: University of Florida Press, 1964.

———. *History of Jacksonville, Florida and Vicinity*. St. Augustine: Florida Historical Society, 1925.

Dixon, Frank, and Julius Parmelee. *War Administrations of the Railways in the United States and Great Britain*. New York: Oxford University Press, 1919.

Dodd, Dorothy. "Railroad Projects in Territorial Florida." Master's thesis, Florida State College for Women, 1929.

Doherty, Herbert J., Jr. "Jacksonville as a Nineteenth-Century Railroad Center." *Florida Historical Quarterly* 58 (March 1966): 373–86.

———. *Richard Keith Call, Southern Unionist*. Gainesville: University of Florida Press, 1961.

Dovell, J. E. "The Railroads and the Public Lands of Florida." *Florida Historical Quarterly* 34, no. 3 (January 1956): 236–58.

Dozier, Howard Douglas. *A History of the Atlantic Coast Line Railroad*. Boston: Houghton Mifflin, 1920.

Dressler, Thomas D., and Douglas A. Dressler. "The Seminole Gulf Railway." *Railfan and Railroad Magazine*, September 1995, 38–45.

East Coast of Florida. St. Augustine: Florida East Coast Railway, 1910.

"Evidence and Documents Reported by the Joint Select Committee, To Whom Was Referred the Charges Contained in the Governor's Message against the Florida Rail Road Company." *Florida Senate Journal, 1858*.

Federal Writers' Project. *Florida. A Guide to the Southernmost State*. New York: Oxford University Press, 1939.

Fenlon, Paul E. "The Florida, Atlantic and Gulf Central Railroad." *Florida Historical Quarterly* 32, no. 2 (October 1953): 71–80.

———. "The Notorious Swepson-Littlefield Fraud: Railroad Financing in Florida (1868–1871)." *Florida Historical Quarterly* 32, no. 4 (April 1954): 231–61.

Ferguson, Maxwell. *State Regulation of Railroads in the South*. New York: Columbia University, 1916.

First Annual Report of the Florida Central and Peninsular Ry. Co. for the Year Ending June 30th, 1890. Jacksonville: Da Costa Printing, 1890.

Fischer, Robert F. *Boca Grande, Once a Railroad Town*. Englewood: self-published, 2004.

Fish, Carl Russell. *The Restoration of the Southern Railroads*. Madison: University of Wisconsin Studies, 1919.

Flint, Henry M. *The Railroads of the United States: Their History and Statistics*. Philadelphia: John Potter, 1868.

Florida East Coast Industries 2006 Annual Report. St. Augustine: Florida East Coast Industries, Inc., 2006.

Florida East Coast Railway 1983 Annual Report. St. Augustine: Florida East Coast Railway, 1983.

Florida Laws, 1860–61, section 8, chapter 1, 138 (no. 45), 84.

Florida Rail Plan, 2004. Chevy Chase: Cambridge Systematics, June 2005. This work contains both a freight and passenger train service component.

Florida Railroad Commission. *The Railroads of Florida*. Compiled by Ralph G. Hill and James H. Pledger; project supervisor, J. W. Stickney Jr. Tallahassee: Florida Railroad Commission, 1939.

Florida Senate Journal, 1852. Appendix, 1–24.

Florida Senate Journal, 1858. "Evidence and Documents Reported by the Joint Select Committee, To Whom Was Referred 'The Charges Contained in the Governor's Message Against the Florida Railroad Company, 1–172.

Frailey, Fred W. "That Cool Railroad in Red-Hot Florida." *Trains Magazine*, October 2007: 32–43.

Gallagher, Dan. *Florida's Great Ocean Railway*. Sarasota, Fla.: Pineapple Press, 2003.

Gannon, Michael. *Florida: A Short History*. Gainesville: University Press of Florida, 2003.

Genesee & Wyoming, Inc. Annual Report 2006. Greenwich: Genesee & Wyoming Corporation, 2006.

Gerstner, Franz Anton Ritter von. *Early American Railroads*. Stanford: Stanford University Press, 1997.

Gibson, Charles Dana. *Boca Grande: A Series of Historical Essays*. Boca Grande: Great Outdoors, 1982.

Glades County Commissioners. *Glades County, Florida History*. Moore Haven, Fla.: Rainbow, 1985.

Gluckman, David. *The Official Rails-to-Trails Conservancy Handbook: Florida*. Guilford: Globe Pequot Press, 2001.

Gonzalez, S. J. "Pensacola: Its Early History." Louisville: Louisville & Nashville Railroad Employees Magazine, August 1926: 7–13.

Goolsby, Larry. *Atlantic Coast Line Passenger Service: The Postwar Years*. Lynchburg: TLC, 1999.

Graham, Thomas. "Henry M. Flagler's Hotel Ponce de Leon." In special "Florida Theme" issue of *Journal of Decorative and Propaganda Arts*. Wolfsonian–Florida International University, 1998.

Grant, H. Roger. *Rails through the Wiregrass: A History of the Georgia & Florida Railroad*. DeKalb: Northern Illinois University Press, 2006.

Griffin, William E., Jr. *Atlantic Coast Line, Standard Railroad of the South*. Lynchburg: TLC, 2001.

———. *Seaboard Air Line Railway: The Route of Courteous Service*. Lynchburg: TLC, 1999.

———. *Seaboard Coast Line & Family Lines Railroad, 1967–1986*. Forest, Va.: TLC, 2004.

Grismer, Karl H. *The Story of Sarasota*. Sarasota: Russell, 1946.

Gunning, James. "The Port St. Joe Route." *Railfan and Railroad Magazine*, July 1993: 54–64.

Hallock, Charles. *Camp Life in Florida: A Handbook for Sportsmen and Settlers*. New York: Forest and Stream, 1876.

Haney, Lewis Henry. *A Congressional History of Railways in the United States to 1850*. Madison: University of Wisconsin, 1908.

Hanna, Alfred Jackson, and Kathryn Abbey Hanna. *Florida's Golden Sands*. New York: Bobbs-Merrill, 1950.

Herbert, Hillary A. *Why the Solid South?* New York: R. H. Woodward, 1890.

Hildreth, Charles W. "Railroads Out of Pensacola, 1833–1883." *Florida Historical Quarterly* 37 (January–April 1959): 397–417.

Hilton, George W. *American Narrow Gauge Railroads*. Stanford, Calif.: Stanford University Press, 1991.

Hoeckel, Marilyn, and Theodore B. VanItallie. *Boca Grande*. Charleston: Arcadia, 2000.

Hoffman, Glenn. *Building a Great Railroad: A History of the Atlantic Coast Line Railroad Company*. Richmond: CSX Corporation, 1998.

Holbrook, Steward H. *The Age of the Moguls*. Garden City, N.Y.: Doubleday, 1953.

Iatarola, Louis M., and Siobhan Gephart. *Tacony*. Charleston: Arcadia, 2000.

Ingraham, James Edmundson. Papers 1850–1924. P. K. Yonge Library of Florida History, Smathers Libraries, University of Florida.

Jensen, Oliver. *The American Heritage History of Railroads in America*. New York: American Heritage, 1975.

Johnson, Dudley S. "The Florida Railroad after the Civil War." *Florida Historical Quarterly* 47, no. 3 (January 1969): 292–309.

———. "Henry Bradley Plant and Florida." *Florida Historical Quarterly* 45, no. 2 (October 1966): 118–31.

———. "The Railroads of Florida (1865–1900)." Ph.D. diss., Florida State University, 1965.

Johnson, Paul. *A History of the American People*. New York: HarperPerennial, 1999.

Johnson, Robert Wayne. *Through the Heart of the South. The Seaboard Air Line Railroad Story*. Erin: Boston Mills Press, 1995.

Johnston, William R. *William and Henry Walters, The Reticent Collectors*. Baltimore: Johns Hopkins University Press, 1999.

Joubert, William. "A History of the Seaboard Air Line Railway Company." Master's thesis, University of Florida, 1935.

Journal of the Florida Legislature, House, 9th sess., 1858.

Key, R. Lyle., Jr. *Midwest Florida Sunliners*. Godfrey: RPC, 1979.

King, Joseph. *The Great South*. Hartford: American Publishing, 1875.

King, Leo. "First Coast's First Days." *Trains Magazine*, June 2006, 34–39.

Klein, Maury. *History of the Louisville & Nashville Railroad*. New York: Macmillan, 1972.

Knetsch, Joe. "Madison Starke Perry vs. David Levy Yulee: The Fight for the Tampa Bay Route." *Sunland Tribune*, no. 22 (1997): 13–23.

Laws of Florida, 1852–53, chap. 483, 6.

Laws of Florida, 1853, chap. 482, 31–38.

Laws of Florida, 1855, chap. 729, no. 120, 16.

Laws of Florida, 1855, chap. 735, no. 125, 26–27.

Laws of Florida, 1887, chap. 3746, no. 66, 118–26.

Laws of Florida, 1897, chap. 4549, no. 35, 82–96.

Laws of the State of Florida, 1854–55, chap. 610, 9–19.

Laws of the State of Florida, 1856, Appendix, no. 3, 41–46.

Lawson, Thomas, Jr. *Logging Railroads of Alabama*. Birmingham: Cabbage Stack, 1997.

Levy Yulee, David. Papers. Box 36, 1861–64, Special and Area Studies Collections, George A. Smathers Libraries, University of Florida.

Long, Durward. "Florida's First Railroad Commission, 1887–1891" *Florida Historical Quarterly*, pt. 1, 42 (October 1963); pt. 2, 42 (January 1964).

Lord, Mills M., Jr. "David Levy Yulee, Statesman and Railroad Builder." Master's thesis, University of Florida, 1940.

Mann, Robert W. *Rails 'Neath the Palms*. Burbank: Darwin, 1983.

McCullough, Mildred White. "Legislative Regulation of Florida Railroads from Statehood to 1897." Master's thesis, Florida State College for Women, 1940.

McGrane, Reginald C. *Foreign Bondholders and American State Debts*. New York: Macmillan, 1935.

McQuigg, Jackson. *Tampa Union Station*. Charleston: Arcadia, 1998.

"Memorial of the Tallahassee Railroad Company, Praying Permission to Construct a Railroad on the Public Lands in Florida," 23rd Cong., 2nd sess., 16 December 1834.

Minutes of Proceedings of the Directors of the Pensacola and Georgia R. R. Company with the Reports of the President and Chief Engineer at Their Annual Meeting at Tallahassee on Wednesday, 31st October, 1855. Tallahassee: Office of the Florida Sentinel, 1855.

Minutes of Proceedings of the Stockholders of the Florida, Atlantic and Gulf Central Railroad Company. Jacksonville: C. Drew's Book and Job Printing Office, 1859.

Minutes of the Board of Trustees of the Internal Improvement Fund. Vol. 1. Florida State Library, Tallahassee.

Morris, Allen, and Joan Perry Morris. *The Florida Handbook*. Tallahassee: Peninsular, 2001.

Morrison, Samuel Eliot. *1789 through Reconstruction*. Vol. 2 of *The Oxford History of the American People*. New York: Penguin, 1994.

Murdock, R. Ken. *Outline History of Central Florida Railroads*. Winter Garden: Central Florida Chapter, National Railway Historical Society, 1999.

National Railroad Passenger Corporation, Consolidated Financial Statements, 2006. Washington, D.C.: Amtrak, 2006.

Ninety-second Annual Report of the Atlantic Coast Line Railroad Company for the Year Ended December 31, 1925. Richmond: Atlantic Coast Line Railroad Company, 1926.

Norfolk Southern Corporation Annual Report 2006. Norfolk: Norfolk Southern Corporation, 2006.

Oates, Joseph L. "Ghosts of the Past." *Lines South Magazine* 22, no. 3 (3rd Quarter 2005): 6–35.

One Hundred and Sixteenth Annual Report of the Atlantic Coast Line Railroad Company for the Year Ended December 31, 1949. Wilmington: Atlantic Coast Line Railroad, 1949.

Orenstein, Jeffrey R. "Miami Tri-Rail." *Trains Magazine*, June 1998, 54–59.

Oxford Dictionary of National Biography. Oxford: Oxford University Press, 2004.

Paisley, Clifton. *The Red Hills of Florida, 1528–1865*. Tuscaloosa: University of Alabama Press, 1989.

Parry, Albert. *Full Steam Ahead!* St. Petersburg: Great Outdoors, 1987.

Patterson, Frank M. "The Florida East Coast Extension." *Railway Age Gazette*, 10 May 1912.

Peeples, Vernon E. "Charlotte Harbor Division of the Florida Southern Railroad." *Florida Historical Quarterly* 58, no. 3, (January 1980): 291–302.

———. "Trabue, Alias Punta Gorda," *Florida Historical Quarterly* 46, no. 2 (October 1967): 141–47.

Pensacola and Georgia Railroad Company, Annual Report of 1855. Tallahassee: Florida Sentinel, 1855.

Pettengill, George W., Jr. *The Story of the Florida Railroads*. Bulletin no. 86. Boston: Railway and Locomotive Historical Society, 1952.

Phillips, Ulrich. *History of Transportation in the Eastern Cotton Belt*. New York: Columbia University Press, 1908.

Plant Investment Company Papers to 1888. Miscellaneous Florida Manuscripts Collection, Finder 00–973, Florida Special and Area Studies, Smathers Library, University of Florida.

Porter, Louise M. *The Lives of St. Joseph*. Port St. Joe: St. Joseph Historical Society, 1975.

Powell, Willis B. "Simply Staggering! Says Florida." *Nations Business*, May, 1925.

Prince, Richard E. *Atlantic Coast Line Railroad*. Bloomington: Indiana University Press, 2000.

———. *Seaboard Air Line Railway*. Bloomington: Indiana University Press, 2000.

Proctor, Samuel. *Napoleon Bonaparte Broward, Florida's Fighting Democrat*. Gainesville: University of Florida Press, 1950.

Rail America Annual Report 2005. Boca Raton: Rail America, 2005.

Railroad Facts, 2006 Edition. Washington, D.C.: Association of American Railroads, 2006.

Railway Age: 28 November 1925, "Enormous Increase in Florida Traffic"; 19 November 1927, "Florida Roads Have Experienced a Phenomenal Development"; 26 November 1927, "Florida Roads Spent Millions in Construction during Boom"; 25 December 1948, "Short Line Pulls Itself out of the Mud."

Report of the Internal Improvement Board of Florida Submitted by the Governor to Both Houses of the General Assembly on Friday, December 22, 1854. Washington, D.C.: Congressional Globe Office, 1855.

Report of the President and Directors of the Alabama and Florida Company of Florida to the Stockholders in Convention, July 26, 1856 at Pensacola. Washington, D.C.: 1856.

Report of the Trustees of the Internal Improvement Fund. State of Florida, Appendix, 20 December 1856.

Report to the Directors and Stockholders of the Florida Railroad Company, July, 1855. Washington, D.C.: Congressional Globe Office, 1855.

Reports of the President and Directors of the Pensacola & Georgia Railroad Company at Their Meeting Held in the City of Tallahassee May 1st, 1865. Tallahassee: Dyke and Sparhawk, 1866.

Rerick, Rowland H. *Memoirs of Florida*, Vols. 1, 2. Atlanta: Southern Historical Association, 1902.

Reynolds, Kelly. *Henry Plant, Pioneer Empire Builder.* Cocoa: Florida Historical Society Press, 2003.

Ripley, William Z. *Railroads: Finance and Organization.* New York: Longmans, Green, 1915.

Schwieterman, Joseph. *When the Railroad Leaves Town: American Communities in the Age of Rail Line Abandonment, Eastern United States.* Kirksville, Mo.: Truman State University Press, 2001.

Scudder, H. E. *Recollections of Samuel Breck with Passages from His Notebook, 1771–1862.* Philadelphia: Potter and Coates, 1877.

Shappee, Nathan D. "The Celestial Railroad to Juno." *Florida Historical Quarterly* 40 (April 1962): 329–49.

Shelby, Gertrude Mathews. "Florida Frenzy." *Harper's Monthly Magazine*, January 1926: 177–86.

Shofner, Jerrell H. *Jackson County, Florida: A History.* Marianna: Jackson County Heritage Association, 1985.

———. *Nor Is It Over Yet.* Gainesville: University Presses of Florida, 1974.

Shofner, Jerrell H., and William Warren Rogers. "Confederate Railroad Construction: The Live Oak to Lawton Connector." *Florida Historical Quarterly*, 43 (January 1965): 217–28.

Shrady, Theodore, and Arthur M. Waldrop. *Orange Blossom Special, Florida's Distinguished Winter Train.* Valrico: Atlantic Coast Line and Seaboard Air Line Railroads Historical Society, 2000.

Silcox, Harry C. *A Place to Live and Work: The Henry Disston Saw Works and the Tacony Community of Philadelphia.* University Park: Pennsylvania State University Press, 1994.

Sistrunk, John. "The Atlanta & St. Andrews Bay." *Railfan and Railroad Magazine*, March 1988: 40–59.

Sixth Annual Report of the Florida Central and Peninsular Railroad Company for the Year Ending June 30, 1895. Jacksonville: Da Costa Printing, 1895.

Smith, J. D. "The Construction of the P & A." *Louisville & Nashville Employees' Magazine*, August 1926: 21–40.

Smith, Tommy. *The History of Bay Colony.* Panama City: Bene-Mac, 2000.

Smyth, G. Hutchinson, D.D. *The Life of Henry Bradley Plant.* New York: Putnam's, 1898.

Standiford, Les. *Last Train to Paradise.* New York: Crown, 2002.

Stoeson, Alexander. "Road From Receivership: Claude Pepper, the du Pont Trust, and the Florida East Coast Railway." *Florida Historical Quarterly* 42 (October 1973): 132–56.

Stover, John F. *American Railroads*. Chicago: University of Chicago Press, 1997.

———. *The Railroads of the South, 1865–1900*. Chapel Hill: University of North Carolina Press, 1955.

Sulzer, Elmer, *Ghost Railroads of Sarasota County*. Sarasota: Sarasota Historical Society, 1971.

Taylor, George Rogers, and Irene D. Neu. *The American Railroad Network (1861–1890)*. Cambridge: Harvard University Press, 1956.

Tedder, Russell. "The Perry Cutoff: ACL's West Coast Gateway to Florida." *Lines South Magazine* 20 (4th Quarter 2004): 11–21.

———. "Seaboard's Covington Subdivision: The Tallahassee, Perry & Southeastern." *Lines South Magazine* 20 (1st Quarter 2004): 14–25.

Turner, Gregg M. *Florida Railroads in the 1920s*. Charleston: Arcadia, 2005.

———. *A Milestone Celebration: The Seaboard Railway to Naples and Miami*. Bloomington, Ind.: Author House, 2004.

——— *Railroads of Southwest Florida*. Charleston: Arcadia, 1999.

———. "The Seaboard's Fort Myers-Naples Extension." *Lines South Magazine* 18 (3rd Quarter 2001): 14–29.

———. *A Short History of Florida Railroads*. Charleston: Arcadia, 2003.

———. *Venice, Florida in the 1920s*. Charleston: Arcadia, 2000.

Turner, Gregg M., and Seth H. Bramson. *The Plant System of Railroads, Steamships and Hotels: The South's First Great Industrial Enterprise*. Laurys Station, Pa.: Garrigues House, 2004.

Turner, Gregg M., and Melancthon W. Jacobus. *Connecticut Railroads: An Illustrated History*. Hartford: Connecticut Historical Society, 1986.

Ulmer, Melville J. *Capital in Transportation, Communication, and Public Utilities: Its Formation and Financing*. Princeton: Princeton University Press, 1960.

Veenendaal, Augustus J., Jr. *Slow Train to Paradise. How Dutch Investment Helped Build American Railroads*. Stanford: Stanford University Press, 1996.

Wallace, John. *Carpetbag Rule in Florida*. Jacksonville. Da Costa Printing, 1888.

Warren, Bob, and Fred Clark Jr. *Seaboard Coast Line in Florida: A Pictorial History*. Newton, N.J.: Carstens, 1985.

Watkins, Caroline. "Some Early Railroads in Alachua County." *Florida Historical Quarterly* 5 (spring 1975): 450–59.

Watkins, Hays T., Jr. *"Just Call Me Hays": Recollections, Reactions and Reflections on 42 Years of Railroading*. Jacksonville: R.E.B. Communications, 2001.

Webber, Carl. *The Eden of the South, Alachua County*. New York: C. H. Webber, 1883; reprint, Micanopy, Fla.: Micanopy Publishing, n.d.

Welsh, Joseph M. *By Streamliner, New York to Florida*. Andover: Andover Junction, 1995.

Williamson, Edward C. "William D. Chipley, West Florida's Mr. Railroad." *Florida Historical Quarterly* 25 (April 1947): 333–55.

Willing, David L. "Florida's Overseas Railroad." *Florida Historical Quarterly* 35 (July 1956 to April 1957): 287–302.

Zeiller, Warren. *The Florida Keys Overseas Railway*. Wilton, Conn.: Signature Press, 2006.

Index

Talleyrand Terminal Railroad, 235

Tampa, 27, 125–26

Tampa & Gulf Coast, 152

Tampa & Jacksonville, 178

Tampa Bay Hotel, 126

Tampa Northern Railroad, 152

Tampa Southern Railroad, 158

Tavares, Apopka & Gulf, 178–79

Tavares, Orlando and Atlantic Railroad, 146–47, 179

Tavares & Gulf Railroad, 178, 179–80

Taxes on railroad companies, 105

Timber harvesting, 212–13. See also Logging railways

Tocoi Landing, 67, 86, 87

Tourism, 187

Trabue, Isaac, 124

Tractive effort of locomotives, 20

Transportation system at statehood, 50–51

Tredegar Iron Works, 82

Triay, Edward J., 144

Tri-Rail, 240–41, 240

Tropical Florida Railroad, 115

Tropicana Juice Trains, 227

Tuttle, Julia, 135

Tyler, John, 50

Unions, 24, 220–21

United States and West Indies Railroad and Steamship Company, 149, 151

United States Sugar Corporation, 237

U.S. Railroad Administration, 164

Valdosta Southern Railroad, 173

Van Buren, Martin, 28, 29

Van Weel, Pieter, 117

Venice station, 243

Vose, Francis, 16, 92

Vose, Livingston & Company, 16

Walker, David, 62

Walters, Henry, 155; on boom traffic, 17; Coast Line and, 153, 154–56, 157, 158; death of, 207; FEC and, 193; Flagler and, 137; McAdoo and, 163

Walters, William, 120, 153, 154

Ward, George Morgan, 139

Ward, Michael J., 229

Warfield, S. Davies, 204; death of, 205, 208; Seaboard and, 153, 199, 201, 202, 203–4; Standard Return plan and, 163

Wartime economy, 186–87

Waybill, 26

Waycross Short Line, 122

Wertheim, Jacobus, 93, 107, 114

West Coast Railway, 172–73

Westcott, John, 67–68, 86

Western Railway of Florida, 178

West Florida Railroad Museum, 243

West Palm Beach, 189, 201

White, Joseph, 2

Williams, John Skelton, 146, 149

Williams, William, 30

Wilson, Woodrow, 160, 162

World War I, 4, 160, 162, 162–63, 190

World War II, 5, 212–17

Wright, W. B., 166–67

Yalaha & Western, 127

Yellow fever, 42

Yellow River Railroad, 166–67

Yulee, David, 70; Civil War and, 83, 84–85, 87–88; Florida Railroad and, 76–77, 78, 80; Florida Railway and Navigation Company and, 116; imprisonment of, 92; Internal Improvement Board and, 53; land grants and, 56; life and career of, 69–71; railroads and, 71–75; treason of, 251n.3, 252n.31

Gregg Turner, a former director of the Railway & Locomotive Historical Society at Harvard Business School, has authored or coauthored many books, including: *A Short History of Florida Railroads*; *Florida Railroads in the 1920s*; *The Plant System of Railroads, Steamships and Hotels*; *Railroads of Southwest Florida*; *A Milestone Celebration: The Seaboard Railway to Naples and Miami*; and *Connecticut Railroads, an Illustrated History*, for which he received a United States Congressional Certificate of Merit. His *Venice in the 1920s* recounts how America's oldest and largest railroad union—the Brotherhood of Locomotive Engineers—created the City of Venice, Florida. The author welcomes your questions and comments; he can be reached at greggturner@msn.com.

Frolicking Bears, Wet Vultures, and Other Oddities: A New York City Journalist in Nineteenth-Century Florida, edited by Jerald T. Milanich (2005)

Waters Less Traveled: Exploring Florida's Big Bend Coast, by Doug Alderson (2005)

Saving South Beach, by M. Barron Stofik (2005)

Losing It All to Sprawl: How Progress Ate My Cracker Landscape, by Bill Belleville (2006)

Voices of the Apalachicola, compiled and edited by Faith Eidse (2006), first paperback edition, 2007

Floridian of His Century: The Courage of Governor LeRoy Collins, by Martin A. Dyckman (2006)

America's Fortress: A History of Fort Jefferson, Dry Tortugas, Florida, by Thomas Reid (2006)

Weeki Wachee, City of Mermaids: A History of One of Florida's Oldest Roadside Attractions, by Lu Vickers and Sara Dionne (2007)

City of Intrigue, Nest of Revolution: A Documentary History of Key West in the Nineteenth Century, by Consuelo E. Stebbins (2007)

The New Deal in South Florida: Design, Policy, and Community Building, 1933–1940, edited by John A. Stuart and John F. Stack Jr. (2008)

Pilgrim in the Land of Alligators: More Stories about Real Florida, by Jeff Klinkenberg (2008)

Disorder in the Supreme Court: Scandal and Reform in Florida, by Martin A. Dyckman (2008)

A Journey into Florida Railroad History, by Gregg M. Turner (2008)